AF646949

THE ARYA SAMAJ AS A FUNDAMENTALIST MOVEMENT

The Arya Samaj as a Fundamentalist Movement

A Study in Comparative Fundamentalism

J.E. LLEWELLYN

MANOHAR
2025

First published 1993
Reprinted 2022, 2023, 2024, 2025

© J.E. Llewellyn

All rights reserved. No part of this publication may be reproduced or transmitted, in any form or by any means, without prior permission of the author and the publisher.

ISBN 978-81-7304-015-3

Published by
Ajay Kumar Jain *for*
Manohar Publishers & Distributors
4753/23 Ansari Road, Daryaganj
New Delhi 110 002

Printed at
Replika Press Pvt. Ltd.

In memory of Margaret O'Brien Llewellyn and
Richard H. Llewellyn

ACKNOWLEDGMENTS

This study was initially produced as a Ph.D. dissertation in the Department of South Asian Languages and Civilizations at the University of Chicago. The greatest debt of gratitude that I must express is to my adviser on that dissertation, Dr. Frank E. Reynolds, and to the other members of my committee, Dr. Colin P. Masica and Dr. Edwin Gerow. Their support was essential to my development as a scholar not only while working on this project, but throughout my career as a student at the University of Chicago. I should also acknowledge my other teachers and fellow students at that institution, who provided a stimulating environment in which to study South Asia and the history of religions.

I feel heavily indebted to Dr. Bharat Bhushan Vidyalankar of the Department of Vedic Literature at Gurukul Kangri University, who was my professor while I was doing fieldwork in India from 1985 to 1987. Dr. Bharat Bhushan was very generous with his time, and his family always treated me as one of its members. I would not have been able to establish myself at the Gurukul Kangri had it not been for the gracious assistance of Dr. Satyaketu Vidyalankar, who was the chancellor of that University when I arrived in India in 1985 and who has since passed away. When Dr. Satyaketu died the Arya Samaj lost a prolific scholar who was also a fine gentleman. I am grateful to the faculty and staff of the Gurukul Kangri for their help to me during the time of my residence there.

There were two other Arya institutions in the area around Hardwar that welcomed me to take part in their community life, the local Arya Samaj chapter at the Arya Samaj Mandir in Hardwar and the Ārya Virakt (Vānprasth + Sannyās) Āśram of Jwalapur. It is through day-to-day interaction with these ordinary Arya Samajists that I have learned about the practical realization of the Samaj's theories.

I was assisted in this research on the Arya Samaj by Dr. Bhawani Lal Bhartiya of Panjab University and Dr. Kenneth W. Jones of Kansas State University. Both of these scholars of the Arya Samaj read an early draft of the third chapter of this book, and their suggestions have made that chapter better. They are, of course, not responsible for any errors contained in that chapter.

The fieldwork upon which this study is based was made possible by a doctoral dissertation research fellowship from the American Institute of Indian Studies. I am grateful not only for this financial assistance, but also for the logistical support provided by the staff of the Institute in United States and in India.

Several administrators and faculty members at Bob Jones University graciously consented to be interviewed by me when I visited the university in May of 1990. I want to express my gratitude especially to Dean Thurman Wisdom, Mr. M. Bruce McAllister, Dean James Berg, and Dr. David Beale.

In the study of fundamentalism I was aided first by Dr. Bruce B. Lawrence of Duke University. Dr. Lawrence generously gave me a copy of the manuscript of his book *Defenders of God*, a ground breaking work in comparative fundamentalism. My attempt to comprehend fundamentalism across cultures was greatly advanced by the Fundamentalism Project of the American Academy of Arts and Sciences. I am especially grateful to the Project's Director Dr. Martin Marty and the Associate Director Dr. R. Scott Appleby. Dr. Appleby was kind enough to read an early draft of chapter one. I only regret that I was not able to pursue all the recommendations that he gave me with regard to the study of North American Protestant fundamentalism. There is one more scholar of comparative fundamentalism whose name I must mention, that is Dr. James Chancellor of Colorado Baptist University. Dr. Chancellor gave me a copy of his dissertation "A Comparative Approach to Religious Fundamentalism: Egyptian Sunni Islam and American Protestant Christianity." I learned much from this fascinating study.

I also wanted to express my personal gratitude to Kailash Jha and his family. They opened their home in Delhi to me, which made doing research far from the United States much less difficult.

Over the past year I have begun to discharge my debt to all of these educators and friends by sharing some of what I have learned with others. I am grateful to my colleagues in the Department of Religious Studies at Southwest Missouri State University and to my students for facilitating my schooling as a teacher.

My family provided moral support throughout my time in graduate school, which was essential to my success there. In recent years I have been sustained by the love of my wife Eileen and our daughter Margaret. This is a debt which I will never be able to express, much less to repay.

LIST OF TABLES

Table

CONTENTS

INTRODUCTION

On 13 September 1986 on the front page of the *Hindustan Times*, an English-language daily newspaper published in Delhi, an article appeared with the title "PM for New Ways to Combat Rise of Fundamentalism." The "PM" referred to here is the then Prime Minister of India, Rajiv Gandhi. The piece reports on the remarks of Mr. Gandhi and other important Indian political figures at a day-long meeting of the National Integration Council. According to this source the Prime Minister and others spoke out at this gathering against the increasing prominence of fundamentalism and communalism in Indian public life.[1]

It is significant that this article is silent as to who these fundamentalists are. In *Language, Religion and Politics in North India* Paul Brass has argued that one of the "rules" which has regulated the attitude of the government of India to pleas for greater regional autonomy is that "regional demands based on language and culture will be accommodated, but that regional demands which are explicitly based on religious differences will not be accepted."[2] The trauma that was the partition of India and Pakistan along religious lines when those two nations became independent in 1947 has given rise to a real fear in India that when political causes become identified with religious communities, there is a threat to the unity of the nation.[3] The abstention of the author of this article from mentioning specific examples of fundamentalism or communalism is a reflection of the attitude of the government of India. It attempts to ignore these issues out of a belief that government attention will only lend an air of legitimacy to individuals whom it condemns as extremists.

An important insight into the interpretation of fundamentalism in India is suggested by the following paragraph:

> Let me state at the outset that fundamentalism has the connotation of community orientation and communal assertion. In that sense it is essentially [a] socio-political

> phenomenon. It should not be mistaken with the tendency of reviving religion and adhering to pre-modern ideology. It certainly aims at utilising religion, tradition, traditional or mythical past and medieval conflicts to respond to the contemporary needs and to meet the challenge of [a] secular-democratic polity. The source of the phenomenon is not religion and religious traditions. One can explain this kind of fundamentalism in terms of [the] operation of [the] existing economic system and the realities of Indian political life.[4]

It is perhaps not surprising that an article in a leftist journal would tend to find the origins of fundamentalism in economic and political factors rather than religious ones. Still, significant consequences arise from such an analysis, and one of them should be noted here. When fundamentalism is regarded as an economic or political phenomenon, then it is easy to dismiss the religious claims of fundamentalists. By reasoning that is clearly circular, one moves from an assertion that fundamentalism is economic or political and not religious to the conclusion that the religious appeals of fundamentalists are therefore illegitimate. Following this logic, there are certainly many in India who would argue that fundamentalists are politicians who use rhetoric based on religion to win a mass following. From this standpoint fundamentalism is not a valid manifestation of religion, but a cynical manipulation of it.

A similar logic seems to lie at the base of the journalistic usage of fundamentalism, particularly with respect to the Muslim world. In many news accounts there seems to be no difference between "Muslim fundamentalists," "Muslim fanatics," and "Muslim terrorists." Some of the more reflective individuals among the journalists who generate these reports might define a fundamentalist movement as one led by venal politicians who use religious symbols to manipulate the masses. This is not the way that fundamentalism will be presented in this book.

Another kind of fundamentalism suggests itself when we consider the North American Protestant movement for which the term was coined. Because of the recent emergence of the New Christian Right as a force in public life, some Americans now think of fundamentalists as political. But for most of their history Protestant fundamentalists have not been so prominent in the public sphere. Fundamentalists have been torn in their evaluation of the larger culture. They condemn the United States as a nation which has turned away from its Christian mission in the world, but they also try to call America back to its original values.

North American Protestant fundamentalism has not been primarily a political movement, but a religious one.

THE COMPARATIVE STUDY OF FUNDAMENTALISM

Clearly our comparison of fundamentalist movements in different cultures is going to be shaped by how we understand fundamentalism in our own. If we begin with the notion that North American Protestant fundamentalism is a kind of right-wing political extremism, then we will be led to select similar extremist movements in other cultures as comparable. By the same token, if we take Christian fundamentalism to be a religious movement which has been involved in politics only intermittently, then the groups which suggest themselves for comparison will be more religious than political. From the outset some definition of fundamentalism must inform any comparison, and it is appropriate to make that definition explicit.

For our definition of fundamentalism throughout this study we will rely on a recent article by Martin Marty, the director of the Fundamentalism Project of the American Academy of Arts and Sciences. Before indicating some of the things that fundamentalism is, we will follow Marty in pointing out some of the things that fundamentalism is not. Marty begins his characterization of fundamentalism by setting aside nine elements which have often been erroneously regarded as definitive of it. (1) Fundamentalism "is not the same thing as conservatism, traditionalism, classicism, or orthodoxy, though fundamentalists associate themselves with such concepts." Here Marty is concerned to carve out a semantic realm for fundamentalism separate from that occupied by other conservatisms. Fundamentalists organize their traditions in a new way, which often puts them at odds with conservatives.

(2) Fundamentalism "does not refer to fossilized elements, to static relics, mutations or throwbacks." One of the most noteworthy features of many fundamentalist movements is that, though they advocate a return to the past, they are still a dynamic response to the contemporary situation. (3) Marty maintains that "fundamentalisms generically have nothing to do with biblical inerrancy or, for that matter, any other substantive elements, any doctrines or tenets of particular faiths." On this point Marty is trying to get away from the close identification of fundamentalism with the North American Protestant case, especially the doctrine of biblical inerrancy that has

been so important for Christian fundamentalism. Obviously if there are fundamentalisms in other religious traditions, they will not agree with the specific theological formulations of Christianity. This is not to say that parallels cannot be drawn between the doctrines of fundamentalist movements from different religions.

(4) Fundamentalism "is also not the only significant popular movement of thought and action to depart from conventional norms of secular rationality." It seems that Marty wants to place fundamentalism within the context of other departures from conventional norms in order to reduce its marginality. (5) Fundamentalists "do not conceive of themselves as being antiscientific or antirational on their own terms." The bias of the liberal critic of fundamentalism may be to dismiss its arguments as utterly and self-consciously irrational, but this would be wrong. If one accepts its presuppositions, the fundamentalist position is often marked by an inexorable logic. (6) To this must be added the observation that "fundamentalists are seldom opposed to technology as such, or to many of its specific artifacts." On the contrary, they have often used modern technology to put their message across. Apparently fundamentalists are able to separate technology from the philosophical underpinnings of the science that has produced it.

(7) According to Marty "fundamentalisms are not declining, fading, likely to go away, as many observers two or three decades ago thought that they were fated or doomed to do." Theories about the necessary capitulation of conservative religion in the face of modernism do not seem adequate to explain the current vigorous growth in fundamentalist groups. (8) "Fundamentalists are not always activists, militants, belligerents, or terrorists." As we have already maintained for the North American Protestant case, the use of the term 'fundamentalism" should not be limited to those groups whose activism makes them notorious. And (9) "Fundamentalists are not always poor, uneducated people who rationalize their hopeless lower-class circumstances through a religious movement." "Deprivation theories" do not account for the persistence and even growth of fundamentalist movements. Very often those who are drawn to fundamentalism are college-educated professionals, individuals who are not thought of as disadvantaged ordinarily. These are some of the things that fundamentalism is not.[5]

Having rejected some of the characteristics which are mistakenly predicated of fundamentalism, Martin Marty goes on to identify twelve elements which might properly be ascribed to it. (1) "Fundamentalism is always reactive, reactionary." Fundamentalism emerges in response to what people see as a critical threat to their tradition. A movement is constituted to defend the tradition from outside attack. (2) "Fundamentalisms engage in what Karl Rahner called 'selective retrieval,' picking and choosing certain 'fundamentals,' 'basics,' or 'essences.'" Fundamentalists reach back to the golden age of their tradition to identify its core. This is the irreducible minimum which they must protect from their enemies at all costs. (3) "The serviceable fundamentals tend to have a 'scandalous'—in the Greek etymological sense—character: 'of the nature of, or causing, a 'stumbling-block' or occasion of offence. . . .'" Fundamentalists grasp just those fundamentals to uphold which are being compromised by their opponents. The fundamentals are a shibboleth which separates the fundamentalist from all others.

(4) "The result is always an exclusive or separatist movement." A fundamentalist community is liable to have very distinct borders. It will not cooperate with other groups in lasting coalitions, it will not brook ecumenism. (5) "A corollary of exclusivism in all cases is the aspect of fundamentalisms as oppositional." The party of the fundamentalist is set against all others. Those who do not support the fundamentalists' position are as bad as those who openly oppose it. (6) "We never see the term fundamentalism applied to movements which are not absolutist." Fundamentalist movements are exclusive and oppositional, because their adherents perceive themselves as the sole defenders of a single, clear, and complete truth. (7) "With absolutism comes authoritativeness or authoritarianism." The fundamentalist version of the truth is often backed up by an unimpeachable authority. Marty's formulation here is deliberately vague as to what that authority might be. A text, a code of law, or an individual could qualify.

(8) Marty writes that "religious fundamentalisms are all, in my observation, antievolutionary or antidevelopmental." This rubric covers the opposition of North American Protestant fundamentalists to Darwin's theory of evolution, but it does not stop there. Fundamentalists tend to oppose any evolutionary theory which makes chance events central to history. (9) Also "fundamentalisms are uniformly antipermissive." A rising tide of vice is a sign of the attack on their values which fundamentalists fight against. Fundamentalists tend to hold themselves to a high standard of morality. (10) "In relation to the texts of a tradition, fundamentalism is consistently antihermeneutical." To clarify his point Marty defines hermeneutical as the idea "that all interpretation occurs inside a circle wherein the presuppositions one brings color the meanings one takes away." In

contradistinction to this, fundamentalists maintain that the message of their authorities is plain, regardless of the perspective of the audience. The truth speaks for itself, so that no contextual analysis is called for.

(11) "Fundamentalists, whether militant or not, uniformly see themselves as agents of the sacred power, person, or force which gives life to their group." Their exclusive grasp of the truth gives fundamentalists a special mission in the world. The organization of their group reflects this mission. (12) "Related to this, finally, is a teleological understanding." Since North American Protestant fundamentalists are mostly millenarians, they have a very concrete view of the future. There is a general tendency to understand history as having an end or a purpose even in fundamentalist movements which are not explicitly millenarian. These are the elements that are often found in fundamentalist movements according to Martin Marty.[6]

This book will be dedicated to comparing groups from the Christian, Islamic, and Hindu traditions with the aid of Marty's definition of fundamentalism. One problem with this project relates not so much to the content of the definition as to the appropriateness of the word "fundamentalist." William Shepard has argued that the term "fundamentalist" in journalistic and academic writing has such a strongly pejorative connotation that its use should not be extended to other cultures by scholars who aspire to objectivity.[7] To a large extent this objection is met by the relatively value-neutral definition of fundamentalism just presented. It is important to realize that "fundamentalism" is a term that is gaining currency in the mass media. Rather than being put off by the promiscuous way that the word is being used in that context, scholars have a responsibility to study fundamentalism cross culturally, precisely in order to introduce some rigor into the discussion.

Even if we accept that "fundamentalism" is an idea which can be applied across cultures, there still might be disagreements about what movements should be characterized as fundamentalist. It is not possible to say simply that those groups which fit Marty's definition are fundamentalist, while those which do not are non-fundamentalist. It will be argued in the body of this study that a couple of the points in Marty's definition seem to be more appropriate to describe North American Protestant fundamentalism than movements in other religious traditions. We might want to eliminate these elements from our definition in future cross cultural studies of fundamentalism. Even if we accept all of the definition, scholars could well come to conflicting conclusions about whether any one of its elements can be predicated of a given movement.[8] And there may be groups which possess some of the elements of fundamentalism, but not others. How should they be characterized?

Jonathan Z. Smith offers a helpful model for classifying religious phenomenon in his book *Imagining Religion.* Relying upon recent scholarship in plant taxonomy, Smith contrasts monothetic and polythetic classification. The classical Linnaean taxonomy, a monothetic system, "held that all members of a given taxon invariably shared common features while differing from other, closely adjacent taxa by a single, definitive feature."[9] More recent studies of plant taxonomy, using statistical methods, have dispensed with the notion of single, necessary differentiating characteristics. According to this new, polythetic mode of classification "a class is defined as consisting of a set of properties, each individual member of the class to possess 'a large (but unspecified) number' of these properties, with each property possessed by a 'large number' of individuals in the class, but no single property to be possessed by every member of the class."[10] Such a polythetic approach might be adopted in the classification of fundamentalist movements across cultures. No one characteristic would thus be necessary in order to identify a group as fundamentalist. Rather a substantial number of features from a set of elements common to different fundamentalist movements would be required in order to apply the label. This approach would allow some flexibility in developing an understanding of fundamentalist movements in various cultures around the world, without abandoning the important task of being explicit about what these groups have in common and how each is unique.

In just the past few years scholarly studies have begun to appear on comparative fundamentalism. A pioneering work is *Studies in Religious Fundamentalism*, edited by Lionel Caplan.[11] This book, based originally on a series of seminars at the School of Oriental and African Studies at the University of London, suffers to a degree from the unevenness which is often characteristic of collections of essays by different authors. It is not clear that the various contributors are talking about groups which are comparable. More successful is *Fundamentalism Observed*, a set of essays based on a somewhat more coherent notion of fundamentalism.[12] Comparative studies of fundamentalism by a single author offer the promise of greater consistency in the analysis of various groups. An important contribution is Bruce Lawrence's fascinating *Defenders of God.*[13] Another interesting work has recently been completed by a younger scholar, James Chancellor.[14] A study of fundamentalism in different cultural contexts, this book extends the range of comparison to include the Hindu tradition.

It must be admitted at the outset that the comparative study of fundamentalism in this book would not be acceptable to fundamentalists themselves. As was noted in the above definition, members of fundamentalist groups tend to be exclusive, regarding themselves as the sole defenders of the truth. There is no place in the fundamentalists' self-understanding for an acknowledgement that there are other movements in very different theological contexts which are comparable.[15] This suggests an interesting problem for the history of religions as a discipline. In studying various religions one encounters a welter of mutually contradictory claims about the nature of humanity and divinity. Historians of religions have thus far not been successful in attempting to come to grips with these claims.[16] From the comparative study of fundamentalism it is obvious that if we ignore these conflicting truths, then we must leave out of account an important element in religion.

This must suffice for a preliminary discussion of the comparative study of fundamentalism. The next section will concern the Hindu movement which is the main focus of this book, the Arya Samaj (Ārya Samāj). In this introduction we will not analyze the Samaj in terms of Martin Marty's definition of fundamentalism—that task will be left for the body of the text. Rather we will offer only a brief description of the group to acquaint the reader with it.

THE ARYA SAMAJ

The Arya Samaj is a Hindu revivalist movement which was founded in 1875 by Swami Dayanand Sarasvati (Dayānand Sarasvatī, 1824-1883). Swami Dayanand was from a Brahman family in Gujarat in India, and his upbringing from all accounts was quite traditional. Still, the message of the Arya Samaj appealed most to an emerging English-educated elite in the northwestern part of the South Asian subcontinent. Dayanand's teaching represents a reversal of what comes to mind for most people when they think of Hinduism. He rejected the notion of polytheism, believing in one omnipotent and omniscient God. It would be tempting to claim that this idea was born of Dayanand's interaction with missionaries, but this is not the explanation that he himself gave. Rather the swami claimed that this God is described in the Vedas, Hinduism's most ancient texts.

Swami Dayanand attacked not only polytheism, but also idolatry. He did not believe that the Supreme Being could be represented in any image. Dayanand also supported a number of social reforms. He maintained, for example, that in the most ancient scriptures the divisions between castes were not so hard and fast as they are in contemporary India. In opposition to the prevailing practice of attributing caste to children on the basis of the family in which they are born, Dayanand suggested that each person should be assigned to the caste that is most appropriate to his or her own qualities.

What is perhaps most striking about Swami Dayanand's progressive social agenda is that even in this area he claimed that he was only following ancient practice. Dayanand taught that India had once been a very advanced nation, technologically as well as socially. Then there had been a cataclysm in the form of the great war described in the epic the *Mahābhārata*. In that conflict, in which so many virtuous kings and wise sages had lost their lives, the Hindu community suffered a setback from which it has not yet fully recovered. On the basis of this reading of history, Dayanand divided all literature into three classes: (1) the Vedas, which issued forth from God at the time of creation, and which are totally free of error; (2) the *ārṣa* literature, that is the literature that was composed by the ancient sages (the rishis) in the period before the *Mahābhārata* war, which is basically reliable but not perfectly so, and which can be trusted to the extent that it does not conflict with the Vedas; and (3) the *anārṣa* literature, which has been written since the time of the great war, and which is absolutely unreliable.

Swami Dayanand's attempt to derive modern social and religious practices, and even modern technology, from the Vedas represents a radical departure from the ways that those texts have been understood both by traditional Hindu commentators and modern Western scholars. Dayanand explicitly argued that the great medieval Hindu scholiasts were wrong, and so the modern academic works which follow them. The swami claimed that his reading of the Vedas was only based on ancient and authoritative works, unlike these later, degenerate texts. Western academics have not agreed that Dayanand's views can be supported even by this older literature, and have denigrated his Vedic commentaries.

It is striking that although Swami Dayanand was a sannyasi whose life-style was in many ways quite traditional, still his message appealed to a developing class of professionals in north India. Members of this new elite found their faith in Hinduism being undermined by

English education and Christian missionary criticism. To them Swami Dayanand offered a new Hinduism, which was at once consistent with their most ancient and revered tradition and free of some of that tradition's worst excesses.

At every turn one finds a peculiar combination of the traditional and modern in the Arya Samaj. This is apparent not only in the Samaj's beliefs, but also in the very organization of the movement. Though Swami Dayanand was a sannyasi revered for his saintliness, he did not set himself up as the absolute master of his followers in the Arya Samaj, as many gurus in India do. From the beginning the Samaj has been governed by representatives elected by the membership of the organization. This principle was enshrined in constitutions that were written at the founding of the Arya Samaj.

The leaders of the Arya Samaj, especially in the early part of its history, were dynamic individuals who made many significant contributions to the development of modern India. Their most salient work was in the area of education. After Swami Dayanand died in 1883, a school was established in his memory in Lahore, the city in northwest India which would remain the center of Arya Samaj activity until 1947. As this memorial institution was to be a purveyor both of modern Western knowledge and ancient Indian lore it was called the Dayanand Anglo-Vedic School. The D.A.V. School met a crucial need of the Hindu community of Lahore, offering Western education in an environment which was free of the dangers of Christian missionary propaganda. D.A.V. schools and colleges became popular with other Hindus as well as Arya Samajists, and now the D.A.V. network constitutes the largest non-governmental educational system in India.

Another area in which Arya Samajists have had a major impact on Indian life has been politics. Members of the Arya Samaj were active in the Indian National Congress, and many took part in the freedom struggle against the British. Arya Samajists also played a crucial role in the development of an explicitly Hindu politics. Through organizations such as the Hindu Mahasabha Aryas have actively defended what they perceive to be the interests of the Hindu community. This activity has continued in post-independence India.

Although parallels between the Arya Samaj and fundamentalism may have already begun to suggest themselves to the reader, it is important to acknowledge that members of the organization do not accept this designation for themselves.[17] When I began doing fieldwork in India in 1985 I was repeatedly dismayed by the intractability of my Arya Samaj informants. They almost always refused to accept my hypothesis that the Arya Samaj is a fundamentalist movement. Those Arya Samajists in India who recognized the word "fundamentalist" tended to be more educated and to have a more cosmopolitan outlook than the average member of the Samaj. Familiar with the journalistic usage of "fundamentalism" as a negative label for groups which manipulate religion for their own political ends, they naturally would not accept the applicability of the term to the Arya Samaj.

Eventually I began to notice that I received a different and much more hopeful reaction to my thesis that the Arya Samaj is a fundamentalist movement when I discussed my research in Hindi. Since there is no word in the Hindi language that perfectly conveys the meaning of "fundamentalism," I was forced to rely on a number of different translations to explain my interests. Some might render "fundamentalism" into Hindi with the word *rūḍhivād*. A pejorative label that implies a hollow conventionalism, Arya Samajists do not accept this term to characterize themselves. This idea is not consistent with the nature of fundamentalism as we have characterized it anyway, so another approach was called for. When I tried to convey that fundamentalists are concerned with the fundamentals of their tradition (using words like *mūl*, root, or *nīṃv*, foundation), then I got a much more positive response. Translated in this way, Arya Samajists would often agree that the Samaj is fundamentalist. They would argue that the Vedas, Hinduism's most ancient scriptures, are the root or foundation of the Hindu religion.[18] Here again one's preunderstanding of the meaning of fundamentalism is crucial.

In recent decades some very competent scholarly studies of the Arya Samaj have appeared. Indispensable for a student of this subject are Kenneth W. Jones's history of the Arya Samaj, entitled *Arya Dharm*, and J. T. F. Jordens's biography of the founder of the Samaj, *Dayānanda Sarasvatī*.[19] These works are supplemented by more specialized studies such as the remarkable early dissertation by Graham on caste and Thursby's monograph on communal conflict.[20] Still, there is much work to be done in interpreting the Arya Samaj. For example, there has not been adequate inquiry into the Arya Samaj's interpretation of the Vedas. Social historians have regarded this topic perhaps as too narrow to be of any general interest, while students of the Vedas have rejected the Samaj's reading of those texts as too derivative to be of much use. Thus, one of the most original aspects of the Arya Samaj's teaching has not been given sufficient attention. When the scholar looks at the Arya Samaj as a fundamentalist movement, then its interpretation of the Vedas assumes its proper salience. This book makes a contribution to the scholarly understanding of the Arya Samaj by suggesting a new context in which to analyze that movement.

This study represents an improvement over earlier work on the Arya Samaj in that it takes seriously the religious claims of that organization, especially the Arya claims related to the Hindu scriptural tradition. That is not to say that this work exhausts the possibilities for analyzing the Arya Samaj's religious teachings. Over the course of Indian intellectual history many thinkers have maintained that their position is uniquely true because it is based upon a uniquely accurate interpretation of the Hindu scriptures, particularly the Vedas. It would not be helpful to call these earlier scripturalist movements fundamentalist in my judgment. Rather the term "fundamentalist" should be restricted to groups that have grown up in recent centuries in response to the rise of modernism.

Even so, it is no doubt the case that the history of the interpretation of scripture in Hinduism is one of the contexts which might be analyzed in a study of the Arya Samaj. In the fourth chapter of this book there is some discussion of the traditional precedents for the Arya Samaj's position on the Vedas, but there is much more to be said. By looking at the Arya Samaj within the context of fundamentalist movements in other religious traditions, something must be sacrificed in analyzing the Indological background to the Samaj. Yet it is undeniably the case that there is much in the program of the Arya Samaj that is distinctly a response to modern conditions. That is brought out more clearly in a study of the Arya Samaj as a fundamentalist movement than it would be in a study of the Samaj as yet another example of a group that bases itself upon a claim to an authoritative interpretation of the Hindu scriptures. Hopefully future work on the Arya Samaj will serve to further clarify the relationship of the Samaj to earlier Hindu scripturalist movements.

Because Hinduism is often thought of as tolerant, "Hindu fundamentalism" may seem to be an oxymoron. There appears to be a contradiction between the absolutism of fundamentalists and the openness of the Hindu tradition. This contradiction is mitigated to a degree by attending to the nature of Hinduism itself. In recent years Western scholars have become more conscious that "Hinduism" is a label that has been used by outsiders to describe a congeries of differing beliefs and practices. There is a great deal of disagreement among "Hindus" themselves about which of these faiths and actions are most true or most virtuous. Of course, there have been attempts to bring varying forms of Hinduism together in one system, but these syntheses often imply a hierarchical evaluation of the elements that they include. The caste system, for example, does provide a model by which different groups are subsumed into a larger whole, but these groups are not all of equal rank. Priests and kings are higher than farmers and servants generally. Hinduism is a label which includes a great diversity of phenomena, but that does not mean that everyone to whom this label is applied is tolerant of everyone else.

There may be a tendency among Western scholars to prize the pluralism that exists in India as a positive thing, but this evaluation should only be attributed to Indians with some care. This is not to say that the Arya Samaj is not different from other groups within Hinduism on this score. The Samaj's doctrines are much more hard and fast than those of most Hindus. Perhaps this dogmatism has discouraged Western academics from studying the Arya Samaj. Embarrassingly, the Samaj attacks many of the beliefs that are generally understood to be basic to Hinduism. In this way the Arya Samaj represents a challenge to the study of the Hindu tradition. When we re-present Hinduism we must do so in a way that incorporates the plasticity which seems characteristic of the tradition as a whole along with the concreteness of the positions of separate groups like the Arya Samaj.

This book offers a reinterpretation of fundamentalism and the Arya Samaj in two parts. In the first part we will compare Christian, Islamic, and Hindu movements according to the definition of fundamentalism spelled out here in the introduction. The first chapter of this work is dedicated to a study of a North American Protestant fundamentalist institution, Bob Jones University, and an Islamic fundamentalist movement, the Jama'at-i Islami. No effort in this chapter has been made to comprehend every movement in the Christian and Islamic traditions that has been identified as fundamentalist, because that could very well have resulted in a discussion that is too diffuse to be of much interest. We have begun by taking the leap of choosing single exemplars of Christian and Islamic fundamentalism, fully aware that this leaves us open to the charge that much has been left out.

The second chapter will focus on the Hindu group which is our primary concern, the Arya Samaj. Reliance upon scriptural authority is one of the elements that the Arya Samaj shares with other fundamentalist movements. The scripturalism of the Arya Samaj will be the subject of the second part of this book. The third chapter will be devoted to an analysis of authoritative and unauthoritative scripture in the writings of Swami Dayanand. In the fourth chapter we will look more closely at Dayanand's writings about the Vedas, the religious texts which he identified as inerrant. In the conclusion to this study we will return to some of the problems which have occupied us in this introduction.

NOTES

1. "PM for New Ways to Combat Rise of Fundamentalism," *Hindustan Times* (Delhi), 13 September 1986, pp. 1 and back page. Another press report also features the Prime Minister's condemnation of fundamentalism in its title: "PM's Call to Fight Fundamentalism," *Times of India* (Delhi), 13 September 1986, pp. 1 and 9. Two other papers mention fundamentalism in their articles, but not in the titles. "Communalism Must Be Curbed, PM Tells Integration Council," *Statesman* (Delhi), 13 September 1986, pp. 1 and 9; and "PM for Pact to Keep Communalism Out of Electoral Politics," *Indian Express* (Delhi), 13 September 1986, p. 1.
2. Paul R. Brass, *Language, Religion and Politics in North India* (London: Cambridge University Press, 1974), 17.
3. One editor has written that "Any discussion of fundamentalism must start with the premise that the phenomenon in its current manifestation in India is inimical to the development of a healthy Indian polity." H.S. Khare, "Fundamentalism," *Seminar* 322 (June 1986): 14.
4. Moin Shakir, "Rise of Fundamentalism—An Enquiry into its Causes," *Radical Humanist* 50, no. 5 (August 1986): 27.
5. Martin E. Marty, "Fundamentalism as a Social Phenomenon," *Bulletin of the American Academy of Arts and Sciences* 42, no. 2 (November 1988): 17-19. This essay is not to be confused with an earlier article by Marty with the same title. See Martin E. Marty, "Fundamentalism as a Social Phenomenon," in *Evangelicalism in Modern America,* ed. George Marsden (Grand Rapids: William B. Eerdmans, 1984), 56-68.
6. Martin E. Marty, "Fundamentalism as a Social Phenomenon," *Bulletin of the American Academy of Arts and Sciences* 42, no. 2 (November 1988): 20-23.
7. William Shepard, "'Fundamentalism' Christian and Islamic," *Religion* 17 (1987): 367-368. As an alternative to "fundamentalism" Shepard recommends "radical neotraditionalism," a formulation which is less than mellifluous and unlikely to pass into common parlance, I think.
8. For example, in chapter two I have argued that the evidence about the Arya Samaj's authoritarianism is ambiguous.

9. Jonathan Z. Smith, *Imagining Religion: From Babylon to Jonestown,* Chicago Studies in the History of Judaism, ed. Jacob Neusner, William Scott Green, and Calvin Goldscheider (Chicago: University of Chicago Press, 1982), 3.
10. Ibid., 4, quoting M. Beckner, *The Biological Way of Thought* (New York: Columbia University Press, 1959), 22-25.
11. Lionel Caplan, ed., *Studies in Religious Fundamentalism* (Albany: State University of New York Press, 1987).
12. Martin Marty, ed., *Fundamentalism Observed* (Chicago: University of Chicago Press, forthcoming). I am grateful Dr. Marty and to Dr. R. Scott Appleby, of the Fundamentalism Project, for sharing parts of their manuscript with me, and for their general encouragement of my work.
13. Bruce B. Lawrence, *Defenders of God: The Fundamentalist Revolt against the Modern Age* (San Francisco: Harper and Row, 1989). Dr. Lawrence was most generous in showing me his manuscript and discussing his ideas.
14. James Darrell Chancellor, "A Comparative Approach to Religious Fundamentalism: Egyptian Sunni Islam and American Protestant Christianity" (Ph.D. diss., Duke University, 1988). I must confess my gratitude to Dr. Chancellor for giving me a copy of his dissertation.
15. More than once in private conversations with Arya Samajists in India I was told that what they advocate is not a religion, in the sense that the term is applied to Christianity, Islam, and other traditions. These others represent merely the efforts of humans to understand the nature of God and the world. The Vedic faith, by contrast, is based upon God's self-revelation. The strivings of humans, however noble in themselves, cannot equal the perfect divine manifestation in the Vedas.
16. Paul Griffiths has used the term "philosophical apartheid" in condemning the unwillingness of philosophers and historians of religions to attempt to advance some judgment of the relative adequacy of the normative discourses of different cultures. Paul J. Griffiths, "Philosophizing Across Cultures: Or, How to Argue with a Buddhist," *Criterion* 26, no. 1 (winter 1987): 10-14.
17. Outsiders have identified the Arya Samaj as a fundamentalist movement. See, for example, Khare, "Fundamentalism," 17.
18. William Shepard has noted a similar reaction among Muslims. "In my experience Muslims tend to respond to the term ["fundamentalism"] in one of two ways. Either they respond to the root meaning of the term and gladly accept it for all serious Muslims, or they respond to its pejorative connotations and reject

its application to Muslims." Shepard, "'Fundamentalism' Christian and Islamic," 376, note 43.

19. Kenneth W. Jones, *Arya Dharm: Hindu Consciousness in 19th-Century Punjab* (Berkeley: University of California Press, 1976); and J.T.F. Jordens, *Dayānanda Sarasvatī: His Life and Ideas* (Delhi: Oxford University Press, 1978).

20. J. Reid Graham, *The Arya Samaj as a Reformation in Hinduism with Special Reference to Caste* (Ann Arbor: University Microfilms, 1965; photomechanical reproduction of a Ph.D. diss., Yale University, 1942); and G. R. Thursby, *Hindu-Muslim Relations in British India: A Study of Controversy, Conflict, and Communal Movements in Northern India, 1923-1928*, Studies in the History of Religions (Supplements to *Numen*), vol. 35 (Leiden: E. J. Brill, 1975).

PART I

THE COMPARISON OF FUNDAMENTALIST MOVEMENTS

1

CHRISTIAN AND ISLAMIC FUNDAMENTALISM

In his brief but seminal work *Islam Observed* Clifford Geertz criticizes the comparative study of religions for its tendency to pigeonhole, to regard the labelling of diverse religious phenomena as a sufficient explanation of them. This criticism is voiced by Geertz as a prologue to his description of the classical religious styles of Morocco and Indonesia. Geertz draws attention to beliefs and practices which have been called mystical, but he does not want to allow this common designation to obscure the differences between the two cultures. "If, however, we use a concept like 'mysticism'—or 'mystic' or 'mystical'—not to formulate an underlying uniformity behind superficially diverse phenomena, but to analyze the nature of that diversity as we find it, then pursuing the different meanings the concept takes in different contexts does not dissolve its value as an ordering idea but enriches it."[1] The author strives not for abstraction that submerges differences in detail, but for a grasp of particularity that relates fruitfully to more general notions.

Though the reader will not find much mysticism in this chapter, still we will follow Clifford Geertz's suggestion. We will attempt to avoid a Procrustean method which forces specific cases to fit into an ideal type of fundamentalism. Rather we will note in some detail how the individual movements described in this study differ from each other. In the first two sections of this chapter we will analyze two fundamentalist groups, one Christian and the other Islamic. At the conclusion of the chapter we will return to the definition of fundamentalism which was presented in the introduction. The book as a whole will be marked by a similar dialectical movement from concrete to abstract in an attempt to develop a well grounded and productive understanding of fundamentalism.

CHRISTIAN FUNDAMENTALISM BOB JONES UNIVERSITY

The reader might anticipate that within the context of the discussion of Christian fundamentalism the choice of an exemplary fundamentalist movement would be a simple matter. The label "fundamentalist" has only very recently been applied to movements in other religious traditions, but it has been used in connection with Christian groups for decades. Even for Christian fundamentalism a judgment must be made in choosing a single movement, however. Christian fundamentalism is an umbrella term which covers a number of different organizations only loosely tied to each other by common ideals and united action. In fact, Christian fundamentalists sometimes disagree among themselves about the groups and individuals that may be properly characterized as fundamentalist.

In this chapter no effort will be made to include all of the North American Protestant groups who would be identified as fundamentalist by themselves or by others. Rather we will focus on one Christian fundamentalist institution, Bob Jones University. It must be acknowledged at the outset that there are some who would place Bob Jones University beyond the pale of fundamentalism. For example, Bob Jones on occasion has been labeled "ultrafundamentalist."[2] Despite these disputes, recent studies of fundamentalist institutions have testified to the important role that Bob Jones University plays in fundamentalist communities throughout the United States.[3] Bob Jones University has been one America's leading fundamentalist educational institutions for over six decades.

FUNDAMENTALISM AS REACTIONARY

Bob Jones University was founded in 1927 by Bob Jones, Sr. (1883-1968).[4] The 1920s were a crucial period in the history of American fundamentalism. At the beginning of this decade conservative Christians appeared to be on the verge of gaining control of a couple of major denominations, but their efforts were ultimately unsuccessful. At the 1922 meeting of the Northern Baptist Convention, conservatives (who by now had been dubbed fundamentalists[5]) proposed that a test of orthodoxy be adopted by the denomination. Finally a substitute resolution was passed to the effect that the Bible should be taken as the basis of the Baptist faith.[6] In the 1924 General Assembly efforts by fundamentalists to impose their brand of orthodoxy on the Presbyterian Church were referred to a committee, which determined that the General Assembly could not adopt a creed without the cooperation of local presbyteries. Since some of the local bodies were dominated by liberals, this had the effect of killing the fundamentalists' initiative.[7] Attempts to gain control of both denominations were defeated because moderates were not willing to join fundamentalists in their divisive conflict with liberals. By the end of the 1920s fundamentalists were being driven out of churches that they had so recently seemed to dominate.

The same decade saw the most widely publicized legal challenge to fundamentalist Christianity. In 1925 John Scopes, a biology teacher in Dayton, Tennessee was tried for teaching evolution in violation of a new state law. The historian George Marsden has argued that in spite of Scopes's conviction (which was later overturned on a technicality), "the Monkey Trial" dealt a serious blow to Christian fundamentalism. The fundamentalist enemies of evolution were characterized by the press as "half-educated yokels." A caricature which has perdured, in spite of the fact that it was not accurate.[8]

The events of the turbulent twenties provide the background to the founding of Bob Jones University. By 1927 Dr. Bob Jones, Sr. had been an evangelist for well over twenty years. From his home base in Montgomery, Alabama Jones traveled around the United States holding evangelistic campaigns in large cities and small towns.[9] In a pamphlet describing the impetus for founding Bob Jones University, Bob Jones, Sr. recounted what he found in his travels. "I have met many young people who went away from Christian homes to colleges and universities and came back not only with their faith shattered but sometimes with their morals wrecked."[10] Jones resolved to found an educational institution that would not produce the same dire results.

The pamphlet quoted in the last paragraph is entitled *Three College Shipwrecks* because it contains the stories of three young people whose lives were wrecked at college. One of the stories was recounted to Jones by a young man who approached him "in a northern city." The man had been very religious as a boy, but encountered derision because of this as soon as he arrived in college.

> The students flocked around me, calling to other students to come see my Bible. "We have a country boy come to town,

> and he has brought a Bible with him!"
>
> "He will get over that," someone said.
>
> "Just give him time. Let him get in biology. The biology prof will fix him. The Bible is all right for country people and for ignorant folks, but we have outgrown that."

As the young man told Jones the story, the predictions of his fellow students came true and he soon found, "I lost my faith." The destruction of this student's faith was quickly followed by the degeneration of his character. The young man told Jones, "I have been drunk for six weeks. I have gambled away the money that Mother saved. I have gone with wicked women, and my faith is all ruined."[11] In this one tale we find the "shattered" faith and the "wrecked" morals that Jones indicates that he encountered among college students all over America.

Reacting against this situation, Bob Jones University would be an institution where students would not find their faith challenged or their morals undermined. As one journalist expressed it, this college would be a place where, "The destructive cult of organic evolution that has saturated the minds of the scientific quidnuncs of the age will be rigidly tabooed and combated with Biblical weapons."[12] In addition to the supportive intellectual environment, Jones worked to create a college where high moral standards would be encouraged. "He decided, too, that the philosophy of discipline for the school would have to be established early and strictly maintained or else the school would easily drift into the current pattern of 'freedom of behavior.'"[13]

In the 1920s conservative Christians banded together into a number of different groups and institutions to combat what they perceived as the rising tide of liberalism in Christian churches and the increasing looseness of American life. Bob Jones University was one such institution. Unlike other colleges and universities, which provided an environment that was intellectually corrosive and morally lax, Bob Jones would be a place where students would be encouraged to live a moral life and to remain true to the fundamentals of the Christian faith. It is to those fundamentals that we will turn our attention in the next section.

SELECTIVE RETRIEVAL OF THE FUNDAMENTALS

The fundamentals of Christianity have been characteristically expressed by North American Protestant fundamentalists in creeds. No one formula has been accepted by all fundamentalists, rather there has been a series of redefinitions of the essential Christian doctrines. The most influential fundamentalist creed was that developed by Presbyterians. Attempts to define the essential doctrines of Presbyterian orthodoxy culminated in the endorsement of five points by the General Assembly in 1910. These doctrines were reaffirmed in 1916 and 1923, but then were abandoned as the General Assembly moved toward greater toleration later in the 1920s. "Summarized, these points were: (1) the inerrancy of Scripture, (2) the Virgin Birth of Christ, (3) his substitutionary atonement, (4) his bodily resurrection, and (5) the authenticity of miracles."[14] George Marsden notes that in the polemic literature surrounding the five points, the premillennial return of Christ was often added to or substituted for the fifth doctrine.[15] This formulation of basic doctrines was accepted by many fundamentalists, not just Presbyterians.

At the very beginning Bob Jones University developed its own version of the fundamentals of Christianity, the essential doctrines upon which there could be no compromise. Bob Jones, Sr. approached Sam Small, a journalist and conservative Christian, and asked him to write out a basic statement of faith for the college that he was about to found. Small's creed, which is a part of the Bob Jones University charter runs as follows:

> The general nature and object of the corporation shall be to conduct an institution of learning for the general education of youth in the essentials of culture and in the arts and sciences, giving special emphasis to the Christian religion and ethics revealed in the Holy Scriptures; combating all atheistic, agnostic, pagan, and so-called scientific adulterations of the Gospel; unqualifiedly affirming and teaching *the inspiration of the Bible (both the Old and New Testaments); the creation of man by the direct act of God; the incarnation and virgin birth of our Lord and Saviour, Jesus Christ; His identification as the Son of God; His vicarious atonement for the sins of mankind by the shedding of His blood on the cross; the resurrection of His body from the tomb; His power to save men from sin; the new birth through the regeneration by the Holy Spirit; and the gift of eternal life by the grace of God.*
>
> This charter shall never be amended, modified, altered, or changed

> as to the provisions hereinbefore set forth.[16]

It would be hard to overstate the importance of this creed in the life of Bob Jones University. Composed before the school first opened in 1927, there was a ceremony in which all of the faculty signed the creed. Assent to the creed is still demanded of faculty, staff, and students. And this affirmation is not expressed only once a year. The students at Bob Jones University are required to attend daily chapel services. At every service all of the students stand and recite the Bob Jones creed. This formulation of the fundamentals of Christianity is drilled into those who attend Bob Jones University.

It is interesting to compare the Bob Jones University creed with the five Presbyterian points detailed above. Although the creed does not use the word "inerrancy," the university shares with other fundamentalists an exalted view of the authority of the Bible. Bob Jones's charter does explicitly affirm the virgin birth, substitutionary atonement, and resurrection of Christ. The miracles of Jesus are not mentioned directly in the Bob Jones statement, although Bob Jones, Sr. would certainly have been willing to acknowledge that they happened just as the Bible says.

It is significant that the Bob Jones University creed does not say anything about the second coming of Christ. Scholars have disagreed in recent decades over whether a particular doctrine about the second coming should be identified as absolutely characteristic of Christian fundamentalism.[17] In a series of sermons on the Bob Jones University creed Bob Jones, Jr. (son of Bob Jones, Sr. and current chancellor of the university) said,

> With regard to the Lord's return, the position of the Administration and Bible faculty of the University is as follows: We believe that God's word clearly teaches that Jesus Christ will come for His Bride *before* the Tribulation—that the church will not go through that terrible time. We believe that the Bible teaches that the Lord will return *before* the Millennium—that He will establish his kingdom on the earth and will bring about the thousand years of peace.[18]

In other words the basic position of Bob Jones University on the second coming is consistent with the dispensational premillennial doctrine which has been characteristic of North American Protestant fundamentalism.[19] Still, Bob Jones, Jr.'s argument from which this statement was taken implies that good Christians might well disagree on details concerning the second coming. So dispensational premillennialism is not enshrined in the Bob Jones creed.

It is also worth noting that the Bob Jones University charter does not include any statement on separation. Later on in this chapter we will see that in recent decades officials of Bob Jones University have argued very strongly that one of the key characteristics of a fundamentalist is that she or he will not cooperate in evangelism with non-fundamentalists. According to Bob Jones III (the grandson of the founder of Bob Jones University and the current president of that institution), "Separation is a biblical doctrine that is found from Genesis to Revelation. It is a major, essential doctrine just like the blood atonement, the bodily resurrection, and the infallibility and inspiration of Scripture."[20] There are historical reasons why separation did not emerge as an important principle in Bob Jones University's fundamentalism until around the 1950s. On this point the creed included in the charter might well be updated, but of course that is not permitted by the terms of the charter itself.

Despite the differences in detail the Bob Jones University creed has a good deal in common with basic statements of the faith that have been developed by other Christian fundamentalist groups. The creed is a function of Bob Jones, Sr.'s attempt to define what the fundamental teachings of Christianity are, teachings which cannot be compromised under any conditions. It is a point of pride with the leaders of the Bob Jones University that these principles have not been compromised in spite of the fact that some of them are no longer in fashion in other Christian groups.

THE FUNDAMENTALS AS SCANDALOUS

It is important to realize that the doctrines which the fundamentalists chose to defend were precisely the ones that they felt were in danger of being surrendered by liberals. It was the polemic with liberal Protestants which defined the content of the fundamentals. This is as true for the creed of Bob Jones University as it was for the better known formulations of the fundamentals.

In his sermons on the university creed, Bob Jones, Jr. mentions several times the alternative understanding of the Christian faith that the creed rules out. To begin with the inspiration of the Bible. By the end of the nineteenth century liberals had begun to believe that a rather substantial reinterpretation of the Christian scripture is called for. The Bible was inspired by God, but it also reflects the limited understanding of the authors of the biblical books. Hence, the liberals reasoned, there is much that is crude in the Bible that must be reworked. Bob Jones University does not accept this position.

> It is fashionable nowadays to say, "I believe the Bible *contains* the Word of God." Beware of anyone who says that. The Bible does not merely *contain* the Word of God; it *is* the Word of God. There is a difference. To say that it contains the Word of God means that there may be parts of it that are not His Words. In such cases man sets his puny mind to decide what is and what is not truth, what is and what is not God's Word.[21]

This analysis of the Bible is not a project that Bob Jones, Jr. is willing to undertake, nor does he believe that it is called for. The liberals are wrong. The Bible does not contain any error.

A similar argument is made in *Fundamentals of Faith* for just about all of the articles of the Bob Jones University creed. The creation of man by God is maintained in opposition to evolutionary theories of human origins.[22] One might argue that the virgin birth is an unimportant feature of Christian doctrine that could easily be dispensed with, but Jones does not agree. "Some men teach that it is possible to be a Christian without believing in the virgin birth. It is not."[23] In the case of the sonship of God, Jones writes, "'Liberalism' teaches that Jesus Christ simply realized His divinity and Sonship, and that all we need to do is recognize our sonship and try to live as a child of God. That is a false doctrine."[24]

We could go on to multiply examples of the points upon which the Bob Jones University creed directly or implicitly attacks the beliefs of others, especially liberal Christians. Yet what has already been written is probably sufficient to convey to the reader the polemic nature of the fundamentals that Bob Jones University has chosen to defend. This creed serves to separate the university from liberalism. In the next section we will review dynamics that have driven a wedge between Bob Jones University and other conservative Christians.

FUNDAMENTALISM AS EXCLUSIVE OR SEPARATIST

In the beginning the fundamentalist movement was a broad coalition of conservative evangelical Christians. The unifying principle of this coalition was opposition to liberalism. With the failure of the fundamentalist bid for control of the Baptist and Presbyterian denominations in the 1920s, it became clear that some members of the coalition were not prepared to completely sever ties with liberals and moderates. From that time fundamentalists have defined themselves as those who will not cooperate with liberals, in contradistinction to conservatives who oppose liberalism but who are not prepared to bar liberals from their churches. With this self-understanding fundamentalists were driven to come out of the denominations of which they had been members. Most North American Protestant fundamentalists today can be found in independent churches that are not a part of any denomination, though they may be loosely tied to other fundamentalist institutions through larger umbrella groups.

Bob Jones University was founded as a non-denominational organization, a university to which students could come from various denominational backgrounds. Assent to certain basic Christian principles has been required (especially those expressed in the Bob Jones University creed), but this requirement has left open large areas of belief and practice in which individuals from differing denominational backgrounds might disagree. This position has been clearly expressed by Bob Jones III.

> A man who is a fair-minded Fundamentalist will allow for differences of Scriptural *interpretation* in areas that may be subject to interpretation. But there are certain basic doctrines that are not subject to interpretation. Among these are the virgin birth, the essential deity of Christ, the blood atonement, the bodily resurrection from the grave, and the verbal inspiration of Scripture. These are not optional. They are cardinal doctrines that are essential to the new birth. But there are some other things that are matters of interpretation. For example, the Baptists have one interpretation of church polity and the Presbyterians have another. A Fundamentalist will not quibble about such matters of interpretation as long as they are not doctrines that are essential to obtaining salvation.[25]

In this paragraph an administrator of Bob Jones University clearly expresses that institution's commitment to being open to fundamentalists from various denominational backgrounds.

Originally Bob Jones University was an institution committed to interdenominationalism, to drawing together people from various denominational backgrounds. As more and more fundamentalists abandoned the major evangelical denominations, with time the university came to attract an increasing number of students from independent churches.[26] Now the position of Bob Jones University might be more accurately characterized as antidenominational rather than interdenominational. Bob Jones, Jr. once wrote that, "There is not a single large, 'historic' denomination that has not gone into apostasy."[27]

The dissolution of the ties of Bob Jones University to the major denominations has not just been an accident of history, but it has also been a matter of principle. In this context 2 Corinthians 6:14 is often cited: "Be ye not unequally yoked together with unbelievers: for what fellowship hath righteousness with unrighteousness? And what communion hath light with darkness?" The purport of this verse is understood to be that Christians should not cooperate in religious activities with those who do not share the same beliefs. The word "Christian" here is being used in the narrow sense to refer to those who have taken a stand on the fundamentals. In recent decades it has been the consistent position of Bob Jones University's leaders that fundamentalists should not involve themselves in religious activities with non-fundamentalists.

This principle has served to separate those associated with Bob Jones University from denominational organizations that they perceive to be increasingly liberal. It has also resulted in division within the conservative camp as well. The doctrine of separation took on an especially great importance in the 1950s when Bob Jones, Sr. and Bob Jones, Jr. publicly condemned the evangelist Billy Graham. Early in his career Graham had maintained close ties with Bob Jones University. He actually attended the college for a few months in his youth, and he was invited back years later to accept an honorary doctorate. But then beginning in late 1950s Bob Jones began to distance itself from Graham.

It was especially the New York campaign of 1957 that elicited the criticism of Bob Jones University, because Graham was sponsored there by pastors who were not fundamental from the perspective of the university. In 1956 Ralph Mitchell, a member of Graham's staff, wrote to Bob Jones University requesting the opportunity to speak there to drum up support for the New York campaign. Bob Jones, Jr. replied in part, "It is our sincere and heartfelt conviction that what Billy is doing in seeking the sponsorship of the liberals and modernists, who repudiate the inspiration of the Scripture and the fundamentals of our faith, is contrary to the plain teaching of Scripture and unfair to the brethren who have stood for the Gospel and endured the attack of these above-mentioned liberals and modernists."[28]

This dispute over principle quickly degenerated into a series of personal attacks coming from both sides. This fusillade of mutual recrimination reached its peak in 1966 when Billy Graham conducted an evangelistic campaign in Greenville, South Carolina, the home of Bob Jones University. At that time Bob Jones, Jr. issued a public statement that concluded, "I think that Dr. Graham is doing more harm in the cause of Jesus Christ than any living man; that he is leading foolish and untaught Christians, simple people that do not know the Word of God, into disobedience to the Word of God. That is wrong, and it is doubly wicked in that he is doing it under the pretext of a soul-winning ministry."[29] A hard-hitting response to this charge came from L. Nelson Bell, Graham's father-in-law, who compared Bob Jones, Jr. to the Pharisees who opposed Jesus of Nazareth.

> Dr. Bob Jones' attack on Mr. Graham is similar to that of the Pharisees. He does not like the company Mr. Graham keeps, nor does he like Christian love being placed above hard orthodoxy. He is typical of the Pharisees of our day—legalists, who forget the greatest of all Christian virtues is love.[30]

Over and above the vitriolic tone of the exchange between Graham's supporters and his detractors, the officials of Bob Jones University have always maintained that there was an important principle at the back of their criticism of Graham: that Scripture demands separation from non-fundamentalists. "The Billy Graham issue is a spiritual issue. It deals with the compromise evangelism in which God's Bible-believing people are being led to join hands with God's enemies to put over a program that violates clear commands and principles of God's Word."[31]

More recently officials of Bob Jones University have felt compelled to speak out again on the principle of scriptural separation in condemning the Moral Majority, the conservative political coalition led by Jerry Falwell. Bob Jones III has written:

> The aim of the Moral Majority is to join together Catholics, Jews, Protestants of every stripe, Mormons, etc., in a common religious cause. Christians can fight on a battlefield alongside these people, can vote with them for a common candidate, but

> they cannot be unequally yoked with them in a religious army or organization.[32]

The stand of Bob Jones University has alienated it from some of the most popular conservative Christian individuals and movements in the past few decades. Be that as it may, Bob Jones has continued to hold to separation as a basic tenet of fundamental Christianity.

OPPOSITIONAL

North American Protestant fundamentalism was first forged in the crucible of conflict. It was opposition to liberalism that drove fundamentalists out of the major evangelical denominations. In the preceding section we saw that in the case of Bob Jones University this polemic has extended to conservatives who are not willing to separate themselves from liberals, including very popular figures like Billy Graham and Jerry Falwell. The controversial literature of the university has not been devoted solely to internecine conflict with very conservative Christians, rather it has extended to other groups as well. In this section we will talk about two of those other groups: Roman Catholics and charismatics.

Most of the literature on Roman Catholicism being produced currently by Bob Jones University Press is composed of the personal testimonies of people who have been Catholics, but who later became fundamentalists. In these autobiographies some themes recur repeatedly. The religious life of the Catholic is focused on lifeless rituals. As one former Catholic priest expressed it, "I was conducting a mechanical ministry because I had grown cold and indifferent."[33] In these testimonies this dryness is interpreted as a consequence of a theological error, a tendency to rely upon works for salvation rather than upon faith in Christ. "All the ceremonies, liturgies, and rubrics that the mind of man can devise cannot solve this problem. Only *God* can cure the universal human disease of sin, and He does it through faith, not good works."[34] Ultimately this insight was attained through searching the Bible. "The Bible must be over tradition, rather than tradition over the Bible, because the Bible was authored by God and not by the Church. Therefore papal authority and tradition must be disregarded when they contradict the teaching of Scripture."[35]

In general the witness of ex-Catholics published by Bob Jones University Press is critical of the Roman Catholic Church, but still respectful of it. In other contexts the language of Bob Jones University officials is not so temperate. Bob Jones, Jr. once wrote, "The Roman Church is not another Christian denomination. It is a satanic counterfeit, an ecclesiastic tyranny over the souls of men, not to bring them to salvation but to hold them bound in sin and to hurl them into eternal damnation. It is the old harlot of the book of Revelation—'the Mother of Harlots.'"[36] Implied in this quotation is an interpretation of the prophecies of the book of Revelation in the New Testament which speak of a great harlot. This harlot has been identified by some Protestants as a metaphor for the Roman Catholic Church. Although the language that Bob Jones, Jr. uses here is much more powerfully negative than that of the testimonies discussed in the last paragraph, the difference is more one of style than of substance. All of the authors would be willing to share in condemning the Roman Catholic Church.

An even more popular object of the controversialist literature currently published by Bob Jones University Press than the Roman Catholic church is the charismatic movement.[37] In a television address Bob Jones III advanced four arguments to prove that charismatic Christianity "is not of God:" (1) that charismatics emphasize the wrong person of the Trinity (the Holy Spirit rather than Jesus); (2) that the charismatic movement places too much emphasis on signs; (3) that the charismatic movement "minimizes the importance of the Word of God;" and (4) that charismatics tend to embrace ecumenism. This last argument ties into the criticism of Roman Catholicism that we have already discussed, since Jones objects to the prominence of Catholics in charismatic circles.[38] Ultimately Jones argues:

> In closing I ask: If Jesus Christ is not the god of the ecumenical church, the god of the charismatic movement, who is? Satan is their god. According to John 16, the Holy Spirit leads all men into all truth—the Bible. A spirit that leads men contrary to God's truth is not God's Spirit. It is not the Holy Spirit but the spirit of Satan which empowers the charismatic movement.[39]

In this quote charismatic Christianity is not just criticized as wrongheaded, rather it is condemned as demonic.

When Bob Jones University has attacked the Roman Catholic Church it has repeated themes that are as old as the Protestant Reformation. The charismatic movement, on the other hand, is a relatively new phenomenon. Undoubtedly charismatics have attracted the ire of the officials of Bob Jones University in part because charismatic preachers have in recent decades won a large following through very popular (and prosperous) television ministries. And there may be some of the internecine animus described in the last section of this study. Charismatic Christians regard their movement as biblical, and some have vociferously attacked liberals. Within this context Bob Jones may have thought it necessary to draw attention to its differences from the charismatic movement.

In this section we have focused on only two examples of the groups against which Bob Jones University has opposed itself. Many other cases might be added to this discussion. Yet perhaps these two instances are sufficient to suggest the oppositional character of the university.

ABSOLUTIST

Much has been said here already about the way that fundamentalists have separated themselves from other Christians. Implicit in this separatism is absolutism. For strict fundamentalists there is no room for cooperation with non-fundamentalists. There is not the sense that because a non-fundamentalist church is Christian—or because it is Protestant, or because it is evangelical, or even because it is conservative—it has much in common with fundamentalism. Only fundamentalists are right, all others are wrong. The fundamentalist perspective on the world is profoundly dualistic. Christians can be divided into the true and the false. There is no residual category.

The dualism between true and false Christians corresponds to a much more basic polarity between God and the devil. Consider the number of times Satan is invoked in the writings of the leaders of Bob Jones University in condemnation of their enemies. The Roman Catholic Church is characterized as "a satanic counterfeit, an ecclesiastic tyranny over the souls of men."[40] About charismatic Christians and ecumenists Bob Jones III has written that "Satan is their god."[41] In another context the same preacher warns, "Some of you attend liberal churches where the voice of antichrist, the voice of Satan, speaks to you."[42] Those who would reinterpret the creation story of the book of Genesis are harshly upbraided. "All this modernistic effort to tear out the first lines of the Bible is a satanic conspiracy to wreck the faith of men in the authority of the only Book which offers salvation to a lost world."[43] Modern translators of the Bible are not just wrong: they are demonic. "The Fundamentalist will also oppose the devilish origin and deception of paraphrases and perversions of the Holy Scriptures."[44] Quoting John 14:30 and 2 Corinthians 4:4 Bob Jones III argues, "This suggests that the Devil rules the world through wicked men, through deceivers, through such men as Hitler, Mussolini, Mao Tse-tung, Stalin, Lenin, and perhaps several presidents of our own country."[45] Even the United Nations is stigmatized as a "satanic and Communist-dominated organization."[46]

The reader of these quotes should not assume that words such as "satanic" are being used here in a metaphorical sense. Bob Jones University stands solidly behind belief in a very real devil. As Bob Jones III has written:

> In the title we asked, "Is there a literal Devil?" The answer is "Yes." The Scriptures we have presented describe the Devil's work and instruct Christians how to be successful in wrestling against him. If you accept the fact of a literal Christ Who came from Heaven's glory and took the form of man and died for the sins of mankind, you must also accept the fact of the literal Devil; for the same Bible tells about both.[47]

The author makes it clear that this devil appears not only in the world but also in churches. "It is possible that the preacher in your pulpit is an emissary of the Devil instead of a servant of the Lord."[48] How can a person discern if the pastor upon whom she or he relies is a man of God?

> Certain questions can be asked and the true character of "the angel" manifests itself. "What do you think of Jesus Christ? Was He virgin-born? Was He God incarnate? Did He die a vicarious, substitutional death on the cross? Did He rise again from the dead? Is it necessary to be born again in order to be saved? Is the Bible the inspired Word of God?"[49]

These questions are a shibboleth that can be used to divide the divine from the demonic.

It is no coincidence that the test for the discernment of spirits involves several of the principles included in the Bob Jones University creed. The leaders of the university do not just separate themselves from a wicked world, but also from false churches. In the end it is only those who cleave very closely to the planks of the Bob Jones creed who will be accorded the status of true Christians. The truth is not ambiguous; it is clearly expressed in the creed. Those who accept it are on God's side; those who reject it belong to the devil. It is hard to imagine a stance more absolutist than that.

AUTHORITATIVENESS OR AUTHORITARIANISM IN FUNDAMENTALISM

North American Protestant fundamentalism has been characterized by a struggle for authority on at least two levels. First and foremost fundamentalists ground their selective retrieval of the Christian fundamentals upon the authority of the Bible. On another level this retrieval of biblical Christianity has depended upon the preaching of evangelists who have often been quite authoritarian in the way that they direct their churches. Within the context of Bob Jones University, let us begin with the authority of the Bible and then turn our attention to the leadership of Bob Jones, Sr. and his descendants.

The first element of the Bob Jones creed is "*the inspiration of the Bible (both the Old and the New Testaments).*"[50] Bob Jones, Jr. has explained that the priority of this principle is not a matter of coincidence. "The opening statement, *I believe in the inspiration of the Bible, both the Old and New Testaments*, is all-important; indeed, upon its truth depends the truth of all the other statements. . . . Undermine faith in its infallibility, its authority, and its divine inspiration, and the whole house will crumble, because His Word is the foundation upon which all rests."[51] Here the Bible is understood to be the basis upon which Bob Jones University stands.

In this same sermon on the Bob Jones creed Jones went on to describe in more technical terms exactly what is meant by "the inspiration of the Bible."

> Our belief in this doctrine goes still deeper: we believe in the *plenary* or full inspiration of the Word; i.e., that the book—all of it—is equally and fully inspired. Moreover, we subscribe to the *verbal* inspiration of Scripture, which is to say that in the original Hebrew manuscripts which the Old Testament writers wrote, and in the original Greek manuscripts which the New Testament writers wrote, God Himself chose the *very word* that should be put down to convey exactly what He meant to convey. This precludes any possibility of human personality intruding upon and interfering with what God had to say.[52]

Jones goes on to explain that this does not mean that the university holds to a dictation theory, that God made the authors of the biblical books "a typewriter upon which His fingers played."[53] Rather each man was allowed to express the revelation that he received from God in language that was natural to himself. And yet God led those that he inspired to the "right word and illustration so that His truth might be preserved in the writing."[54]

Scholars at Bob Jones University admit that the inspiration of the Bible only extends to the original manuscripts and not to English translations.[55] But doubts about translation should not divert the average Christian from faith in the Bible. Bob Jones III has written:

> When we say the Bible is without error, we are referring to the original manuscripts—the Greek, Hebrew, and Aramaic manuscripts—not the various translations of the Bible. Copyists make errors. But God-fearing scholars have brought translations to a high state of accuracy, so that the form in which we have the Bible today is substantially identical with the original manuscripts.[56]

This does not mean that every translation is equally accurate. On the contrary, Bob Jones University has openly condemned translations produced by scholars who were not conservative Christians. "I refer to *Good News for Modern Man*, *The Living Bible*, *The Revised Standard Version of the Bible*, and *The New English Bible*; these are not translations of the Hebrew and Greek, but perversions that would water down the gospel and rob God's Holy Word of its fundamental truths."[57] In general in its chapel services and in its publications Bob Jones University uses the King James Version of the Bible.

For the reader who is not familiar with debates over the authority of the Bible some of the preceding discussion may seem to be scholastic, but that is certainly not the perspective of Bob Jones University. In a world full of uncertainty the Bible is the solid rock upon which Christians can stand, and any doubts about its inspiration, even in the smallest detail, threaten to undermine that rock. As Bob Jones III has argued:

> The Bible is in contrast to the uncertainty of all ordinary books. If it is not without error, this book must be classified with every other book in the world. If it is not *all* true, what part of it is true and what part is false? Are you willing to make that judgement?

> Is it ninety percent true and ten percent false?. . . If you are not willing to take all of the Bible as His Word, you must decide which part is true and which is false. That makes you the judge of the book which claims to judge you. This book then becomes subordinated to the standard against which its truth is measured. If the Bible is what it claims to be, it must be all true and therefore all trustworthy.[58]

The Christian must accept the absolute authority of the whole Bible or else face an ambiguity which Jones clearly regards as unbearable.

The inspiration of the Bible is not just a matter of narrow religious dogma at Bob Jones University, rather it is a living reality that pervades all areas of life. The publications of Bob Jones University Press give some idea of the breadth of contexts in which the Bible might be used. For example, science is not beyond the reach of the scriptures. In biology[59] and geology[60] the evidence of the Bible is worthy of consideration. Ammunition from the Bible is used in pamphlets condemning morally degrading television[61] and homosexuality.[62] The frequent quotation of the Bible in just about all of the publications put out by Bob Jones University is an indication of the pervasive effort to interpret every area of life in terms of the Bible.

The people who have been responsible for discerning how the Bible relates to practical problems at Bob Jones University have been its officials, especially Bob Jones, Sr., Bob Jones, Jr., and Bob Jones III. One of the striking facts of the history of this university is that the leadership has remained in the hands of one family. Bob Jones, Sr. was the founder of the university and its first president. Very soon after graduating from Bob Jones University with a B.A. Bob Jones, Jr. (born in 1911) began his administrative career at the university with an appointment as vice president in 1931. In 1947 Bob Jones, Sr. resigned as president of the university, but stayed on as chairman of the board of trustees. Bob Jones, Jr. was appointed president in his father's stead. Bob Jones III (born in 1939) received a B.A. from Bob Jones University in 1959 and an M.A. in 1961. In 1964 Bob Jones, Sr. resigned as chairman of the board of trustees of the university. Bob Jones, Jr. took over the chairman's office and remained president of the university. In the same year, after serving in other capacities, Bob Jones III was appointed vice president of the university. In 1971 the new post of chancellor was created which Bob Jones, Jr. occupied. Bob Jones III took over as president of the university. Bob Jones, Jr. remains chairman of the board of trustees and chancellor of Bob Jones University up to the present. Bob Jones III is still the president of the university.

Despite his death on 16 January 1968, Bob Jones, Sr. is still a commanding presence at Bob Jones University. An extensive body of material that could almost be described as hagiographical has grown up around him. This is perhaps most clearly evidenced by the relish with which the productions of the university recount stories of the founder's humble beginnings in a poor farm family.[63] Bob Jones, Sr.'s sermons were punctuated by phrases which he enjoined his audience to remember such as, "*For a Christian, life is not divided into the secular and the sacred. To him all ground is holy ground, every bush a burning bush, and every place a temple of worship.*"[64] Some of these sayings are inscribed on the walls of Bob Jones University. And they pepper the conversation of Bob Jones officials.[65] Finally it must be said that Bob Jones, Sr. is still physically present on the campus of the university that he founded. In the middle of the fountain in front of Rodeheaver Auditorium at Bob Jones University is an island which contains the graves of Bob Jones, Sr. and his wife.

Despite the imposing presence of Bob Jones, Sr., his son, and grandson which looms over Bob Jones University, other officials there maintain that none of these individuals is (or was) particularly authoritarian when it comes to his managerial style.[66] Yet it is important to realize that these are officials who have come to share in the vision of the Jones family for how Bob Jones University should develop. Within this context it is significant that a substantial proportion of the administrators at Bob Jones attended the university at some point during their career as students.[67] In their education these individuals began to conform themselves to the rules by which Bob Jones University is run, including respect for the authority of superiors.[68]

There is one question which this section seems to pose, but which has not been answered. What is the relationship of the authority of the Bible and the authority that has been exercised by the leaders of Bob Jones University, especially the Jones family? The literature that is published by the university does not make any claim to a special status for Bob Jones, Sr. or his descendants. It does not say that the Joneses have been inspired by God to lead a new religious movement. Rather Bob Jones University has always maintained that it is simply attempting to live up to the standard established by the Bible. The authority of the Bible is self-consciously embraced. The authority of the Jones family is played down in favor of the authority of the Bible.

FUNDAMENTALISM AS ANTIEVOLUTIONARY

Opposition to the teaching of Darwinian evolution was one of the distinctive positions of Bob Jones University at its founding, and it remains the official policy of the university up to the present. In recent decades Bob Jones University has worked to clearly articulate its views on evolution and other matters of science in connection with the growing Christian school movement. Beginning in the 1970s more and more fundamentalist Christians have become discontented with public school systems around the United States. Many parents have felt compelled to take their children out of those schools in favor of an environment more consistent with their religious beliefs. This trend has led to a dramatic increase in the number of schools run by and for fundamentalist Christians. Bob Jones University has been at the forefront of this movement, not only training educators for Christian schools but also trying to work out what those schools should be like.

Consistent with this general effort Bob Jones University has published several pamphlets expressing what the Christian philosophy should be in teaching in a number of different subjects. *The Christian Teaching of Science* presents the university's stand on evolution and in other areas as well. The pamphlet begins by emphasizing the importance of the Bible in all areas of human experience.

> The Christian teaching of science requires not only a good command of basic subject matter, but also the spiritual perception to discern truth from error in a great variety of contexts. As a prerequisite for this, the Christian teacher of science must be thoroughly grounded in the Word of God. Moreover, he must have firmly implanted in his mind a biblical framework of truth which serves as the touchstone for decision making. True science will fit that framework; anything that fails to fit the biblical framework must be rejected as erroneous.[69]

It is the Bible which must be used as the standard of truth. Any scientific theory which fails to measure up to that standard "must be rejected as erroneous."

The Christian Teaching of Science goes to great lengths to emphasize the limitations of science.[70] Many people in America believe that "science potentially holds the answer to every human problem."[71] Students develop an undue reverence for scientists. "This is most unfortunate, for the public statements of the typical unregenerate scientist are often arrogantly evolutionary and anti-God in their tenor."[72] The science teacher in the Christian school must work to disabuse students of their naive faith in the power of science.

In dealing with evolution specifically *The Christian Teaching of Science* rejects the theory.

> We live in an evolution-crazed world. We are told that everything we see—stars, galaxies, planets, and living organisms, including man himself—has evolved spontaneously out of primordial self-existent matter, is still evolving, and will continue to evolve in the future. This in essence is the view called atheistic evolution. Such fanciful theorizing is both unscriptural and unscientific.[73]

The text goes on to quote several passages from the Bible which state or imply that God created human beings (Genesis 2:7 and 22, Matthew 19:4, Mark 10:6, 1 Corinthians 15:45, 2 Corinthians 11:3, and 1 Timothy 2:13). *The Christian Teaching of Science* argues not only that evolutionary theory is "unscriptural" but also that it is "unscientific," maintaining that "From a scientific standpoint, evolution is at best an unsupportable and unworkable hypothesis, at worst a reprehensible lie that has misdirected the thrust of both theoretical and experimental science for over a century."[74] The pamphlet goes on to state that there is evidence from genetics, thermodynamics, and paleontology that disproves evolutionary theory. So evolution is rejected not only on religious but on scientific grounds as well.[75]

In its materials for Christian schools Bob Jones University has not limited itself to basic statements of philosophy, rather it has gone on to publish a number of textbooks as well. *Biology for Christian Schools* is Bob Jones University Press's basic high school biology textbook. In this work many of the themes of *The Christian Teaching of Science* are repeated. The section on "Theories of Evolution" begins by saying, "Christians who believe that the Bible is the inspired Word of God need not wonder about the beginning of life. The beginning of the physical universe is clearly outlined in Genesis 1 and 2."[76]*Biology for Christian Schools* argues that behind the theory of biological evolution there is a philosophy of evolution which begins with the assumption that there is no God and culminates in the conclusion that "There can be no moral code except that which man sets up and agrees to follow."[77] As an alternative to this atheistic and humanistic philosophy this text offers biblical creationism, the view that scientific evidence supports the biblical account of the creation of the world by God.

From the evidence presented in this section we can see that Bob Jones University has been implacably opposed to the biological theory of the evolution of life. In recent decades this opposition has been expressed in support for an alternative theory of the origin of species (creationism) in alternative, Christian schools. In spite of the wide diffusion of evolutionary theory in biology and in other areas of the thought in the United States over the past century, the fundamentalists of Bob Jones University are not on the defensive. Rather they continue to actively combat evolution not only in the university but wherever the voice of Bob Jones University is heard.

ANTIPERMISSIVE

Bob Jones University was founded not only with an intellectual agenda that included opposition to Darwinian evolution, but with a moral agenda as well. At the time of the founding of the university over a half a century ago fundamentalism was a powerful force in American life, urging the United States to return from wickedness to morality. As an evangelist Bob Jones, Sr. would often attack immorality in his sermons, singling out liquor and loose women as special objects of condemnation.[78] When Jones created Bob Jones University he built into it a high standard of morality. It is in the rules by which its students must live that the antipermissive character of Bob Jones University is clearly expressed.

Outside observers have often remarked on the very strict rules that govern student life at Bob Jones University.[79] For instance, unchaperoned dating is not permitted at the university.[80] Students may date on campus chiefly in dating parlors: large rooms filled with sofas through which chaperones circulate. Young men and women can only date off campus if accompanied by an escort, usually in organized dating outings. Bob Jones University punishes infractions of these rules and many others with a system of demerits. "One hundred demerits restrict a student to campus, and 150 demerits automatically expel a student."[81]

According to published reports the disciplinary system covers not only dating, but many different aspects of a student's life.[82] All single students who are under twenty-three years old must reside on campus, unless they live with close relatives in the Greenville area.[83] Because Bob Jones University believes that much of what is broadcast on television is not edifying, television sets are not permitted in dormitory rooms.[84] Students may have radios, but they not permitted to listen to rock and roll or country and western music, or even Gospel music in rock or country style. They may tune into classical, light classical, and easy listening music.[85] Bob Jones University has one radio station exclusively for the campus that is wired into the dormitories, and another station (WMUU-FM) that broadcasts over the air waves. The rules at Bob Jones cover not only what a student may watch and listen to, but also how a student may look. Men must have hair that does not extend over the collar, and beards and mustaches are not allowed. Women must wear skirts or dresses that cover the knee (slacks are not permitted), and hose are mandatory. Men must sport shirts and ties until after lunch.[86] The disciplinary system at Bob Jones University even extends to punctuality, with students receiving demerits for being late to class or for cutting classes.[87]

Officials at Bob Jones University maintain that the point of the system of student discipline is not simply to penalize miscreants, but to encourage all students to live a life in accord with the Bible. The university works hard to convince students to willingly embrace the morality reflected in the rules. Students must attend chapel services not only on Sunday, but Monday through Friday as well. There are also nightly prayer meetings in the dormitories which all residents must take part in. The university places in every dorm room a person of proven spiritual maturity (usually an upperclass man or woman). There are hall leaders paid by the university, who conduct the dormitory prayer meetings, and who are responsible for general order in their section of the dorm. Over the hall leaders is the resident supervisor. Assisting the resident supervisor in every dormitory is a resident counsellor, who works with students who have discipline problems or other emotional concerns. There is an elaborate hierarchy at Bob Jones University devoted to persuading every student to accept the university's moral code.[88]

In articles about Bob Jones University this code of conduct is sometimes described in strongly negative terms. "It's like being in jail," according to one disaffected Bob Jones graduate.[89] But that does not seem to be the experience of most of the students at the university. According to another reporter the majority of the young people at Bob Jones University are glad to be able to live apart from an immoral world. "I already know the world is wicked and no good. . . . I've seen what it does to people, how they're always unhappy, always unsatisfied, always searching. To go out and get drunk and come back all bombed out, what's so appealing about that?"[90] In a world that is seen as all too permissive Bob Jones University is a bastion of moral decency.

ANTIHERMENEUTICAL

North American Protestant fundamentalism arose at a time when scholars were starting to rethink the Bible. In the early decades of this century the higher criticism that had become dominant at some universities in Germany was just beginning to make inroads in the United States. Following the higher critics students of the Bible were breaking down the biblical books and reorganizing them in order to more clearly sketch the outlines of the history of the ancient Israelites. Fundamentalists rejected this analysis in favor of a simple common sense faith in a literal reading of the Bible.[91]

In the publications of Bob Jones University there are no long, abstruse discussions which outline the Bob Jones method for interpreting the Bible. The university's leaders do not recognize the need for any hermeneutical theory, because they believe that they are merely bringing out the plain sense of the text. As an example of this argument let us look at one sermon that was preached by Bob Jones, Sr. on 26 October 1952. This is a sermon that concerns the second coming of Christ.

Jones admits in his remarks that there are some liberal Christians who have argued that the images of the second coming contained within the Bible must be reinterpreted. Surely we cannot expect to see Jesus riding down from heaven on the clouds, the liberals argue. What this crude image portends, according to the liberals, is that good will win out over evil in the long run. Yet this will be accomplished not by Christ's literal return, but by the growing influence of Christian principles around the world. Bob Jones was not willing to accept the liberal reinterpretation of the second coming of Christ. "You know, come to some of our liberal thinkers today, every time you mention something like this, 'Why,' they say, 'Jesus is coming all the time. It's figurative.' It isn't figurative. It's literal. He came literally." In fact, Jones implies that these liberal thinkers are motivated by bad faith. "Let's just think clearly about this thing. Let's don't listen to these men that say what they want to say to express their own lack of faith in the absolute authority of the Bible."[92]

As alternative to the liberal method of reading the Bible figuratively, Bob Jones, Sr. embraces a solid literalism.

In studying the Word of God keep this in mind now. If you don't

> know a thing couldn't be literal [rather, if you do know a thing could not be literal], make it figurative. Somebody said one time, 'What about the earth where it says, "The hills clapped their hands"?' Well, you know that's poetic. The hills have no hands to clap. That's a poetic expression. But unless you know a thing could not be literal—then it's figurative, alright—but when it can be literal in the Bible, it's literal. Let's remember that.[93]

Some might object that this just sounds too easy. Are there no passages where it is hard to tell whether the Bible is being literal or not? Are there no passages that are ambiguous? In another context the founder of Bob Jones University admitted very readily that some things in the Bible are difficult. "There are many things in the Bible that I cannot understand either. There are things that are too deep, too high, and too broad for me." But then Jones goes on to maintain that these dense passages do not affect the essential outlines of human salvation. "It is a blessed thought that everything that I really need to know is made plain in the Bible. The plan of salvation is clear."[94] And Jones affirms the same principle in his sermon on the second coming. "Now, you know people talk about obscurity in the Bible. There is no obscurity about that. That's as simple as language can put it. And the great fundamental truths in the Bible are always clothed in simplicity."[95]

A liberal might still be left unsatisfied by this argument. After all some Christians might regard the idea of Jesus returning to the earth upon the clouds as just as absurd as the notion that mountains can clap. But Bob Jones, Sr. does not detain himself with these subtleties. The significance of repairing to a literal reading of the Bible is that it obviates the necessity of engaging in wrangles over just what it is that the text means. If the principles of biblical Christianity are debatable, then the fundamentalist faith is not grounded upon an unimpeachable authority. In the writings by the leaders of Bob Jones University that possibility is not entertained.

FUNDAMENTALISTS AS AGENTS IN HISTORY

From published statements it is clear that the leaders of Bob Jones University have always believed that their institution has a role to play that has been assigned to it by God. Bob Jones, Jr. once wrote:

> As I am writing this during the fifty-eighth anniversary year of

> Bob Jones University, I know beyond the shadow of a doubt that God has raised up this institution for this day. The saints of God in hard places around the world, the lonely, faithful, and obedient Christians everywhere are turning to Bob Jones University for encouragement, for the clarification of scriptural principles, and for advice and counsel.[96]

Bob Jones University was "raised up" by God with a mission to support fundamental Christians around the world. Although the university vigorously prosecutes this mission, university officials have only modest hopes for what they can accomplish in drawing converts to the cause of Christ. "There is not going to be any national or world-wide revival before the Lord comes back. He asks if, when He returns, He shall find faith in the earth, the implication being that there will be very little."[97] According to the interpretation of the Bible of the leaders of Bob Jones University, the saved will always be few in number.

The university was forced to articulate this belief against the background of the rise of the Moral Majority in the late 1970s and the early 1980s. Jerry Falwell, the most prominent leader of the New Christian Right, maintained that America was on the verge of a great revival. Officials of Bob Jones University interpret the situation very differently. "Jerry Falwell said, 'When you see 30 per cent of the people of America claiming to be born again, we're on the way to revival.' My friend, I told you here at chapel. There's not 3.5 per cent of the people in America that are really born again. God tells you that. 'The way is narrow, the gate is straight, few there be that walk therein.'"[98] In the analysis of Bob Jones, Jr. the United States is not on the verge of a revival of Christianity but of condemnation. "We are not in the midst of a revival in America. We are in the midst of apostasy, and the two cannot occur at the same time. A study of the Old Testament will reveal that God always sent judgment upon apostasy, and God is going to send judgment upon America because of the apostasy of our day."[99] Bob Jones University refused to jump onto Jerry Falwell's bandwagon not only because Falwell allied himself with people who are not fundamental Christians, but also because Falwell touted a coming revival that the people at Bob Jones did not anticipate.

This does not mean that officials at Bob Jones University have always held themselves aloof from politics. Bob Jones, Sr. would frequently condemn the political bosses of a town in which he held a campaign, particularly if he had reason to believe that they had connections with the liquor trade. In the decades since the general rule that conservative Christians tend to support conservative politicians ordinarily has been applicable to those associated with Bob Jones University. In the 1950s the university backed the radical Christian separatist and notorious anticommunist Carl McIntire. Magazine articles in the 1960s highlight Bob Jones's support of the presidential candidacy of the conservative Barry Goldwater.[100] Bob Jones University has also helped conservatives in local elections in South Carolina.[101] Still, the emphasis at the university has been on winning souls, not winning elections.

> Biblical Fundamentalists recognize the importance of the voting booth, but we stress the necessity of the prayer closet. We believe in taking vigorous political action and speaking out on everything that concerns the welfare and freedom of America, but we major in the preaching of the gospel and the proclamation of God's Word. We repudiate the idea that moral reform will produce revival but recognize that sin, immorality, and crime will bring God's judgment upon our country.[102]

As an agent of God in history Bob Jones University is in a paradoxical position. The university must take a stand for fundamental Christianity and try to build up the church of true Christians. And yet the leaders of Bob Jones believe that this battle is necessarily going to be a loosing one, since the Bible asserts that in any generation God's people will be few. In the end the fundamentalists of Bob Jones University remain confident that God will vindicate their stubborn refusal to compromise. It is to that end, the end of history, that we will now turn our attention.

FUNDAMENTALISM AS TELEOLOGICAL

Scholars have argued that it is in prophecy conferences of the late nineteenth century that the roots of fundamentalism can be found.[103] Other historians have maintained that these conferences were only one of the streams that fed fundamentalism at its origins.[104] Certainly interpretation of biblical prophecy, especially prophecies that have to do with the end of time, was one of the chief concerns of conservative Christians in the latter half of the last century. Back of this concern was a widely held conviction that we are living near the end of the drama of human history. Most fundamentalists have resisted the temptation to try to fix precisely when the world will end. This is partially because of the embarrassment of figures such as the Adventist William Miller, with whose prediction of the second coming in 1844 God did not cooperate.[105] And yet a concern with the end times remains a characteristic concern of fundamentalist Christianity, and this is also true for Bob Jones University.

In a sermon preached on 16 April 1985 Bob Jones, Jr. identified the events that will come to pass at the end of time. This will be a drama in two acts. In the first act Christians both living and dead will be taken up into the air to meet with the returning Christ. This is known as the rapture. Following this will be the seven-year reign of the antichrist upon the earth. This will culminate with Christ returning to earth, defeating the forces of the antichrist in the battle of Armageddon, which is the second act of the drama of the end of history. When Christ has defeated evil there will be a millennium of his just reign upon the earth, after which the world will be destroyed.[106]

There are several points in this description of the end of time that are significant. First the officials of Bob Jones University have always been premillennialists. Some liberal Christians near the end of the nineteenth century argued that Christ's second coming would only come at the end of a thousand-year period of justice and peace. Some even argued that this millennium has already begun. Premillennialists believe that Christ's return will come before the millennium. It is not through some gradual transition that the age of righteousness will begin, but through the cataclysmic return of Christ.

Secondly, the leaders of Bob Jones University have always maintained that these events will take place even as they are described in the Bible. Liberal Christians have reinterpreted the image of the second coming of Christ as it is described in the scriptures. Perhaps the things described there will not happen with the literal return of Jesus, but rather with the gradual spread of Christian teaching throughout the world. That is not how the problem is understood by the people at Bob Jones University. As the founder of the university once said, "He's coming back personally, literally, bodily, visibly."[107]

The reader should not read this concern about the second coming as a scholastic debate over obscure predictions in the Bible. Rather the leaders of Bob Jones University are concerned with earth shattering events that they understand to be imminent. Listen to the words of Bob Jones, Sr.:

> As I went around the world, wherever I went I found just one thing and that is that people under all flags are looking for something to get hold of quickly to save them from the crash of civilization and the crumbling of empires. Wherever I went if you tell them that Jesus died for them, it looks to me like God Almighty is in a hurry now to gather them for the glorious day of the consummation of all things when Jesus comes again.[108]

This does not mean that Christians can fix the date of when the final drama of history will begin, because the Bible does not allow that. "Now these disciples were like lots of people today. They were so eager to know when it was going to be. And He said, 'It's not for you to know the times and the seasons.'"[109] Still, there are some signs that we are near the end.

For Christians past history, especially the history recounted in the Bible, is not a meaningless jumble of facts but a record of how God has dealt with human beings. In the same way, the future can only be understood as the time when Jesus will save those who have been faithful to him. In the first act of this final drama Christians will go up to meet Jesus in the air in the rapture. By doing this they will escape the terrible suffering that is to befall the world during the reign of the antichrist. And those associated with Bob Jones University count themselves among those who will be so saved.

ISLAMIC FUNDAMENTALISM THE JAMA'AT-I ISLAMI

In the last section we analyzed one North American Protestant fundamentalist institution with the aid of Martin Marty's definition. Now we turn to one example of Islamic fundamentalism, the Jama'at-i Islami.

There are several different groups in varied cultures in the Muslim world which have been dubbed fundamentalist, groups with diverse characteristics. In this section we have decided to focus on only one example, on the assumption that a general survey of all the Islamic fundamentalist movements would be less helpful than a more detailed examination of just one. The Jama'at-i Islami has been identified as a fundamentalist movement by scholars.[110] The Jama'at's formula for the revitalization of Islam has had an impact on other Muslim radical groups.[111] So it is appropriate to take it as our Islamic case.

FUNDAMENTALISM AS REACTIONARY

The Jama'at-i Islami arose in reaction to the growing popularity of Western ideals in the Muslim community in South Asia especially in political life. In the absence of an effective response by traditional religious leaders to the challenge of Westernizing Muslims, the Jama'at emerged to defend a specifically Islamic politics. The Jama'at-i Islami ("Islamic Society") was founded on 26 August 1941 in Lahore at a meeting called by Maulana S. Abu'l-A'la Maududi. Maududi (1903-1979) was a Muslim publicist who had attracted a large following through his journal *Tarjuman al-Qur'an* ("Interpreter of the Qur'an"). He had been critical of the political parties who claimed to represent Muslims, and he announced this meeting to establish an organization that would work towards a truly Islamic state.

According to Maududi what makes an Islamic state distinctive is that it affirms the sovereignty of Allah over humans. By way of contrast, in democracy, for example, sovereignty is said to vest in the people, but in Islam it is reserved for Allah. Having admitted Allah's sovereignty, it naturally follows that his dictates must govern all aspects of life. Allah has revealed his commands to humans in the Qur'an and the Sunna of the Prophet Muhammad. "So long as we claim to believe in Islam and to accept it as our way of life, our System of Government should be essentially based on the fundamentals prescribed by the Qur'an and by the Holy Prophet Muhammad (blessings of Allah be with him for all times to come)."[112] It is these prescriptions as codified in the Shari'a which must be the basis of the laws of the Islamic state.

Before independence on the basis of his Islamic ideology Maududi was critical of the British rulers of India, because their state was based on the sovereignty of the crown and not of Allah. The Maulana also rejected the secular nationalism of the Indian National Congress. Maududi's harshest criticism was reserved for the Muslim nationalism of the Muslim League.

> Being a Muslim I am not at all interested that Muslim governments are formed in areas where Muslims are in a majority. For me the most important question is whether in your Pakistan the system of government will be based on the Sovereignty of God or on popular sovereignty based on western democratic theories. In the case of the former it will certainly be Pakistan otherwise it will be as 'na-Pakistan' (unholy land) as the other areas where according to your scheme, non-Muslims will rule. But in the eyes of God it will be much more reprehensible and unholy than even that. Muslim nationalism is as reprehensible in the Shariah of God as Indian nationalism.[113]

Even if the Muslim League was ready to adopt the Islamic ideology, its Westernized leaders, unacquainted with the Islamic sciences, would not be in a position put it into practice.[114]

On the other extreme Maulana Maududi also attacked the ulama, the traditional religious scholars. Busy with narrow sectarian disputes, the ulama were ineffective in public life. They were not open-minded enough to see the relevance of Islam to contemporary political debates.[115] Most of the ulama would not be able to contribute to the drafting of an Islamic constitution, for example, because they would not be able to get beyond the details of the Shari'a to consider the basic principles of Islamic law.[116] The Jama'at-i Islami had to advocate the Islamic ideology in public life, because the ulama, who were supposed to be the representatives of Islam, failed to do so.

Despite the opposition of the Jama'at-i Islami, the Muslim League did succeed in winning a Muslim state in the Indian subcontinent in 1947. This did not shake the basic commitment of the Jama'at. Rather the organization turned to advocating the Islamization of the state of Pakistan through the constitution. In an early statement Maududi demanded that the constitution declare:

> (i) That the severeignty [*sic*] in Pakistan belongs to God Almighty alone and that the Government of Pakistan shall administer the country as His agent;
>
> (ii) That the basic law of the land is the Islamic Shari'ah which has come to us through our Prophet Muhammad (peace be

on him).

(iii) That all those existing laws which may be in conflict with the Shari'ah shall in due course be repealed or brought into conformity with the basic law and no law which may be in any way repugnant to the Shari'ah shall be enacted in future.

(iv) That the State, in exercising its powers, shall not be competent to transgress the limits laid down by Islam.[117]

These are the principles for which the Jama'at-i Islami would fight for the next few decades, fielding candidates for election to advance its cause.[118] Although the formulation of the demands would change from time to time in the future, the substance would remain the same.

So the Jama'at-i Islami was reactionary. It was first and foremost a reaction against the spread of Western political ideals in the Muslim community especially under the aegis of the Muslim League.[119] At the same time it criticized the ulama, the religious scholars who were not meeting the challenge of Western ideals.

SELECTIVE RETRIEVAL OF THE FUNDAMENTALS

Since the Jama'at-i Islami is primarily a political movement, it is appropriate to begin here with its retrieval of Islamic law. Maududi's most radical and insistent demand is that the Shari'a, the traditional law of Islam, be taken as a basis for legislation. This is not to say that the Maulana did not recognize that some adjustment in Shari'a would be necessary for the modern Islamic state. Maududi's discussion of how the Shari'a might be applied in the modern period gives us an insight into the logic behind his call for the reimposition of the Shari'a.

In *The Islamic Law and Constitution* Maulana Maududi identifies four sources for developing an Islamic constitution under modern conditions : the Qur'an, the Sunna (the traditions about the sayings and deeds of the Prophet Muhammad), the conventions of the rightly guided caliphs (the *Khilafat-e-Rashidah*), and the rulings of great jurists of the past. A traditional qadi might identify the same sources for the Shari'a as it currently exists, but this is not what Maududi has in mind. The ulama generally regard the decisions of past jurists to be comprehensive, so that independent legal reasoning, or *ijtihad*, is no longer appropriate. Maududi wanted to throw open the gate of *ijtihad*, arguing that original thinking is necessary if Islam is to deal effectively with the modern world.

The basis for this new legal reasoning will be overwhelmingly the Qur'an and the Sunna. The Maulana writes that "the only Source of guidance and inspiration for an ideological movement for the renaissance of Islam in this age are the Book of Allah and the *Sunnah* of His Prophet."[120] Maududi looks basically to the early Islamic community for the model for his Islamic state. "In effect, he is asking for an intellectual short-circuit of the entire course of Islamic history from the death of the prophet's fourth successor to the present."[121] Maududi aspires to reconstruct the political system of the early years of Islam.

The fundamental demand that Maududi makes is for reimposition of the Shari'a. Ultimately the hope behind this demand is that the political life of the early Islamic community might be reproduced. Of course the period of Muhammad and the rightly guided caliphs is an ideal one for all Sunni Muslims. The retrieval of the Shari'a as a return to the golden age of the prophet had a great appeal for the Maulana's audience.

THE FUNDAMENTALS AS SCANDALOUS

The very notion that the Shari'a might be made the basis of the government of a nation-state is scandalous to many Muslims in the modern world. How could such an antiquated system be reimposed? Certain provisions of the Shari'a, which Muslim modernists regard as particularly odious, are cited by them as the proof that Islamic law is worthless. Maududi embraces even these parts of the Shari'a. He passionately defends purdah, the restrictive rules of movement and dress for women. Similarly Maududi refuses to abandon jihad, or holy war. And he insists that the Qur'an does allow polygamy.

Maududi admits that some of the punishments mandated in Shari'a might appear barbaric when taken out of the context of the whole of Islamic law. When the Islamic social system is fully realized, however, they are not so extreme. For example, cutting off the hand of a thief seems like strong medicine. But Maulana Maududi's vision of the ideal society includes a network of charity which would guarantee freedom from want. With poverty eliminated as an extenuating circumstance, stealing should be punished more vigorously, making mutilation a reasonable sentence, or so the Maulana argues.[122] Maududi defended whipping and stoning as punishments for fornication and adultery by much the same logic.

Muslim modernists tend to embrace the secularist ideal of a state in which every citizen enjoys equal rights regardless of religious affiliation. Instances of tolerance toward minorities in Islamic history are highlighted; provisions in the Shari'a which mandate special restrictions on non-Muslims are de-emphasized. Maududi is not prepared to give up the special rules for minorities (or dhimmis) in the Shari'a. Where the rights of dhimmis are restricted, this is wholly appropriate. For example, dhimmis are not allowed to hold some political posts in the Islamic state. Since the dhimmis do not share the Islamic ideology, they cannot be trusted to be in charge of implementing it.[123]

Muslim modernists have come to reject the limitations placed by the Shari'a on lending money at interest as a hindrance to economic development. Maududi does not agree that the provisions of the Shari'a should be abrogated in line with modern economic practices, and he holds that earning interest should still be forbidden.[124]

Beyond embracing the scandalous notion that the Shari'a could be made the basis of the law of a modern nation, Maulana Maududi defends just those provisions of the Shari'a that were a source of deep embarrassment to Muslim modernists. Clearly if some adjustments are to be made in the Shari'a in Maududi's system, they will not be in the direction of making the law more palatable to Westernized Muslims.

FUNDAMENTALISM AS EXCLUSIVE OR SEPARATIST

The position of the Jama'at-i Islami is ambiguous with respect to separatism. On the one hand the movement has been careful to define who its members are, and to draw them away from commitments other than to the Jama'at. On the other hand the Jama'at-i Islami has been willing to endorse constitutions which are in conflict with its ideology, and it was quick to join with other groups in temporary political coalitions in order to accomplish some limited end.

The compromises of the Jama'at-i Islami in the very long and tortuous process of framing a constitution for Pakistan are most striking. The Jama'at-i Islami, in the organization's original constitution, forbids its members from working for a government which does not acknowledge the sovereignty of Allah. Though Pakistan has never accepted the full Islamic ideology, still the Jama'at has generally been willing to admit that it is an Islamic state within which its members can work. The breakthrough in this area came with the passage of the Objectives Resolution by the Constituent Assembly of Pakistan in 1949, which reads at the outset:

> WHEREAS sovereignty over the entire universe belongs to God Almighty alone and the authority which He has delegated to the State of Pakistan through its people for being exercised within the limits prescribed by Him is a sacred trust;
>
> This Constituent Assembly representing the people of Pakistan resolves to frame a constitution for the sovereign independent State of Pakistan; . . .[125]

The Jama'at-i Islami was quick to embrace this commitment in principle to the sovereignty of Allah, and to proclaim Pakistan an Islamic state. The first Constituent Assembly was dissolved in 1954 by Governor General Ghulam Muhammad, who became martial law dictator. Nonetheless when a new constitution was adopted for the government in 1956, the Jama'at accepted it.[126] In fact, the Jama'at-i Islami endorsed every constitution which was imposed during Maududi's lifetime.[127]

The Jama'at-i Islami has engaged in coalitions with other opposition political parties during election campaigns, parties that in no way advocated the Islamic ideology.[128] The most difficult decision of this kind involved supporting Fatima Jinnah as a presidential candidate in 1965 against Ayub Khan. The Combined Opposition Parties, of which the Jama'at-i Islami was a member, picked Ms. Jinnah as a candidate partly because they hoped that as the sister of the late Muhammad Ali Jinnah she would be immune from arrest by the repressive Ayub regime. Maududi had always maintained that the highest offices in an Islamic state should be reserved for men, but he still supported Ms. Jinnah, arguing that electing a woman was a lesser evil than allowing the corrupt Ayub government to continue in power.[129] This was a controversial decision, and it alienated some important Jama'at leaders.[130] Yet it was consistent with the general pattern of compromise on principle in the face of intractable political realities.

The Jama'at-i Islami was separatist in its organizational structure, relying on a small circle of devoted followers. In political life the Jama'at proved quite capable of compromise, accepting constitutions at variance with its ideology and engaging in coalitions with groups to which in was opposed in principle. In this the Jama'at-i Islami is similar to other cadre-based parties. Maintaining the ideological purity of its membership, the party postpones imposing this ideology on others while it concentrates on the struggle for political power. Once power has been obtained then the ideology can be promulgated generally. Of course the last phase of this plan has not been realized by the Jama'at-i Islami.

OPPOSITIONAL

In considering the Jama'at-i Islami as oppositional it is appropriate to turn to the place of jihad in Maulana Maududi's works. In Islam jihad is the ultimate struggle against one's opponents. It is a principle in Islam which has been de-emphasized by Muslim modernists, but which Maududi defends.

Maulana Maududi's first book was *al-Jihad fi 'l-Islam* ("Jihad in Islam"), which was published in 1930.[131] Up to this time Maududi had much in common with modernist Muslims. The Maulana did not receive the standard education of an alim (a member of the ulama), nor did he dress as one as a young man.[132] For Leonard Binder *al-Jihad fi 'l-Islam* marks a turning point in Maududi's life, when his interests began to shift from current events to Islam.[133] It is significant that in this transformation Maududi looked first to jihad.[134]

A slightly more mature presentation of Maududi's views on jihad can be found in his *Fundamentals of Islam*, which was first published in Urdu in 1940. This is a collection of sermons by the Maulana. The bulk of the text is devoted to explaining the duties which are required of every Muslim: declaration of faith in Allah as God and Muhammad as his prophet, daily prayer (salah), fasting during the month of Ramadan, annual alms (zakat), and pilgrimage (hajj). The last chapter is on jihad. Though jihad is not included among the duties incumbent on every Muslim, the Maulana places jihad at the center of his version of Islam.

> Briefly speaking, it would be enough to state that the real objective of Islam is to remove the lordship of man over man and to establish the government of One God. To stake one's life and everything else to achieve this purpose is called *Jihad* while *Salah*, fasting, *Hajj* and *Zakat* are all meant as a preparation for this task.[135]

Muslim modernists have tended to identify jihad with the individual struggle of each Muslim to better him or herself or with the social struggle of Muslim communities to reform themselves. War against infidels has not been emphasized. The Maulana does not hesitate to affirm that jihad includes armed conflict, along with these less dramatic efforts.[136] Maududi admits that some Muslims will not have the opportunity to participate in a holy war. "But now I tell you that all the '*Ibadaat* [the required duties] of that person are meaningless in whose heart there is no intent of *Jihad* and who does not keep in view this purpose of *Jihad.*"[137] A Muslim who does what is required with reservations, without being willing to give up everything for Islam, will gain nothing thereby.

Though some will not have the opportunity of participating in a jihad, still the spirit of struggle must pervade the life of every Muslim. All the other sacrifices required in Islam are merely a preparation for jihad. They must inculcate a willingness to sacrifice everything for the propagation of Islam. Hence Maududi's Islam is ultimately intensely oppositional.

ABSOLUTIST

The absolutism of the Jama'at-i Islami is revealed in the writings of Maulana Maududi. In several contexts it is clear that in Maududi's thought there is a black and white difference between Muslims and non-Muslims, without any room for shades of gray. The choice for Islam must be a total one. Those who attempt to compromise in this choice are little better than non-Muslims.

In the first chapter of his *Towards Understanding Islam* Maulana Maududi contrasts Islam and *kufr*. Islam is submission to Allah, and the Muslim is one who submits. *Kufr* is infidelity to Allah, the kafir is an infidel. Throughout the chapter these are the only two options—no choice other than Islam or *kufr* is presented. The characteristics of the kafir and the Muslim are diametrically opposed. The kafir is ignorant, tyrannical, rebellious, ungrateful, and unfaithful. "The inevitable consequence of this revolt and denial of Reality is failure in the ultimate ideals of life."[138] Intellectually, morally, politically, socially—in every sphere of activity—the efforts of the kafir are doomed to be ineffective.

In contrast to the failure of the kafir, Maududi paints a brilliant picture of the success which accompanies the Muslim.

> Such a man will always choose the Right Path in every field of knowledge and action. The man who knows God with all His attributes knows the beginning as well as the ultimate end of

> Reality. He can never be led astray, for his first step is on the right path, and he is sure of the direction and destination of his journey in life.[139]

The Muslim philosopher is able to probe the secrets of life without giving in to despair. The Muslim scientist advances human understanding of nature without hubris, leading to discoveries which are not self-destructive. Morally the Muslim is a paragon of virtue. Because of these perfections, the Muslim is naturally indomitable. "He is bound to prevail and no power on earth can overwhelm him or subdue him."[140]

Maududi affirms that the commitment to Islam over other systems of life must be total in *Fundamentals of Islam*. The Maulana explains his point through a subtle redefinition of the words *din*, Shari'a, and '*ibadat*. Din is an Arabic word which is often translated "religion." Maududi defines *din* here as obedience to some sovereign entity. Shari'a is the term used for Islamic law, but in this context Maududi takes it as that law which is imposed by the sovereign whom one accepts in one's *din*. Finally the '*ibadat* are usually the actions that are required of Muslims, but here Maududi defines them as service of the sovereign of one's *din*. In life one must follow one *din*, and embrace the Shari'a and the '*ibadat* which are consistent with that *din*.

> You may say that there can be another method. . . that in the matter of belief we can accept one ruler while in reality we obey another; we offer worship to one while we do servitude to another; we affirm faith with our heart in one law while in practice the affairs of our life are regulated by another law. In reply to this I shall say: "No doubt this can be done, and in fact it is being actually done, but this is Shirk. . . . and this Shirk is sheer falsehood."[141]

The individual who chooses Islam must go beyond accepting it as a philosophy. One must also govern one's life by Islam and direct one's actions toward the service of Allah.

Here we see that the choice that the individual must make must not only be clear, but it must also be total. Simple assent to Islam is not sufficient unless all of the provisions of Islamic law are realized. There are several contexts in his writings where Maududi attacks those who do not make a clear and total decision in favor of Islam. As will be noted below, with regard to purdah, for example, the traditional Islamic restrictions on the dress and movement of women must be adopted without reservation. In this case and in others in the Maulana's writings those who do not accept his definition of the injunctions of Islam are regarded by him as basically non-Muslims.

In his most general works Maulana Maududi seldom discusses the role of the Jama'at-i Islami: many of his major works were written before the founding of that organization. Yet there does seem to be a tendency to identify the membership of the Jama'at with true Muslims. For example, in the beginning the primary ritual of initiation in the Jama'at-i Islami was the affirmation of faith required of all Muslims that there is no God but Allah and Muhammad is his prophet.[142] It would seem that to become a member of the Jama'at is to become a Muslim. To the extent that the members of the Jama'at-i Islami are the only true Muslims the boundary between the Muslim and non-Muslim, between right and wrong, would be the boundary between the Jama'at and everyone else. The thought of Maulana Maududi is absolutist in that within it there is a clear and total distinction between right and wrong, a distinction which is homologous to the division between Muslims and non-Muslims and even to an extent to that between members of the Jama'at and non-members.

AUTHORITATIVENESS OR AUTHORITARIANISM IN FUNDAMENTALISM

The ultimate authority over the Jama'at-i Islami is Allah, whose will has been communicated in Islamic religious writings. Practically it was Maulana Maududi's authoritarian leadership that directed the Jama'at for most of his lifetime. First we will take up the question of scriptural authority.

The most important Islamic scriptural authority is the Qur'an. About it the Maulana writes, "belief in the Qur'an should be of the nature that *it is purely and absolutely God's own words*, that *it is perfectly true*, that *every word of it is preserved*, that *everything mentioned therein is right*, that *it is the bounden duty of man to carry out in his life each and every command of it*; and that *whatever be against it must be rejected*."[143] Beyond such exalted asseverations of the perfection of the Qur'an, Maududi also testifies to its authority implicitly in his writings. The Maulana's most massive work is a six volume commentary on the Qur'an entitled *Tafhim al-Qur'an* ("The Meaning of the Qur'an") which he worked on for almost three decades.[144] In his other writings also frequent quotations from the Qur'an attest to the

Maulana's reliance upon its authority.

Another source which Maududi quotes frequently in his works is Hadith, which are traditions about the words and actions of the Prophet Muhammad and his companions. Unlike the Qur'an, according to Maududi, the transmission of Hadith has not been perfect. Some Hadith do reflect the practice of the early Islamic community, others were written later then attributed to the early community to add to their authority. No one body of Hadith associated with an individual school can be unqualifiedly accepted. An effort must be made to separate the spurious Hadith from the genuine ones on the basis of the reliability of the chain of transmission of a given tradition and its inclusion in the earliest collections. The authority of a corpus of Hadith, no matter how carefully considered, will never be as great as that of the Qur'an. Nonetheless, enough certitude is possible so that Hadith can be an aid in understanding the Qur'an and the basis for legislation in areas where the Qur'an provides no guidance.

Through most of the history of Islam the Qur'an has been accepted as absolutely perfect while Hadith has been taken as generally reliable. Maulana Maududi's basic theory on the authority of these works is not unusual. His insistence that the Shari'a is still authoritative is more original. While many Muslims have come to the conclusion that the Shari'a can no longer be imposed on the community, Maududi insists that it must be the basis of law even in the modern Islamic state. This is not to say that the Shari'a is a perfectly reliable text in the way that the Qur'an is. In fact the Shari'a is only a text in the broadest sense. It would be more accurate to describe the Shari'a as the collective legal wisdom that has accumulated over the centuries in the Islamic world. The source of the Shari'a is ultimately the Qur'an and Hadith, but the substance of the Shari'a is the legal decisions that have been reached over time. Because Maududi supports renewed *ijtihad*, original decisions are still possible and the Shari'a is open-ended. The Shari'a is not a limited text like the Qur'an, and it does not enjoy authority equal to the Qur'an. Nevertheless, a generally reliable codification of the Shari'a should be possible as the basis for law in a modern Islamic state.

It is the injunctions of these authoritative religious writings as interpreted by Maulana Maududi which are the basis of the life of the Jama'at-i Islami. Maududi founded the Jama'at. He was the author of its first constitution. Maududi was the head of the Jama'at, the Amir, for most of his life.[145] The constitution of the Jama'at-i Islami provides for a body of representatives (called the Majlis-i-Shura), elected by the membership, to advise the Amir.[146] Generally the Majlis-i-Shura supported Maududi during his lifetime.[147] Practically it was his authoritarian leadership which formed the Jama'at-i Islami.

As a cadre-based party the Jama'at-i Islami emphasizes heavily the importance of obedience. Members are also bound to the Amir by pecuniary considerations. A significant proportion of the members of the Jama'at are paid full-time employees.[148] These individuals depend upon the Jama'at for income and might be reluctant to criticize it. During Maududi's lifetime the proceeds from the sale of his books was a significant part of the total revenue of the Jama'at, which increased his hold over the organization.

During the period of the Maulana's leadership, several influential figures in the Jama'at-i Islami resigned in protest from the organization.[149] Kalim Bahadur has argued that with the elimination of these dissidents the Jama'at-i Islami became dominated more and more strongly by Maududi. In the beginning the membership roles of the Jama'at included some respected religious and political leaders whose authority was independent of the Maulana. By the time of Maududi's death a younger generation held most of the influence in the Jama'at. These younger officers had been brought up in the Islamic ideology by Maududi, and they were much less likely to oppose him.[150]

It was only near the end of his life, when the Maulana was partially incapacitated by illness, that control of the Jama'at-i Islami was wrested from him. For most of the period from 1941 to 1979 he totally dominated the organization. Through his writings he trained his disciples in his understanding of the Qur'an, as well as in political matters. It was with the authority of Maulana Maududi that they were to understand the dictates of the Qur'an, which was theoretically a higher authority.

FUNDAMENTALISM AS ANTIEVOLUTIONARY

Though Maulana Maududi condemned Darwin's theory, he does imply that there was an evolution in the history of the human community. Yet this development came to an end with the Prophet Muhammad. Because this evolutionary process does not continue into the present, its significance is limited.

First let us consider evolution in the narrow sense of Darwin's theory in the writings of Abu'l-A'la Maududi before moving on to more general evolutionary patterns. In *Maududi: Thought and*

Movement Syed As'ad Gilani quotes a passage by the Maulana in which he criticizes Charles Darwin's notion of the origin of species. Specifically Maududi rejects the idea of natural selection as the mechanism that determines evolution. It is really social Darwinism that Maududi criticizes, the idea that "the survival of the fittest" should control the relations between human individuals and groups. "The aggression which used to qualify as cruelty, has now become the basic right of the mighty."[151] Given that Maududi repeatedly tries to prove that his Islamic social system is based upon natural law, it is not surprising that he would be quick to judge Darwin's version of the laws of nature in terms of its impact on the human community.

In spite of Maududi's refutation of Darwin, there are evolutionary schemes in his work. For example, in *Towards Understanding Islam* the Maulana describes the development of human religious consciousness in terms similar to those which were used by Western historians of religions when evolutionary theories were dominant in the discipline. In their powerlessness primitives deified the forces of nature. Gradually an understanding developed of personal entities behind the natural world. Finally in the face of mounting discontent with a multiplicity of spiritual entities, monotheism dawned.[152]

Alongside this general theory of the evolution of religious consciousness Maududi presents a special theory of unfolding revelation. When Allah created Adam he revealed to him a religion which is basically the same as Islam, but most of the descendants of the first man eventually turned away from that revelation. Through history Allah occasionally propagated his religion through other messengers. Each time the community which had been blessed with a glimpse of the truth eventually lost it, covering it over with beliefs and practices that are contrary to Islam. A certain spiritual improvement did endure nonetheless, which became the basis of a final, more lasting revelation through the Prophet Muhammad. "The Prophets, thus, prepared the mental attitude of their respective people in such a way that a universal religion could be safely introduced—a religion which is quite in consonance with the nature of man, which embodies all that is good in all other creeds and societies, and which is naturally and commonly acceptable to the entire mankind."[153] Despite the repeated rejections of Allah's message in history before the prophet of Islam, Maududi seems to divine a growing moral consciousness and a developing technical capacity, which prepared the ground for the final, complete revelation through Muhammad.

Maududi does describe an evolution in history, but we have access to the evidence of this process only through Islam. There have been many prophets, but Muslims only "have to believe positively in those of the Prophets whose names have been mentioned in the Qur'an."[154] With regard to the others, "we are not in a position to be definite about a particular person outside the list of Prophets named in the Qur'an, whether or not he was a Prophet, for we have not been told anything definite about him."[155] Maududi says the same for the scriptures revealed by these other prophets. Only those must be held in reverence which are mentioned in the Qur'an.

There is no authentic account of the content of earlier scriptures except in Islam. The problem is that these scriptures no longer exist in their pristine form. The Qur'an mentions the Torah of Moses, the Psalms of David, and the Gospel of Jesus, but these documents are not the same as anything in the Jewish or Christian scriptures. Rather in the Hebrew scriptures and the New Testament the original revelation has been perverted by interpolations which reflect religious practices contrary to Islam.[156] The other scriptures mentioned in the Qur'an are even more obscure. In this situation the Qur'an and the Sunna of the prophet are the only sure guide to Allah's message.

Maududi maintains that only the prophecy of Muhammad is complete, while the messages of other prophets were limited by the situation in which they lived. Muhammad's revelation clearly supersedes the teaching of other prophets. It is as if Allah has said, "Now We cancel all the previous modes. From now on whosoever wants to serve Us must follow the system which We are now promulgating through Our last prophet."[157] Maududi suggests that Muhammad's version of the truth will be lasting. "His teachings stand uncorrupted and are uncorruptible."[158] This is implicitly an argument in favor of the traditional Islamic doctrine that Muhammad is the seal of the prophets, that is, that there will be no other prophet after him.

So the evolution in history is only clearly testified to in the Qur'an and Sunna of the Prophet Muhammad. There is nothing of worth that can be gleaned from the study of the previous prophetic teachings that is not included in the more complete revelation of Muhammad. And there need never be, and can never be, another prophet after Muhammad. An evolutionary theory of history is important if it describes a process that is ongoing, a process that includes the present. But Maududi's evolutionary theory is only concerned with fossils. It accounts for a process which effectively came to an end with the prophet of Islam. In this sense the thought of the founder of the Jama'at-i Islami is antievolutionary. Regardless of what has gone on in the past, we are not a part of any continuing evolution.

ANTIPERMISSIVE

The Jama'at-i Islami is antipermissive. The members of the Jama'at are held to a strict moral code. Of them one Western scholar has written, "Perhaps nowhere else in Pakistan could one find a group of men with the dedication and moral excellence of the Jama'at-i-Islami."[159] Also the Jama'at-i Islami is critical of the permissiveness of the world beyond its members.[160] Its attack on permissiveness is most clear in Maulana Abu'l-A'la Maududi's book *Purdah and the Status of Woman in Islam.*

In defending the social system which restricts the movements and dress of women in Islam, Maududi goes on the offensive against the status of women in Western nations. Maududi argues that the role of women throughout history in different societies has tended to develop from a primitive state in which women are slaves to a decadent one in which they are sexual playthings. The author substantiates this theory with reference to ancient Greece. In Greece women were oppressed in the age before civilization dawned. When the culture was vigorous, according to Maududi, women were dominant in the domestic sphere, but not active in public (in fact, a kind of purdah). Finally there was a period so degenerate that the machinations of prostitutes came to influence public life.[161]

Similarly, in the Middle Ages European Christianity condemned women as a source of sin. In the eighteenth century the status of women began to improve, but by the twentieth things had gone too far. The West had advanced from the position that women should have the same basic human rights as men to the idea that women should adopt the same behavior. The breakdown of the separate roles of the husband and wife is weakening the stability of the family. The constant interaction of men and women in the workplace has led to titillation, and an increase in adultery. "This disease is eating fast into the very vitals of Western nations."[162]

Maududi recounts at great length and in lurid detail the "tragic consequences" of the sexual license which is running riot in the West.[163] Taking France, the United States, and England as examples, Maududi quotes his sources on the rise of pornography, prostitution, sexually transmitted diseases, divorce, contraception, and abortion. After a particularly grisly description of a mother killing her own child Maududi writes:

> A nation that develops such hatred and hostility against its own offspring cannot be saved from annihilation even by a miracle. New generations are necessary in order to continue the physical existence of a nation. If it turns against its own seed it is in fact turning against itself; it is committing suicide.[164]

The prevailing sexual practices of the Western nations that Maududi describes are leading to self-inflicted genocide.

Nowadays the licentiousness of the West is spreading to the Islamic world as well according to Maududi. The author quotes modern Urdu literature in which young women scorn restrictions on premarital sex and adultery. While many ridicule purdah without serious examination of the values which underlie it, a few attempt to show that purdah was not characteristic of Islam in its golden age. Maududi argues that purdah was enjoined in Islam at the very beginning. Those who say otherwise are attempting to disguise the values that they have acquired from the West with an Islamic facade. To Maududi such logic is unacceptable. The Maulana demands, "before they go the Western way they will have to declare their desertion of Islam so that they may no longer use it to deceive people and their misdeeds do not reflect on Islam and Muslims."[165]

The decision between purdah and Western practices is an absolute one for Maududi. No mixture of the two is possible, because their underlying values are inconsistent with each other. "People who are treading this path [combining Islamic and Western practices] should clearly understand that the beginning they have made may not bring them to grief, but it will surely lead their children or the children of their children to grave consequences."[166] The only answer is to adopt the Islamic system in *toto*.

> But before they choose the way of Islam they will have to give up all desire for material gains and sensual pleasures that has been created by the fascinations of Western civilization; they will have to cleanse their mind of all those concepts and ideas that they have borrowed from Europe; and they will have to cast off all those principles and ideals that they have imbibed from the Western culture and way of life.[167]

In contrast to this decadence, the ideal status for women is one between oppression and libertinism, according to Maududi. Women should enjoy the same basic rights as men, and they should be allowed to develop themselves within limits, but the roles of women and men should remain separate.[168] Men should dominate in the public sphere, and be trained for that responsibility.[169] The activities of women are limited to the home, and even in domestic affairs the wife must submit to the direction of her husband.[170] It is not necessary to invent a system to maintain this balance between freedom and excess. Such a system has been mandated by Allah in purdah, Maududi argues.

The Jama'at-i Islami is antipermissive, maintaining a high moral standard for itself and using that standard to judge the world at large. From the Jama'at's perspective Western nations are particularly decadent. This degeneracy is spreading to the Islamic community as well, as Muslims rush to adopt Western mores. In morality as in politics the Jama'at-i Islami strives to check the erosion of Islamic values by Western ones. So the antipermissiveness of the Jama'at-i Islami is just one part of the larger polemic.

ANTIHERMENEUTICAL

Maulana Maududi is antihermeneutical in his approach to the Islamic scriptures which he takes as authoritative. In his commentary on the Qur'an, for instance, Maududi usually gives only one gloss of the verse in question, rather than discussing the various ways the verse has been understood by previous commentators.[171] This is not to say that the meaning of the verses of the Qur'an is so self-evident that no interpretation is required. In "Maulana Maududi on Quranic Interpretation" Freeland Abbott reproduces a series of questions which he submitted in writing to Maududi, along with the Maulana's written responses. One of Abbott's questions was:

> The clear revelations—*Āyāt-i-Muḥkamāt*—because their meaning is clear, need no interpretation. Is this true? Is it assumed that the same verses are clear to everyone? If so, does this imply that everyone thinks alike, or possesses the same degree of intelligence?[172]

Maududi's response is as follows:

> A reply to this question becomes redundant after the explanation given above [of clear and allegorical verses]. Verses of established

> meaning do not signify that they are verses "which do not call for any interpretation at all." On the contrary, the Qur'ān, by forbidding indulgence in symbolical verses, diverts man's attention towards these verses in so far as these, to the exclusion of the symbolical verses, are the proper objects to which all efforts at meditation, contemplation, probing and research should be directed.[173]

Clearly some interpretation is permitted.

The Maulana in this same article, however, implies that restrictions must be placed on the latitude of permissible interpretation. This is clear in Maududi's discussion of Qur'an 4.3. Abbott's question begins:

> Is Surah iv.3 on (polygamy) [*sic*] allegorical? Is it a clear revelation? If it is clear, why should it be so disputed, and so variously interpreted?[174]

The Quranic verse referred to has generally been understood to allow polygamy as long as each wife is treated equitably. Nineteenth-century Muslim modernists, interested in putting down polygamy, interpreted this verse as requiring that the husband feel equal attachment for each spouse. Since such affective equality is difficult to maintain, the modernist argued, polygamy is actually discouraged in this verse. It is this dispute, between allowing polygamy and forbidding it, that Abbott refers to in his question.

Maulana Maududi responds that there really has been no dispute in interpreting this verse. The ulama have always maintained that it permits polygamy while requiring "justice in treatment and rights." As for the nineteenth-century idea that "equal attachment" is enjoined, Maududi writes, "these are not 'interpretations,' but 'distortions of meaning,' which cannot be given place within the limits of the term 'interpretation' of the Qur'ān."[175] This distortion reflects an attempt to twist the meaning of the Qur'an to fit Western values. Those who engage in such readings would be more honest to admit that they have chosen Western mores over Islamic ones and to sever their ties to Islam. Apparently interpretation of the Qur'an is allowed, but the Maulana reserves for himself the right to decide what qualifies as interpretation. Those who are judged to be engaging in distortion rather than interpretation are thrust beyond the pale of Islam by this determination.

The problem of acceptable interpretation has great practical consequences when it comes to the Shari'a, since the Shari'a is the basis of law in Maududi's system. Here, too, the Maulana admits some argument is possible among Muslims of good faith.[176] But woe to the individual who attempts to reinterpret Shari'a on the basis of Western values. In the case of purdah discussed above, such a faithless Muslim would be better off renouncing his or her hypocritical adherence to Islam. Again the Maulana is the arbiter of acceptable interpretation.

For the religious texts of the Islamic tradition which he takes as authoritative, Maulana Maududi does admit that some interpretation is permissible. Nonetheless, Maududi attacks interpretations which differ from his own in terms that imply they are absolutely illegitimate. It seems that the only interpretation that Maududi finds permissible is his own. The idea that different interpreters bring different perspectives to a text which are all valid but limited seems very foreign indeed.

FUNDAMENTALISTS AS AGENTS IN HISTORY

Despite the small size of their organization, the members of the Jama'at-i Islami struggle to change the course of history. In Maulana Maududi's philosophy there is some hope that their goal might be achieved by the will of Allah. The working model for the Jama'at-i Islami is cadre-based parties like the communists and fascists.[177] The members of the Jama'at are expected to be totally dedicated to it and they are discouraged from joining other organizations.[178] They become members only after a period of probation. The training of those in the Jama'at includes a camp where members go for a couple of weeks during which they are completely immersed in the Islamic ideology. If an individual strays from the party line in spite of this training, then he or she can be kicked out. There is a regular system for review of the commitment of party members, and expulsion from the party is very common.[179] Because of these stringent requirements, the total membership of the Jama'at-i Islami has never been large.[180]

The structure of the Jama'at-i Islami closely reflects Maududi's thinking. Based on the writings of the Maulana it would seem that the Jama'at-i Islami is bound to succeed in its mission to make Pakistan a truly Islamic state, and ultimately to become dominant in the world. He is confident that, "if there is an organized group superior to the rest of the world in its possession of both Islamic moral qualities and the basic human moral qualities and which also does not lack material means, then it is in no way possible that any other group should exercise leadership and control over it."[181] Because Allah loves virtue and will always reward it, the virtuous will naturally come to the fore.

This Islamic organization will not come to power overnight, however. "It must be remembered that the mere coming into being of such a group will not of itself effect a change in the system of leadership so that corrupt and evil men will be dethroned, as it were with the assistance of angels, and the righteous group instantaneously and easily be established in their place."[182] Real struggle is required, and not many are willing to make the necessary sacrifices. "*Jihad-fi-sabilillah* [jihad in the cause of Allah] is the function of only those persons who have the will to carry out this onerous task, and such persons are always few in number."[183] Only a small number will be prepared to prosecute the struggle, but if this group is perfectly virtuous then it is bound to prevail. The vast majority of people are willing to accept whatever system of life is dominant. Once the virtuous minority accedes to power, then the majority will go along with their program, just as they have run to vice when the vicious have been in power. "If the leadership and power of command are vested in God-fearing and righteous people, then it is inevitable that the entire system of life should proceed in terms of fear of God, goodness, and righteousness."[184]

The Jama'at-i Islami is just such a small organization of virtuous Muslims. The members of the Jama'at are few in number, but they are sternly righteous. In the long run their cause is destined to be vindicated because Allah favors the good. So Maududi's followers struggle on, enduring failures in the short run but confident of victory in the end.

FUNDAMENTALISM AS TELEOLOGICAL

The view of future history of the Jama'at-i Islami is profoundly teleological, but it is not marked by any fervent eschatological expectation. On the most general level, in his writings Maulana Maududi repeatedly expresses his faith in a judgment day. At the appointed time this world will come to an end. All the men and women who have ever lived will be resurrected. Allah will judge each on the basis of his or her deeds. Those who have done good will go to heaven to enjoy eternal bliss. Those who have done evil deeds will go to hell to suffer endless punishment.[185] The belief in a day of judgment at the end of history is not peculiar to Maududi's philosophy but is generally accepted by Muslims.

In *A Short History of the Revivalist Movement in Islam*

Maududi presents theories about an aspect of future history which has been the subject of some dispute among Muslims—the coming of the Mahdi. Some Muslims, especially Shi'ites, hope for the emergence of a messianic figure known as the Mahdi near the end of history who will draw the whole world to Islam. Maududi articulates his own view of the Mahdi with reference to the following Hadith:

> Your Religion [presumably the Prophet Muhammad is speaking to his companions] originates from prophethood and Allah's mercy and this will remain among you as long as Allah wills. Then Allah will recall it and replace it by "Caliphate after the pattern of Prophethood". Then Allah will bring this to an end.
>
> Then it will be succeeded by tyrant kingship which will continue as long as Allah wills. Then Allah will bring it also to an end.
>
> Then there will be the reign of terror which will remain as long as Allah wills. Then Allah will bring it also to an end.
>
> Then will return the same "Caliphate after the pattern of Prophethood" which will administer the affairs of people according to the *Sunnah* of the Prophet, and Islam will take root in the earth. This rule will please those who belong to the heavens and also those who belong to the earth. When it comes the heavens will generously shower their blessings and the earth will divulge all its treasures.[186]

Maududi admits that he is not prepared to defend absolutely the authenticity of this Hadith, but its general sense is the same as other Hadith on the same topic and can be taken as basically trustworthy.

According to these Hadith from the time of the prophet forward history will advance in five stages: (1) the period of the prophet himself; (2) the period of the "Caliphate after the pattern of Prophethood," that is, the age of the four rightly guided caliphs; (3) the period of tyrant kings; (4) the period of the reign of terror; and (5) the return of the "Caliphate after the pattern of Prophethood," which will be ushered in by the Mahdi. Maududi writes that we are currently in the fourth stage.

> As to the fifth stage mentioned in the prophecy there are clear signs to show that human history is fast heading towards it. All the man-made 'isms' have been tried out and seen to collapse. Now man in his utter disappointment has been left with no other

choice than to turn to Islam.[187]

This passage would seem to indicate that Maududi looks forward to an imminent eschatological event.

In mitigation of this impression it is important to underscore that Maududi attempts to demythologize the usual messianic image of the Mahdi. For example, the Maulana is skeptical about the common understanding of the emergence of the Mahdi. Many are of the opinion that the Mahdi, when he begins his public work, will proclaim himself to be the Mahdi. The ulama will examine the claimant to determine if he has the characteristics which have been prophesied.[188] If not, the claimant will be discredited. If so, then the Mahdi will go ahead with his work of reestablishing the glory of Islam. In contradistinction to this Maududi writes the Mahdi will most likely not proclaim his identity, he will probably not even be aware of it. It might only be after his death that people will realize, on the basis of his having established the "Caliphate after the pattern of Prophethood," that this must have been the Mahdi.[189]

This issue becomes critical when one considers what Maududi regarded his own role to be in the revival of Islam. In the second edition of *A Short History of the Revivalist Movement in Islam* Maududi added appendixes containing articles published in his journal *Tarjuman al-Qur'an* in response to questions raised after the publication of the original edition. One of the appendixes concerns allegations that Maududi himself claimed to be a *mujaddid* (a reviver of Islam) or even the Mahdi.[190] In this appendix the Maulana asserts unequivocally that he never claimed such status. Here the Maulana does not explicitly deny that he is a *mujaddid*. M.R. Khan, a violent detractor of Maududi, maintains that by stopping short of writing, 'I am not a *mujaddid*,' Maududi is implicitly encouraging his followers to embrace such claims for him.[191] But this misses the point. Maududi argues that the determination of whether or not one is a *mujaddid* or a Mahdi must be left up to history. Just as it is impossible for an individual to ascertain that he himself is a *mujaddid*, so it is impossible to establish that he is *not* one. Maududi wanted to encourage his reader to go ahead with the practical work of reviving Islam, rather than becoming involved in divisive debates about the Maulana's own status as a reviver of Islam.

Certainly history has an end in the philosophy of Maulana Maududi in the day of judgment, but in a way this is an event which comes after the termination of time. Before judgment day Maududi hopes for a complete revival of Islam by the coming Mahdi, an event which he regards as imminent. Nonetheless it would be misleading to place too much emphasis on eschatological fervor in the Jama'at-i Islami. The Mahdi does not appear frequently in Maududi's writings. The Maulana expresses the opinion that belief in the Mahdi is not incumbent upon Muslims.[192] In his discussion of *mujaddids* and the Mahdi, Maududi's focus is not on the portents that will accompany their appearance in history, but on their mission to revive Islam. To the extent that the Jama'at-i Islami advances that revival it participates in the eschatological enterprise, but the emphasis is on the work and not its culmination.

A COMPARISON OF BOB JONES UNIVERSITY AND THE JAMA'AT-I ISLAMI

To conclude this chapter we will compare Bob Jones University and the Jama'at-i Islami. The organization of the presentation of the two movements here has served to underline their similarities. Both groups arose to defend their traditions against attacks that were perceived to be critical. In both cases there has been a retrieval of some of the fundamentals of the tradition, which were established in the golden age, but which are being abandoned now. There has been a tendency for the leaders of Bob Jones University and of the Jama'at-i Islami to see themselves as the exclusive adherents of an absolute truth, in opposition to all others. Both movements argue that they are uniquely supported by sources of indubitable authority. The Jama'at and Bob Jones have fought against relativizing understandings of those authorities, along with laxness in morality. Both have a distinctive grasp of a purposive history which gives them a role to play in it. Neither Bob Jones University nor the Jama'at-i Islami are prepared to surrender history to randomness. To that extent both are antievolutionary.

Though the two movements have much in common, some of the dissimilarities are also striking. There is a significant difference in the relationship between religion and politics in these two fundamentalist groups. The Jama'at-i Islami was created to have impact on public policy. After Pakistan became independent the Jama'at put up candidates for election like any other political party. Officials of Bob Jones University have focused more on religious than political issues. In spite of occasional forays into the public realm, for most of its history the university has held itself aloof from the rough and tumble of politics.

It might be argued that this difference between Bob Jones

University and the Jama'at-i Islami on politics is a reflection of the choice of the analyst which does not have any general significance for the study of Christian and Islamic fundamentalism. If one began with the Moral Majority as a test case on the Christian side, for example, one might well contend that North American Protestant fundamentalism is basically political. On the other hand, it would also be possible to assert that fundamentalism in the Islamic world is not necessarily political, citing a movement like the Jama'at-i Tabligh in Pakistan. Both of these arguments are undermined by the peculiarity of the evidence upon which they rely. Political activism like that of the Moral Majority has not been salient in North American Protestant fundamentalism through most of its history. The quietism of the Jama'at-i Tabligh has not been characteristic of most of the Islamic movements that are generally recognized to be fundamentalist. Here the author of this study has followed more general trends in the scholarship on fundamentalism. This an issue that we will come back to in the conclusion of this book.

There is a significant contrast between the Bob Jones University and the Jama'at-i Islami with regard to scripture, which is tied in with broader issues in the Christian and Islamic traditions. Almost all Muslims agree that the Qur'an is wholly reliable. It contains only what Allah communicated to the prophet, and all that Allah communicated to the prophet. It has been handed down faithfully, so that the Qur'an that we have today is the same as the one that Muhammad recited in the seventh century A.D. When Maulana Maududi says that the Qur'an is inerrant, he is not making a radical claim. Many Christians in the modern period believe that their scripture is only an imperfect record of God's revelation. There are interpolations in the Bible, which have altered its contents. Some would even allow that the biblical books were not a complete reflection of God's perfect wisdom in the beginning, because of the limitations of the human authors of those books. To maintain that the Bible is inerrant, as the leaders of Bob Jones University have, is to make a very radical claim indeed.[193]

In addition to an inerrant Qur'an, Maududi also allows a limited authority to Hadith as well, which is not uncommon in the Islamic tradition. It is only when we come to his views on the Shari'a that we reach the point where Maududi is defending the authority of a religious text (a tradition really) that others would dispute.[194] Even though we are dealing with a more complicated body of authoritative religious texts in the case of the Jama'at-i Islami, there is a debate about one authority which distinguishes the movement. On this point Bob Jones and the Jama'at are both similar and different.

Among a number of other contrasts in detail between Bob Jones University and the Jama'at-i Islami, two are important enough to bear mention here. In general the polemic of the Jama'at has been directed more against Westernization than against modernization or liberalization. It is interesting that some Christian fundamentalists, especially in the South, present liberalism as a set of values that is being imposed on them by outsiders ("the eastern establishment"). Still, the dispute in America between fundamentalists and non-fundamentalists is basically a family feud within one culture. For the Jama'at-i Islami the battle is between two cultures.

Another difference has to do with the idea that fundamentalism is antievolutionary. While it is true that Maulana Maududi does not attach any great weight to randomness in history, it should be acknowledged that an offensive against evolution does not occupy an important or distinctive place in his thought. In the West, especially in America and England, Darwin's theory of evolution became the crux of a furious debate. For conservatives with Darwinian evolution science allied itself with liberalism in an attack on traditional ways of thought. When a Western scholar attends to the same debate in non-Western cultures, he or she hears only a deafening silence. Evolution simply has not taken on the same role as the spearhead of science against tradition in most non-Western societies. So non-Western fundamentalisms are not likely to be so desperately antievolutionary as Bob Jones University is, certainly the Jama'at-i Islami is not.[195]

Finally there are two interesting ways that the fundamentalist movements which we have dealt with so far are similar—likenesses not suggested by Marty's characterization of fundamentalism. In both the Jama'at-i Islami and Bob Jones University there is a paradoxical but powerful combination of universalism and particularism. The friends of Bob Jones remain an embattled minority on the religious scene in the United States. Nonetheless, these fundamentalists are convinced that they hold the real truth and that their position will eventually be vindicated by none other than God himself. In a similar way, though the Jama'at has been massacred at the polls, still its followers nurse the hope that Pakistan and the world can be won over to their stance, because they alone are right. Both movements must rely on a small number of supporters, but both harbor staggeringly grandiose dreams.

Another fundamentalist pattern is revealed by these two movements which is worthy of consideration. In the case of Bob Jones University and the Jama'at-i Islami there is a definite tie between the authorities from the tradition upon which they rely and the authorities in the group who provide leadership. The be all and end all of Christian fundamentalism is the Bible, but it is the evangelist who has been key figure in developing and propagating the fundamentalist understanding of the Bible. The Bible is a polysemous text, but there is a tradition of evangelical interpretation which guards the individual believing reader from too much ambiguity. Similarly, it is Maulana Abu'l-A'la Maududi who has proved to the members of the Jama'at-i Islami that the Shari'a must be reimposed, and he has guided them in intermediate steps for its reimposition. Maududi did not accord himself any special metaphysical status, he certainly did not claim to be uniquely inspired by Allah. And yet he is the author of the Jama'at's Islamic ideology—his authority has been crucial in establishing the authority of the Shari'a. In both movements there is a close tie between the authority of their leaders and the authority of the tradition.

In the introduction to this book a basic definition of fundamentalism was proposed. In this chapter two fundamentalist movements have been analyzed in terms of that definition, one Christian and one Islamic. We have also begun to suggest ways that our original definition might be altered in light of the evidence. We will return to these conclusions again at the end of the next chapter, in which we will apply the same definition of fundamentalism to the movement which is the central focus of our concern, the Arya Samaj.

NOTES

1. Clifford Geertz, *Islam Observed: Religious Development in Morocco and Indonesia* (Chicago: University of Chicago Press, 1971), 24.
2. Bob Jones University has returned the favor, dubbing some who call themselves fundamentalists "pseudofundamentalists." Bob Jones, Jr., *Pseudo-Fundamentalism* (Greenville, S. C.: Bob Jones University, 1977), audio cassette of a sermon delivered on 15 November 1977. Included among the pseudofundamentalists in this sermon are New Evangelicals, pentecostals, and Jerry Falwell.
3. Nancy Ammerman identifies Bob Jones University as part of "The Larger Fundamentalist Network" of a fundamentalist church in the northeastern United States. Nancy Tatom Ammerman, *Bible Believers: Fundamentalists in the Modern World* (New Brunswick, N.J.: Rutgers University Press, 1987), 117. Alan Peshkin speaks of "the pervasive influence Bob Jones University has on BBA," a Christian academy that he studied located in Illinois. Alan Peshkin, *God's Choice: The Total World of a Fundamentalist Christian School* (Chicago: University of Chicago Press, 1986),

87.

4. In the early years the university was known as Bob Jones College. The college was located first near Panama City, Florida. In 1933 Bob Jones College moved to Cleveland, Tennessee. Finally in 1947, changing its name to Bob Jones University, the school took up its present location in Greenville, South Carolina. For the sake of simplicity, throughout this study I will talk about Bob Jones University, even in contexts where it would more accurate historically to say Bob Jones College.
5. By Curtis Lee Laws, a Baptist publicist, in 1920. George M. Marsden, *Fundamentalism and American Culture: The Shaping of Twentieth-Century Evangelicalism: 1870-1925* (Oxford: Oxford University Press, 1980), 159.
6. Marsden, 164-175.
7. Ernest R. Sandeen, *The Roots of Fundamentalism: British and American Millenarianism, 1800-1930* (Chicago: University of Chicago Press, 1970), 250-260.
8. Marsden, 184-189.
9. For an extended description of these campaigns see R.K. Johnson, *Builder of Bridges: A Biography of Bob Jones Sr.* (Greenville, S.C.: Bob Jones University Press, 1982 [first published in 1969 by Sword of the Lord]), 63-167.
10. Bob, Jones, Sr., *Three College Shipwrecks* (Greenville, S.C.: Bob Jones University, n. d), n. p.
11. Ibid.
12. Article by Sam Small, no publication information, quoted in Melton Wright, *Fortress of Faith: The Story of Bob Jones University* (Greenville, S.C.: Bob Jones University Press, 1984), 42.
13. Wright, 36.
14. Marsden, 117.
15. Ibid., 262, n. 30.
16. *Bulletin: Catalog & Announcements*, vol. 64 (Greenville, S.C.: Bob Jones University, 1990), 15. The italics are in the original.
17. Especially at issue is the doctrine known as dispensational premillennialism. In his *The Roots of Fundamentalism*, Ernest Sandeen has presented the fundamentalist movement as an outgrowth of British and American millenarianism. George Marsden has argued that Sandeen's characterization of fundamentalism is too narrow. It is true today, Marsden admits, that all most all fundamentalists are dispensational premillennialists. But in the 1920s and before, the fundamentalist coalition included conservatives who did not accept dispensational theory. Marsden, 5.
18. Bob Jones, Jr., *Fundamentals of Faith* (Greenville, S.C.: Bob

Jones University Press, 1964), 60.

19. Marsden simply explains the outlines of this very complicated theory on pp. 48-55.

20. Bob Jones III, *What is a Fundamentalist?* (Greenville, S.C.: Bob Jones University Press, 1985), 1. This is a reprint of an article that originally appeared in *Faith for the Family*, October 1985.

21. Bob Jones, Jr., *Fundamentals of Faith*, 9. Italics in the original.

22. Ibid., 14-21.

23. Ibid., 28.

24. Ibid., 31.

25. Bob Jones III, *Biblical Answers to Bothersome Questions* (Greenville, S. C.: Bob Jones University Press, 1981), 28.

26. M. Bruce McAllister, Associate Director of Extension and Ministerial Training at Bob Jones University, interview by author, Tape recording, Greenville, South Carolina, 30 May 1990.

27. Bob Jones, Jr., *Cornbread and Caviar* (Greenville, S.C.: Bob Jones University Press, 1985), 163.

28. Bob Jones, Jr. to Ralph W. Mitchell, 7 November 1956, quoted in Johnson, 284

29. "Bob Jones Says Billy Graham Doing More Harm to the Cause of Christ than Any Living Man," *Greenville (S.C.) News*, 4 March 1966, 38, quoted in Johnson, 298.

30. "Billy Graham's Father-In-Law Attacks Critics," *Greensboro (N. C.) Daily News*, 6 March 1966, sec. A, p. 9.

31. Johnson, 273.

32. Bob Jones III, *The Moral Majority* (Greenville, S.C.: Bob Jones University, 1980), 2. This is a reprint of an article that originally appeared in *Faith for the Family*, September 1980.

33. Bartholomew F. Brewer with Alfred W. Furrell, *Pilgrimage from Rome*, new ed. (Greenville, S.C.: Bob Jones University Press, 1986), 74.

34. *Catholics Now at Peace* (Greenville, S.C.: Bob Jones University, 1987), 3-4. Italics in the original. This pamphlet contains the testimony of four former Roman Catholics who at the time of publication were employees of Bob Jones University.

35. *Catholics Now at Peace*, 10.

36. Bob Jones, Jr., *Romanism and the Charismatic Movement* (Greenville, S.C.: Bob Jones University, 1981), 1. This pamphlet is a reprint of an article that originally appeared in *Faith for the Family*, July-August 1981.

37. A distinction must be made here between current charismatic groups and the early pentecostal movement. Bob Jones University Press has published works by O. Talmadge Spence, which criticize contemporary pentecostals but allow, "that in the body of Christ

there are Pentecostals." O. Talmadge Spence, *A Pentecostal Speaks to Pentecostalists* (Greenville, S.C.: Bob Jones University Press, 1973), 1. This pamphlet is a reprint of an article that was originally published in *Faith for the Family*, September-October 1973.

38. This is of course also the theme of the pamphlet cited earlier by Bob Jones, Jr., *Romanism and the Charismatic Movement.*
39. Bob Jones III, *The Charismatic Movement: Is It of God?* (Greenville, S.C.: Bob Jones University, n. d.), not paginated. This pamphlet is a transcription of a sermon presented on Bob Jones University's television program *Show My People.*
40. Bob Jones, Jr., *Romanism and the Charismatic Movement,* 1.
41. Bob Jones III, *The Charismatic Movement: Is It of God?* n. p.
42. Bob Jones III, *Biblical Answers to Bothersome Questions,* 61.
43. Bob Jones, Sr., *Comments on Here and Hereafter,* selected and arranged by Grace W. Haight (Greenville, S.C.: Bob Jones University Press, 1942), 107.
44. Bob Jones III, *Biblical Answers to Bothersome Questions,* 30. The "devilish" translations identified are the Good News for Modern Man, the Living Bible, the Revised Standard Version, and the New English Bible.
45. Idem, *A Sermon a Day Keeps the Devil Away* (Greenville, S.C.: Bob Jones University Press, 1980), 4.
46. Bob Jones, Jr., *Cornbread and Caviar,* 201.
47. Bob Jones III, *A Sermon a Day Keeps the Devil Away,* 5-6. This quote occurs in a chapter entitled, "Is There a Literal Devil?'
48. Ibid., 4.
49. Bob Jones, Sr., *Comments on Here and Hereafter,* 84-85.
50. *Bulletin: Catalog & Announcements,* 15.
51. Bob Jones, Jr., *Fundamentals of Faith,* 3. Italics in the original.
52. Ibid., 4. Again the italics are in the original.
53. Ibid.
54. Ibid., 5.
55. Bob Jones University does not agree with some conservative Christians that the King James Version of the Bible is uniquely inspired by God. Thurman Wisdom, *Light on the Bible Text Debate* (Greenville, S.C.: Bob Jones University Press, 1984), 1-2.
56. Bob Jones III, *Biblical Answers to Bothersome Questions,* 5.
57. Ibid., 30.
58. Ibid., 2-3. Italics in the original.
59. Stewart Custer quotes Isaiah 40:13, 22, and 26 in *Problems of Evolution* (Greenville, S.C.: Bob Jones University, 1988), 1.
60. George Mulfinger cites Job 38:4, Genesis 2:1, 2 and a number of other verses in *How Did the Earth Get Here?* (Greenville, S.C.: Bob

Jones University Press, 1972), 4, 5, and elsewhere.

61. Genesis 6:5, Matthew 12:34, and other quotations in Elmer L. Rumminger, *X-Rated TV* (Greenville, S.C.: Bob Jones University Press, 1973), 2, 3, and elsewhere. This pamphlet is a reprint of an article that originally appeared in *Faith for the Family*, March-April 1973.

62. Ezekiel 18:20, Genesis 19, and other citations in Dan Olinger, *Homosexuality*, 2d ed. (Greenville, S.C.: Bob Jones University Press, 1989), 3, 5, and elsewhere.

63. The official history of the university devotes its first twenty-four pages to describing Bob Jones, Sr.'s life as a child and young man. Wright, 1-24. The first film produced by the Bob Jones University film department was an illustrated sermon of Bob Jones, Sr. called *Light of the World,* which includes a dramatic reenactment of a couple of incidents from the founder's childhood. The most extensive discussion of Bob Jones, Sr.'s youth is in Johnson, 3-59.

64. Wright, 280.

65. For example, the apothegm just quoted was recited by Thurman Wisdom, Dean of the School of Religion at Bob Jones University, interview by author, Tape recording, Greenville, South Carolina, 29 May 1990.

66. Current administrators disagreed over how important the Jones family is to the university. Dean Wisdom told me that he did not think that it would make much difference if in the next generation there was no longer someone from the Jones family to take over the reins, as long as another leader could be found with "the same vision, the same beliefs." Wisdom, interview by author. Mr. McAllister, on the other hand, said that he thought that many people would be concerned if there were no Jones to head up the university in the future. McAllister, interview by author. Yet both men maintained that the Joneses have not been authoritarian leaders.

67. In 1990-1991 eighteen of the twenty-six deans of schools and chairpersons of undergraduate divisions were listed in the catalog as having had at least a part of their education at Bob Jones University. *Bulletin: Catalog & Announcements.*

68. Apparently in the early 1950s an effort was made to unseat Bob Jones, Sr. as chairman of the board of trustees led by an administrator named Ted Mercer. This coup was unsuccessful and Mercer was forced to leave the university. He later became president of Bryan College in Dayton, Tennessee. (Wisdom, interview by author). Unfortunately I have not been able to collect much information on this incident.

69. *The Christian Teaching of Science* (Greenville, S.C.: Bob Jones University Press, 1981), 1.
70. The pamphlet actually spells out eight ways in which science is limited: that science is fallible, for example, and that it is changeable. *The Christian Teaching of Science*, 9-12.
71. *The Christian Teaching of Science*, 12.
72. Ibid., 13.
73. Ibid, 14. Theistic evolution is also rejected, the idea that God created the world but used evolution in that process.
74. *The Christian Teaching of Science*, 15.
75. George Marsden has pointed out that in their scientific criticisms of evolution fundamentalists have tended to rely upon a taxonomic model of science which emphasizes the disciplined observation of facts and which is suspicious of grand theorizing. Marsden, 212-221.
76. William S. Pinkston, Jr., *Biology for Christian Schools*, rev. ed. (Greenville, S.C.: Bob Jones University Press, 1987), 176.
77. Ibid., 178.
78. For one example of the offensive against bootleggers see Johnson, 126-128. On "Women on Road to Ruin," see Johnson, 68-71.
79. See, for example, Lynn Darling, "Bob Jones University: Safe and Saved in South Carolina," *Washington Post*, 9 May 1982, sec. H, pp. 1 and 4.
80. Interracial dating is also forbidden, since the university believes that the Bible does not allow interracial marriage (Wright, 377-389). Up until 1970 when the Internal Revenue Service threatened to cut off Bob Jones University's tax exempt status, the university did not admit African American students. Bob Jones changed its policy so that African Americans might be enter the university, but that still did not satisfy the I.R.S. In 1976 the tax exempt status of the university was revoked by the I.R.S. with the argument that Bob Jones University's rules against interracial dating are racially discriminatory. The university appealed the case all the way to the Supreme Court, charging that the decision of the Internal Revenue Service was a violation of religious freedom. In spite of losing this appeal, Bob Jones University still forbids interracial dating, and it is still not tax exempt. For a general discussion of the Bob Jones tax case see Dean M. Kelley, "The Supreme Court Redefines Tax Exemption," in *Church-State Relations: Tensions and Transitions*, ed. Thomas Robbins and Roland Robertson (New Brunswick: Transaction Books, 1987), 115-124. The implications of the case are debated in Dean M. Kelley and Donna Demac, "What's the Issue at B.J.U.?" *Christianity and Crisis*, 1 November

1982, 331-336. See the text of the high court's ruling in "Text of U.S. Supreme Court Decision: *Bob Jones University* v. *United States* and *Goldsboro Christian Schools, Inc.* v. *United States*," *Journal of Church and State* 25 (1983): 605-628.

81. *Bulletin: Catalog & Announcements*, 231.
82. These rules are codified in the *Student Handbook* given to every new student at Bob Jones University. In order to adequately portray the university's discipline I tried to obtain a copy of the *Handbook*, but was unsuccessful. Bob Jones IV, who works in the Public Liaison office, explained that in the past the university has not been fairly represented by journalists who have quoted rules out of context from the *Handbook*. As a consequence of this experience Bob Jones University only gives the *Student Handbook* to students, and not to anyone else. So I will be forced to rely here on published reports and interviews with university officials.
83. *Bulletin: Catalog & Announcements*, 231.
84. James Berg, Dean of Students at Bob Jones University, interview by author, Notes, Greenville, South Carolina, 31 May 1990. The case against T.V. is made in the pamphlet by Rumminger already cited.
85. James Berg, interview. The beat of rock and roll music is condemned as inspiring sensuality. Bob Jones III, *Idols, Rock Music, and Elvis Presley* (Greenville, S.C.: Bob Jones University, n. d.), audio cassette of a sermon.
86. Lyn Nabers Riddle, "Bob Jones: A Mystery to Outsiders," *Greenville (S.C.) Piedmont*, 23 February 1981, sec. 2, p. 1. This article is based upon the 1980-1981 *Student Handbook*.
87. James Berg, interview.
88. Ibid.
89. J.H. Powell, "Unrequited Spring," *Atlanta Weekly*, 4 April 1982, n.p.
90. Darling, sec. H, p. 4. The author is quoting Don Unruh, a ministerial student at the university.
91. Sandeen, 103-131.
92. Bob Jones, Sr., *The Second Coming of Christ* (Greenville, S.C.: Bob Jones University, 1977), audio cassette of a sermon delivered on 26 October 1952.
93. Ibid.
94. Bob Jones, Sr., *Comments on Here and Hereafter*, 108.
95. Bob Jones, Sr., *The Second Coming of Christ*.
96. Bob Jones, Jr., *Cornbread and Caviar*, 175.
97. Ibid., 204. The quote refers to Luke 18:8.
98. Bob Jones, Jr., *Pseudo-Fundamentalism*. The quote is Matthew 7:14.

99. Bob Jones, Jr., *Revival and Morality* (Greenville, S.C.: Bob Jones University, 1981), 2. This pamphlet is a reprint of an article that originally appeared in *Faith for the Family,* May-June 1981.
100. Larry L. King, "Bob Jones University: The Buckle on the Bible Belt," *Harper's Magazine,* 8 June 1966, 53, 57-58.
101. Jean Daskais, "Religion and Politics: Fundamentalists Helped Build Area's Republican Party," *Greenville (S.C.) Piedmont,* 14 November 1984, sec. A, pp. 1, 14 and 15.
102. Bob Jones, Jr., *Cornbread and Caviar,* 197.
103. This is the thesis of Sandeen's book *The Roots of Fundamentalism.*
104. This seems to the position of David Beale, a church historian and faculty member at Bob Jones University, when he writes "Fundamentalism does have 'roots,' but Sandeen has only treated *a* root, i. e., millenarianism." David O. Beale, *In Pursuit of Purity: American Fundamentalism Since 1850* (Greenville, S.C.: Unusual Publications, 1986), 400. Italics in the original.
105. For a discussion of Millerite Adventism, see Sandeen, 49-55.
106. Bob Jones, Jr., *The Return of the Lord* (Greenville, S.C.: Bob Jones University, 1985), audio cassette of a sermon delivered on 16 April 1985.
107. Bob Jones, Sr., *The Second Coming of Christ.*
108. Ibid.
109. Bob Jones, Jr., *The Return of the Lord,* quoting Acts 1:7.
110. For example, Leonard Binder, *Religion and Politics in Pakistan* (Berkeley: University of California Press, 1961), 70-75, and Sheila McDonough, *Muslim Ethics and Modernity: A Comparative Study of the Ethical Thought of Sayyid Ahmad Khan and Mawlana Mawdudi,* Comparative Ethics Series, vol. 1 (Waterloo, Ontario: Wilfrid Laurier University Press for the Canadian Corporation for Studies in Religion, 1984), 94-98.
111. For example, Emmanuel Sivan, *Radical Islam: Medieval Theology and Modern Politics* (New Haven: Yale University Press, 1985), 22-23.
112. Maulana S. Abu'l-A'la Maududi, *The Islamic Law and Constitution,* trans. and ed. Khurshid Ahmad, 2d ed. (Lahore: Islamic Publications, 1960), 270.
113. Idem, *Musalman aur Maujudah Siyasi Kashmakash* (Pathankot: n. p., 1942), 3: 76, quoted in Kalim Bahadur, *The Jama'at-i Islami of Pakistan: Political Thought and Political Action* (Delhi: Chetana Publications, 1977), 39.
114. Maududi wrote, "A Throng consisting of Socialists, athiests [*sic*], secularists, jagirdars and landlords, carelessly herded together, can

never lead the nation in the right direction." Sarwat Saulat, *Maulana Maududi* (Karachi: International Islamic Publishers, 1979), 15.

115. Maududi, *The Islamic Law and Constitution*, 44.
116. Ibid., 117-118.
117. Ibid., 107.
118. Islamization became more popular with the government after General Zia seized power in 1977. Before that the Jama'at's record in Pakistan's infrequent elections was dismal. In the 1951 provincial elections only one of the Jama'at's fifty-three candidates was elected. In the 1970 elections the Jama'at-i Islami could capture only four out of three hundred seats in the National Assembly. Bahadur, 64 and 125.
119. The Jama'at-i Islami was critical of the spread of Western ideas and practices in other areas of life as well, though politics was paramount.
120. Maulana S. Abu'l-A'la Maududi, *A Short History of the Revivalist Movement in Islam*, trans. al-Ash'ari, 2d rev. ed. (Lahore: Islamic Publications, 1972), 114-115.
121. Charles J. Adams, "The Ideology of Mawlana Mawdudi," in *South Asian Politics and Religion*, ed. Donald Eugene Smith (Princeton: Princeton University Press, 1966), 385.
122. Maududi, *The Islamic Law and Constitution*, 55-56. For the same argument by Egyptian fundamentalists see James Darrell Chancellor, "A Comparative Approach to Religious Fundamentalism: Egyptian Sunni Islam and American Protestant Christianity" (Ph.D. diss., Duke University, 1988), 178-179.
123. Maududi, *The Islamic Law and Constitution*, 293-321.
124. McDonough, 64.
125. *Constituent Assembly of Pakistan Debates*, vol. 5 (7-12 March 1949): 1-2.
126. The text of the resolution of the Majlis-i-Shura of the Jama'at-i Islami, which was moved by Maududi, in support (with some reservations) of the 1956 constitution can be found in Maududi, *The Islamic Law and Constitution*, 405-411.
127. This includes the constitution imposed in 1962 by Ayub Khan and in 1973 by Bhutto. Sarwat Saulat, 54 and 85.
128. With the Combined Opposition Parties in 1964, with the Pakistan Democratic Movement in 1967, and with the Pakistan National Alliance in 1977. Sarwat Saulat, 60, 63, and 94.
129. The members of the Consultative Assembly, as well as the Head of State, should be male. Maududi, *The Islamic Law and Constitution*, 260-261.
130. Bahadur, 105-112.

131. Although the details are confused in many of the sources, it is clear that the occasion that prompted Maududi to write the book was the controversy surrounding the murder of the Arya Samaj leader Swami Shraddhanand. On *al-Jihad fi 'l-Islam*, see Binder, 81-82. For the murder of Shraddhanand, see J.T.F. Jordens, *Swāmī Shraddhānanda: His Life and Causes* (Delhi: Oxford University Press, 1981), 166.
132. The Maulana only adopted the dress and appearance identified with the ulama after 1937, when he was appointed to a religious post by Muhammad Iqbal. Before that Maududi wore Western-style clothing.
133. Binder, 82.
134. Bruce Lawrence has underlined the tendency of Islamic fundamentalists to emphasize jihad, to the extent that it is often added to the traditional 'five pillars' as required of every Muslim. Bruce B. Lawrence, *Defenders of God: The Fundamentalist Revolt against the Modern Age* (San Francisco: Harper and Row, 1989), 216-217.
135. Maulana S. Abu'l-A'la Maududi, *Fundamentals of Islam* (Lahore: Islamic Publications, 1975), 243.
136. Not every war in which Muslims fight non-Muslims is a jihad. For example, for years the Maulana refused to accept that Pakistan's undeclared guerilla war with India over Kashmir was a holy war. Maududi did proclaim the 1965 Indo-Pakistan War a jihad, however. Bahadur, 55-58, 113-114.
137. Maududi, *Fundamentals of Islam*, 253.
138. Idem, *Towards Understanding Islam*, trans. and ed. Khurshid Ahmad, 14th ed. (Lahore: Idara Tarjuman-ul-Quran, 1974), 10.
139. Ibid., 13.
140. Ibid., 19.
141. Idem, *Fundamentals of Islam*, 255. The ellipses are in the original. *Shirk* is the sin of associating other entities with Allah which is tantamount to polytheism.
142. Bahadur, 13.
143. Maududi, *Towards Understanding Islam*, 112. Italics in the original.
144. Sarwat Saulat writes that Maududi began *Tafhim al-Qur'an* in 1943 and published the last volume in 1972. Sarwat Saulat, 85-88, 186.
145. Maududi occasionally vacated the post of Amir when in prison (he was jailed three times, 1948-1950, 1953-1955, and 1967), sick, or traveling overseas, but he did not finally surrender it until late in his life.
146. On the constitutional powers of the Amir and the Majlis-i-Shura, see Bahadur, 139-140.
147. See Bahadur, 57, for an instance when the Majlis-i-Shura failed to

support the Amir.

148. In 1965 one out of every fifteen of the members of the Jama'at-i Islami was a paid worker. Bahadur, 145.

149. Bahadur, 17-18, 87-93, and 109-112.

150. Ibid., 143-146.

151. Maulana S. Abu'l-A'la Maududi, *Musalmanon ka Mazi va Hal aur Mustaqbil keli'e La'ihah-yi 'Amal* (no publication information), quoted in Syed As'ad Gilani, *Maududi: Thought and Movement*, trans. Hasan Muizuddin Qazi, 5th ed. (1st English ed.) (Lahore: Farooq Hasan Gilani, 1978), 291.

152. Maududi, *Towards Understanding Islam*, 88-98.

153. Ibid., 45-46.

154. Ibid., 113.

155. Ibid., 114.

156. Ibid., 108-109.

157. Idem, *Fundamentals of Islam*, 86.

158. Idem, *Towards Understanding Islam*, 80.

159. Adams, 380.

160. It should be noted that, though we will concentrate here on sexual licentiousness, Maududi condemns raging permissiveness in the Islamic world in areas beyond the sexual. In the sermons collected in *Fundamentals of Islam* the Maulana paints a very dark picture of the laxness of his hearers with regard to the basic duties of Muslims. For example, pp. 12-14.

161. Maulana S. Abu'l-A'la Maududi, *Purdah and the Status of Woman in Islam*, trans. and ed. al-Ash'ari, 2d ed. (Lahore: Islamic Publications, 1975), 1-6.

162. Ibid., 15.

163. "Tragic Consequences—I" and "Tragic Consequences—II" are the titles of the two chapters which contain this tale of woe in Maududi, *Purdah*, 37-83.

164. Maududi, *Purdah*, 56.

165. Ibid., 82.

166. Ibid., 81.

167. Ibid., 82.

168. Ibid., 112-113.

169. In the modern nation-state women should not be allowed representation in the legislative assemblies, rather separate bodies should be established made up entirely of women to represent women. Maududi, *The Islamic Law and Constitution*, 345-346. This policy has its parallel in the Jama'at-i Islami where women are permitted to become members, but are represented by a separate Majlis-i-Shura, which reports to and is directed by the male Amir. Bahadur, 149.

170. Maududi, *Purdah*, 121-122.
171. McDonough, 68.
172. Freeland K. Abbott, "Maulana Maududi on Quranic Interpretation," *The Muslim World* 48 (1958): 8. The author's name is actually spelled Abbot here, but this is apparently incorrect. In this quote Abbott is referring to the distinction between clear and allegorical verses in Qur'an 3.7, which he brought up in the question preceding this one.
173. Abbott, "Maulana Maududi on Quranic Interpretation," 13.
174. Ibid., 8
175. Ibid., 14.
176. Maududi, *Fundamentals of Islam*, 86-87.
177. Adams, 375. The Jama'at imitates these groups only in party structure, Maududi claims that it is free of the dictatorial and repressive tendencies of the communists and fascists.
178. Though our focus here is on the members, there are a number of ways that the influence of the Jama'at-i Islami spreads beyond the membership. The Jama'at formally recognizes a body of sympathizers (*muttafaqin*), who support the Jama'at's ideology but are unwilling to accept the severe discipline imposed on its full members. The Jama'at's public image is enhanced by its commitment to social service, providing free medical care to the indigent, for example. An active publishing program carries the message of the Jama'at to non-members in Pakistan and beyond. (In the Middle East the Ikhwan al-Muslimun were influenced by Maududi's works as early as the 1940s.) Also the Jama'at-i Islami sponsors front organizations that work with students, laborers, farmers, and the ulama.
179. Before the first all-India conference of the Jama'at-i Islami in 1944 three hundred members, out of a total of seven hundred, were purged. Bahadur, 19.
180. In 1963 the number of members was reported to be 1605, with 43,000 registered sympathizers. Bahadur, 103.
181. Maulana S. Abu'l-A'la Maududi, *Tahrik-i-Islami ki Akhlaqi Bunyaden*, 5th ed. (Karachi and Lahore: n. p.), 1954, quoted in Aziz Ahmad and G.E. von Grunebaum, eds., *Muslim Self-Statement in India and Pakistan, 1857-1968*, (Wiesbaden: Otto Harrassowitz, 1970), 166. The translation of this passage in this anthology is by Charles J. Adams.
182. Ibid.
183. Maududi, *Fundamentals of Islam*, 263.
184. Maududi, *Tahrik-i-Islami ke Akhlaqi Bunyaden*, in Ahmad and von Grunebaum, 158.
185. See, for example, Maududi, *Towards Understanding Islam*, 116-

117.

186. Maududi, *A Short History of the Revivalist Movement in Islam*, 40. Maududi indicates that this version of the Tradition is derived from Shatibi in *Muwaflqat* and Maulana Isma'il Shahid in *Mansab-i-Imamat*.

187. Maududi, *A Short History of the Revivalist Movement in Islam*, 40.

188. There are elaborate Hadith about how the Mahdi will be recognized. Maududi speculates that they are not utterances of the prophet, but were developed to bolster false claims to being the Mahdi that had been made by individuals in the past especially among Shi'ites. Maududi, *A Short History of the Revivalist Movement in Islam*, 139-140.

189. Maududi, *A Short History of the Revivalist Movement in Islam*, 41-44.

190. Ibid., 135-139.

191. M.R. Khan, *The Delusion of Grandeur: An Analysis of Maulana Maudoodi and his Jamaat* (Karachi: Lahore Book House, 1964), 125-142.

192. Maududi, *A Short History of the Revivalist Movement in Islam*, 142-143.

193. A similar argument can be found in William Shepard, 'Fundamentalism' Christian and Islamic," *Religion* 17 (1987): 359.

194. Perhaps Marty's characterization of the antihermeneutical interpretation of the textual authorities of fundamentalisms should be extended to non-textual traditional authorities as well. There is a significant sense in which Maududi's interpretation of the Shari'a is antihermeneutical.

195. Consistent with this argument, it seems to me that to include "antievolutionary" among the defining elements of fundamentalism is to skew the discussion in the direction of North American Protestant fundamentalism. There is a view of past and future history which is rather characteristic of fundamentalism. Yet, because the term antievolutionary suggests something very specific for the Christian case which is not important in other cases, it is not an appropriate label for this fundamentalist view of history.

2

HINDU FUNDAMENTALISM

In the previous chapter a definition of fundamentalism was presented and two fundamentalist movements were analyzed in light of that definition. In this chapter we will direct our attention to a Hindu movement which has been characterized as fundamentalist, the Arya Samaj.[1] There are two main sections in this chapter. In the first section the Arya Samaj will be analyzed according to Martin Marty's definition of fundamentalism. The second section will be given over to a presentation of some comparisons of the Arya Samaj with Bob Jones University and the Jama'at-i Islami, the two groups which have already been scrutinized. Then in the next part of this book we will move on to look at the scripturalism of the Arya Samaj in greater depth.

THE ARYA SAMAJ AS A FUNDAMENTALIST MOVEMENT

In this section we will study the Arya Samaj with the aid of the definition of fundamentalism presented in the introduction.[2] Hence our discussion will be divided into twelve headings, which correspond to the twelve aspects of Martin Marty's definition. Although parallels between the Arya Samaj and the movements presented in the last chapter will be obvious, we will only draw out those parallels directly in the next section. The presentation of the Arya Samaj as a fundamentalist movement in this section will provide the basic material for comparison in the next.

FUNDAMENTALISM AS REACTIONARY

The Arya Samaj arose as a reaction against modernist ideas that were just beginning to make headway in India at the time of the founding of the Samaj, and against traditional Hinduism as well. By 1849 the British had taken over the entirety of the province of Punjab. Through interaction with their conquerors the Punjabi elite came to know of the British disdain for many aspects of Indian culture. A response to this criticism was offered by Bengalis who came to Punjab to work for the British in the administration of the province. Already in Bengal liberals were attempting to reform Indian society in light of colonial criticism. The Brahmo Samaj was at the vanguard of this movement. Some of the Bengalis who came to Punjab with the British were Brahmo Samajists; many had been influenced by Brahmo thought.[3]

Yet most of the members of the Punjabi elite came to reject the philosophy imported from Bengal. Many opted instead for the Arya Samaj. The Arya Samaj criticized the Brahmo Samaj for rejecting the good along with the bad in its efforts at reform. At the same time the Arya Samaj was not silent about more traditional aspects of Hindu society, rather it bitterly condemned some common religious beliefs and social practices. The real Hinduism, Arya Samajists argued, has been weighed down with all kinds of objectionable accretions. According to the Arya Samaj, then, the Vedic religion, the true Hinduism, is under attack from two sides. Traditional Hindus have obscured it with a vast body of false ideas and actions. By the same token, modernists, in trying to purify the Hindu tradition, have thrown out the true Vedic faith along with the false accretions. Arya Samajists believe that it is only they who understand the true tradition and can save it from these profound threats.

The Arya Samaj has defended its version of Hinduism from traditionalists and modernists by going on the attack against them.[4] The author of this strategy was Swami Dayanand Sarasvati, the founder of the Samaj. In public debates and in his writings Swami Dayanand very strongly criticized other Hindu sects. The best example of this is the eleventh chapter of Dayanand's book *Satyārth Prakāś*. First published in 1875, a second revised edition of *Satyārth Prakāś* came out in in 1884. This book is the most complete statement of Swami Dayanand's teachings, and it is his most popular work. In the first part of *Satyārth Prakāś* the swami sets forth his own philosophy positively. The second part of the book is devoted to criticism of other religions.

The eleventh chapter of *Satyārth Prakāś*, the first chapter in the critical second part of the book, is dedicated to analyzing Hindu sects. Most of this chapter is concentrated on criticizing traditional practices, but here Dayanand also attacks reform movements, particularly the Brahmo Samaj and the Prarthana Samaj. The swami enumerates sixteen faults of the followers of the other two Samajes. We will not reproduce all sixteen objections here, but a few of the cardinal points are worth noting. Dayanand argues that the modernists feel no attachment to their own country (they feel no *svadeśbhakti*). In place of the ancient sages of India, they praise Jesus and Muhammad. In place of Indian clothing and diet, they have adopted European styles.[5]

Dayanand's point here is most clearly expressed when he criticizes the reformers' tendency to dine with Europeans, Muslims, and Hindus of all castes. Swami Dayanand brings home his argument against interdining with a therapeutic metaphor. Just as medicine is not for the healthy but should be used to cure the sick, so knowledge is meant to be shared with the ignorant. The disease of ignorance is so rampant in India, Dayanand writes, that some have come to regard dietary practices as the soul of religion. The modernists by interdining indiscriminately have become anathema to the ignorant. Thus the knowledge that the reformers possess, salutary as it might be, cannot reach the people who need it most. The modernists by taking too radical a course, not only in matters of diet but in other areas as well, have cut themselves off from the very people whom they should be trying to help.

Swami Dayanand also criticizes the Brahmo view of scripture. It was a tenet of Brahmoism at this time that there is no infallible book.[6] As Dayanand states the theory, just as no human is perfect, so all scriptures produced by humans are imperfect. The swami goes on to point out that by this logic even the statement, "Every human production contains some error," must contain some error. The swami insists that the Brahmo doctrine makes it impossible to ever certainly determine the truth.

> You are not omniscient, just as other humans are not omniscient. By mistake won't you sometimes accept untruth and reject truth? For this reason, for us whose knowledge is limited the assistance of the words of the omniscient highest soul is necessary. . . . When all truth is accessible in the Vedas, in which there is not any untruth, you are only hurting yourselves and others by raising objections to accepting them.[7]

Against Brahmo relativism Swami Dayanand offers the Vedas. It is the swami's belief that the Vedas are the one scripture that was created by God. All other holy books are the compositions of humans, Dayanand admits, and they do contain error, as the Brahmos aver. But the Vedas were composed by God: they are the only sure source of truth in an imperfect world. So Dayanand attacks the beliefs as well as the practices of modernist Hindu organizations.

Though Swami Dayanand does criticize reformers in the eleventh chapter of *Satyāth Prakāś*, most of his attention is directed against traditional beliefs and practices. The swami's argument here is not organized under general headings, rather he concentrates on a series of individual sects, exposing the faults of each in turn. Even so, there are some aspects of traditional Hinduism which are repeatedly attacked. Among these are the worship of images and pilgrimage. With regard to idolatry Dayanand maintains that God is formless and hence cannot be adequately captured by any plastic representation. Ultimately the swami sees image worship as tied to the sectarianism of Hinduism, which he decries.[8] In the section on pilgrimage, Swami Dayanand rejects one by one the miracles associated with various sacred centers. Studying the Vedas, speaking the truth, and so forth, are the only means for reaching a higher world, not visiting holy places.[9]

Dayanand also criticizes some of the scriptures which are held in high regard by traditional Hindus, most notably the Puranas. He argues that although the eighteen Puranas are attributed to the sage Vyāsa, it is impossible that such a wise individual would create such false stories. The Puranas are characterized first of all by mutual contradiction: each text claims that the deity who is its subject is the highest lord (*parameśvara*), while denying this status to other divinities. These competing claims are at the heart of contemporary Hindu sectarianism in the swami's analysis. The Puranas also contain fantastic tales, Dayanand argues, which are opposed to the order of nature as ordained by God. For example, in the *Bhāgavata Purāṇa* it is said that the various classes of animals were born to the wives of Kaśyapa. Birds were brought forth from Vinatā, snakes from Kadrū, dogs and jackals from Saramā, and so forth. Dayanand writes: "From the union of the discharge of a woman and semen of a man only a human can be made, in opposition to the order of creation of the highest lord animals, birds, snakes, and so forth, can never be produced."[10] According to Swami Dayanand the Puranas are not the works of sages but of sectarians, they are mutually contradictory, and contain much that is false.[11]

Despite some constant themes in the analysis of traditional sects in the eleventh chapter of *Satyārth Prakāś*, there is not the sense that Dayanand is criticizing a single unified phenomenon. In fact one of the swami's arguments against the sects that he attacks is that they hold to mutually exclusive beliefs—each is divided against the others. It was really only after Dayanand's time, and partially in response to his criticisms, that organizations emerged at the end of the nineteenth century to defend the congeries of beliefs and practices that is traditional Hinduism. These organizations often called what they were protecting the *sanātana dharma*, or the eternal religion. Hence their leaders have sometimes been called "Sanatanists" by students of modern Hinduism. Arya Samajists occasionally label traditional Hindus *sanātanī*s, but they are much more likely to call them *paurāṇika*s. Some Arya Samajists never use the term *sanātanī* for the defenders of traditional Hinduism, believing that it is a misnomer.[12]

This difference in terminology arises from a debate over history. "Sanatanists" call their version of the Hindu tradition the *sanātana dharma* (the eternal religion) because they believe that it represents the ancient and enduring form of Hinduism. The teaching of the Arya Samaj is, in the opinion of those who hold this view, a pernicious novelty. Arya Samajists on the other hand argue that their formulation of Hinduism is consonant with the most antique, Vedic form of the tradition. Since Vedic times the Hindu religion has changed, according to the Arya theory, most notably with the apotheosis of the deities associated with the Puranas. Arya Samajists claim that the Hinduism which the "Sanatanists" defend is not the ancient religion, but the medieval degenerate cult of the Puranas. This cult and those who uphold it are thus characterized as *paurāṇika*, an adjective which means "of or related to the Puranas." Arya Samajists believe that the religion that they themselves advocate is the real *sanātana dharma*, the real eternal religion.[13]

The first important traditionalist to emerge in defense of Hinduism in Punjab was Pandit Shraddha Ram Phillouri (1837-1881). Shraddha Ram published his major work *Dharma Rakṣā* ("Defense of Dharma") in response to Bengali Brahmo criticism of Hindu practices. After 1877 Swami Dayanand burst upon Punjab, and Shraddha Ram accepted the challenge of the founder of the Arya Samaj. Shraddha Ram and Dayanand never debated face to face, but still the pandit tried to counter the effects of the swami's preaching. During the course of his life Shraddha Ram founded several organizations to propagate his version of Hinduism, including a couple of different schools, but none of those institutions grew into a major movement.[14]

In 1887 a new organization came on the scene which became the center of traditional polemics against the Arya Samaj, the Bharat Dharma Mahamandal (the "Great Association for Indian Dharma"). The Mahamandal was founded in that year in the princely state of Kapurthala through the efforts of Pandit Din Dayalu Sharma. The Mahamandal first won adherents in Punjab among the followers of Shraddha Ram Phillouri. There were debates between the members of the Mahamandal and Arya Samajists on a number of issues stemming from their divergent views of Hinduism—the worship of idols was a frequent topic. The adherents of the Mahamandal went on the offensive through attempts to have Arya Samajists outcasted, but this censure, where it was invoked, usually did not hold for long.[15] The Bharat Dharma Mahamandal was just the first of many traditionalist groups that arose to do battle with the Arya Samaj, a battle that continues to the present.

The Arya Samaj has defended the true faith on two fronts. To the left are the modernists, to the right the traditionalists. Behind this conflict lay the overwhelming force of European ideas which was just beginning to make itself felt in Punjab at the end of the last century. From the perspective of the Arya Samaj, the reformers weaken Hinduism by attacking what is true in it. The traditionalists are not in a position to protect Hinduism either, Arya Samajists believe, because they maintain what is false. In the view of Arya Samajists, it is only they who can defend the true faith, because they alone understand that faith.

SELECTIVE RETRIEVAL OF THE FUNDAMENTALS

Arya Samajists reach back to the Vedic age to determine the fundamentals of the Hindu tradition which they uphold. There have been many influential formulations of the fundamental teachings of the Arya Samaj, but the most important is the ten *niyams*. The ten principles (or *niyams*) of the Arya Samaj were written in Lahore in 1877 as a summary statement of the Samaj's position.[16] Since then assent to the *niyams* has been required of every individual who joins the Arya Samaj, and as such they are a sort of official creed. The *niyams* occupy a prominent place in the lives of Arya Samajists. In many Arya Samaj temples a copy of the principles is prominently displayed. Often the *niyams* are recited at the end of the weekly service, or on other important occasions. They are frequently quoted in the sermons preached at Arya services. Given their significance, it is worth quoting the ten *niyams* in their entirety.

1. The original source of true knowledge and whatever is known through it is the highest Lord ["parameśvar"].
2. The Lord is the very essence of truth, consciousness, and bliss, formless, almighty, just, merciful, unborn, without end, changeless, without beginning, unparalleled, the basis of everything, lord of all, omnipresent, pervading all, ageless, deathless, fearless, permanent, pure, and the creator of the world, only he is worthy of worship.
3. The Veda is the book of true knowledge. To study the Veda and to teach it, to hear and expound it is the highest dharma of all Arya Samajists.[17]
4. All should always be ready to accept truth and reject untruth.
5. All should perform every action consistent with dharma, that is, after reflecting upon truth and untruth.
6. Doing good for the world is the chief goal of this society, that is, improving it physically, spiritually, and socially.
7. One's behavior towards all should be appropriate, consistent with dharma, and loving.
8. All should destroy ignorance and increase knowledge.
9. Each should not be satisfied with his or her own improvement alone, rather the improvement of all should be understood as one's own improvement.
10. All people should be bound in maintaining social principles which affect the welfare of all, and everyone should be free in the principles which affect the welfare of the individual.[18]

Although the ten principles provide some introduction to the fundamental beliefs of the Arya Samaj, they are not a complete guide to its teachings. These *niyams* were intended as an inclusive statement of the position of the Arya Samaj, and there is an emphasis in them on generalities that might win wide acceptance.[19] Many of the most important aspects of Dayanand's teaching are not explicitly spelled out in the ten principles. In the early history of the Arya Samaj there was some debate over whether assent to these *niyams* could be taken as a sufficient confession of faith for new members. Some maintained that more should be required.[20] To understand the full thrust of Swami Dayanand's philosophy, one must look beyond the ten principles of the Arya Samaj.

Perhaps the most important summary of Dayanand's teachings by the swami himself is the epilogue to his book *Satyārth Prakāś*, which is entitled "Svamantavyāmantavya-Prakāśaḥ" ("Light on My Own Beliefs and Disbeliefs").[21] Here Dayanand sets out his position in a set of explanations of key terms, each of which is numbered. The ten principles of the Arya Samaj along with "Svamantavyāmantavya-Prakāśaḥ" provide a solid introduction to the Arya Samaj's fundamentals.

Such an introduction must begin with the Vedas, since Arya Samajists argue that their teaching in all areas is grounded in those texts. In the third *niyam* of the Samaj the Vedas are identified as the source of true knowledge. In "Svamantavyāmantavya-Prakāśaḥ" Swami Dayanand's position on the Vedas is spelled out in greater detail, beginning with his second definition. Dayanand first indicates that when he is speaking of the Vedas he is only concerned with the mantras. There is a vast literature that is called Vedic, but Dayanand makes a distinction between the Vedic mantras (the Samhitas) and the later commentatorial material. The mantras are without error (*nirbhrānt*) and independently authoritative (*svataḥpramāṇ*). The other literature which explains the mantras is *parataḥpramāṇ* (dependently authoritative), that is, its authority is dependent on the Vedas. Only that is to be accepted from the commentaries which is consistent with the Vedas, anything contrary to them must be rejected.[22]

In the next chapter we will discuss the works which are authoritative for the Arya Samaj and those which are not authoritative in much greater detail. Here we need only mention again that the swami did not have any use for many widely regarded books, especially the Puranas. The twenty-third item in "Svamantavyāmantavya-Prakāśaḥ" is *purāṇ*. Here Dayanand affirms that Brahmanas (which he identifies as commentaries on the Vedas) are the real Puranas, not the traditional Puranic literature.[23]

All of the fundamental beliefs of the Arya Samaj are defended on the basis of the Vedas. Perhaps the most distinctive of these beliefs concerns the Samaj's concept of God. The first word that the swami takes up in "Svamantavyāmantavya-Prakāśaḥ" is God ("īśvar"),[24] and his definition is basically consistent with the second principle of the Arya Samaj which has just been quoted. Arya Samajists believe in only one omniscient, omnipresent, and abstract God. Unlike the deities of traditional Hindus the God of the Arya Samaj does not take on human form, which is implied above when it is said that he is "unborn" ("ajanmā"). According to the Arya Samaj this God is formless ("nirākār"). It is common for Hindus to worship their deities as represented in statues, but Dayanand rejects this practice. The twenty-first item in "Svamantavyāmantavya-Prakāśaḥ" is *devpūjā*. This would be understood by traditional Hindus as the worship (*pūjā*) of an image of a god (*dev*). But Dayanand defines *dev* as one who is learned, and *devpūjā* as service to that person. "I understand their images [that is the learned themselves and others who merit respect] to be worthy of worship, and, on the contrary, inert images made of stone and so forth to be totally unworthy of worship."[25]

In the area of practice the Arya Samaj has supported a number of social reforms, arguing that prevailing customs are not consistent with those of the Vedic period.[26] These reforms have been the source of considerable rancor between the Samaj and its detractors. Perhaps that is why they are not spelled out in great detail in either the ten *niyams* of the Arya Samaj or in "Svamantavyāmantavya-Prakāśaḥ." There is, nonetheless, some support for social action even in the ten principles. The sixth *niyam* states very succinctly the purpose of the Arya Samaj, which is to do good. Though the Arya Samaj is a religious organization, it does not limit itself to spiritual questions. This *niyam* specifies that the Samaj is not only for spiritual improvement (*ātmik unnati*), but for physical (*śārīrik*) and social (*sāmājik*) improvement as well. In contrast to the individualistic emphasis of much of Hindu spirituality, the ninth principle directs the attention of the Arya Samajist to the wider world. According to it the individual cannot rest content with his or her own improvement alone (again the word used here is *unnati*), rather each person must understand his or her improvement to lie in the betterment of all.

There is a specific reference to one social reform advocated by Swami Dayanand in "Svamantavyāmantavya-Prakāśaḥ." The sixteenth topic covered there is caste and station in life (varnashrama). Dayanand did not accept the prevailing system of caste determined by birth, rather he argued that the caste of each individual should depend on his or her personal merits. Here he writes, "I believe in varnashrama as based on the worthiness of one's qualities and deeds."[27]

Although on some issues the position of the Arya Samaj has been in consonance with that of modernizing social reformers, it is important to realize that the Samaj does not understand itself to be advocating something new. Rather the Samaj demands a return to the beliefs and practices reflected in the Vedas. According to this theory it is the fundamentals from the normative Vedic period which the Arya Samaj defends.

THE FUNDAMENTALS AS SCANDALOUS

The fundamental beliefs and practices of the Arya Samaj serve to define the boundaries of the movement by alienating traditionalists and modernists. The most crucial point in this regard is the position of the Samaj on scripture. For the Arya Samaj the Vedas are the one infallible authority. Every aspect of the teaching of their organization is based on the Vedas, Arya Samajists argue. There is some other literature worthy of study, but its reliability is contingent on the Vedas. And there are many works which the Samaj has identified as totally unauthoritative.

The Arya Samaj's perspective on the Vedas is strikingly different from that of the traditionalists. In classical Indian philosophy the Vedas were held to be *apauruṣeya* (of divine rather than human origin), and hence perfect. Yet even during the Brahmanical age, when the philosophical schools evolved, the use of the Vedic hymns (the Samhitas) was largely limited to ritual contexts. Since the medieval period the center of popular religious devotion has been bhakti works, some of which explicitly affirm that the religion of the Vedas is not appropriate for our degenerate age. With this history as a background, while traditional Hindus might be willing to accede to the infallibility of the Vedas, the importance of the Vedas to the practice of their religion is in fact quite limited. When the Arya Samaj maintains not only that the Vedas are infallible but also that they should be one's guide in all aspects of life, it is making a claim that sets it apart from Hindu traditionalists.

The Arya Samaj's position on scripture other than the Vedas is even more scandalous for traditionalists. While Swami Dayanand accorded limited credibility to some works other than the Vedas, he also denied all authority to a large library of the literature of the Hindu tradition, most notably the Puranas. The Puranas are texts which are basic to contemporary Hindu devotionalism. The Arya Samaj's condemnation of the Puranas and other works definitely distinguishes it from traditional Hinduism.

Arya theories about scripture have been unacceptable to modernists also. The Brahmo Samaj came to conclusions that are directly opposed to the Arya Samaj's positive assertion that the Vedas are infallible. Scripture has always been a part of the life of the Brahmo Samaj. For example, Rammohun Roy, the founder of the Brahmo Samaj, translated the Upanishads and the *Vedanta Sutras* into Bengali and English to establish that his reformed faith has some basis in traditional Hinduism. Later an intense debate took place over the authority of scripture within the context of an attempt to rationalize the philosophy of the Brahmo Samaj. In 1847 Debendranath Tagore and his contemporaries decided that no scripture can be taken as infallibly true, that every book contains some error. This conclusion is reflected in *Brahmo Dharm*, a work made up of passages selected by Debendranath for Brahmo worship, many from the Upanishads. The texts included could only be accepted by Brahmos after their errors had been excised. The Brahmo Samaj denies that any book is entirely inerrant, including the Vedas.

The Brahmo Samaj has not only rejected the Arya Samaj's positive assertion of the infallibility of the Vedas, it has also resisted the negative Arya claim that most other religious literature is worthless. By the Arya Samaj's reckoning it is only works of the Hindu tradition which demand acceptance, while Brahmos have been more eclectic. Rammohun, who was influenced by Unitarianism, was a universalist in accepting rational religion and condemning superstition wherever he found them.[28] He published a translation of the New Testament, for example, which included Christ's ethical teachings but excluded his miracles. In contrast to this, in the thirteenth chapter of his book *Satyārth Prakāś* Swami Dayanand vigorously criticizes the Bible without identifying any worthwhile teaching in it.[29] In the later history of the Brahmo Samaj while Debendranath's attention was focused largely on the Hindu tradition, Keshub Chandra Sen attempted to return the movement to a universalist orientation. In 1875 Keshub and his followers initiated a systematic study of great leaders from various religions. On the other hand, those in the Arya Samaj who have studied other religious traditions have usually done so in order to attack them. In asserting the infallibility of the Vedas and in denying the authority of non-Hindu scriptures, the teachings of the Arya Samaj have alienated modernist Brahmos.

Among the fundamental beliefs of the Arya Samaj, its view of God has been more congenial to modernists than to traditionalists. Swami Dayanand did not accept that the many divinities of contemporary Hinduism are really gods. He did not believe that God can become incarnate. Dayanand's God cannot be represented in any plastic form, and so the swami attacked the image worship of traditional Hindus. The Brahmo Samaj has also been critical of polytheism and idolatry in Hinduism. Brahmos worship a single, abstract God not unlike Dayanand's own. The theism of the Brahmo Samaj is similar to the theology of the Arya Samaj.

In the area of social practice also the Arya Samaj has been closer to modernism than traditionalism. Both the Arya Samaj and the Brahmo

Samaj are generally identified as advocates of reform, though neither organization has been monolithic in its support for social change. For example, though Swami Dayanand admitted that caste should not be determined by birth, he still maintained that it is reasonable for society to be divided into castes. As we will note below, some later Arya Samajists could not accept this position and demanded more radical reform. On just this issue there was a schism in the Brahmo Samaj in 1866. Young radicals, who had demanded a complete disavowal of caste within the Brahmo Samaj, started their own organization called the Brahmo Samaj of India under the leadership of Keshub Chandra Sen. Older conservatives remained with Debendranath Tagore in the Adi Brahmo Samaj (the "Original Brahmo Samaj").[30] Because the views on social reform of the members of both the Arya Samaj and the Brahmo Samaj have spanned a wide spectrum, strong contrasts might be drawn between individuals from the two organizations. Nonetheless it is true that as a whole the Arya Samaj and the modernists have embraced a similar social reform agenda.

A comparison of the positions of the Arya Samaj and the Brahmo Samaj on social reform not only shows the similarity between the two movements but also brings to light their differences as well. In the area of caste, for example, the bases of the programs of the two organizations are divergent. While Brahmos have attempted to show that social status was less rigid in ancient India, they have also supported caste reform with arguments based on Western values like egalitarianism and social utility. Arya Samajists have been much more reluctant to take refuge in Western principles, contenting themselves with an insistence that their theories are based on Vedic social life. The authority for the Arya Samaj in social reform as in all areas of its teaching is the Vedas. It is the Samaj's distinctive position on scripture which is a stumbling block to modernists and a scandal to traditionalists.

FUNDAMENTALISM AS EXCLUSIVE OR SEPARATIST

It is a commonplace of Indological scholarship that Hinduism stresses orthopraxy rather than orthodoxy. While this is a generalization that should not be pushed too far—Hindus have battled over belief as well as practice—yet there is a very heavy emphasis on proper behavior in the Hindu world. This is especially true when it comes to questions of caste. In the nineteenth century many reformers found that it was in the area of caste that their convictions were most profoundly challenged.

The ostracism attendant upon outcasting drove many back from radical experiments in social reform. Caste is an area in which the exclusiveness of the Arya Samaj has been tested.

Arya Samajists maintain that their movement is not a new sect (not another *sampradāya* or *panth*). Behind this denial is an implicit theory about the fate of reform movements in the Hindu tradition over the centuries. Some groups have moderated their attacks on Hinduism, and then disappeared upon being reabsorbed into the larger Hindu community. Other movements have stuck to their criticisms, but over time have been isolated as separate caste groups. This is particularly liable to be the case when a movement encourages caste breaking behavior among its followers. Once a protest movement is relegated to the status of just another subcaste, its effectiveness must be very greatly limited, since the contacts permitted between individuals of different castes are restricted. In order to keep the channels of communication open with all Hindus, Arya Samajists resist being pigeonholed as just another sectarian group.

This has not been an easy struggle, and in no case has it been more difficult than in the area of caste. Swami Dayanand left to his followers a radical teaching with regard to caste. Dayanand rejected caste based on birth, and he was critical of other aspects of caste observance. For example, traditionally it has been maintained that the *śāstras* (the scriptures) do not allow women and Shudras to study the Vedas, and practically women and members of the lower castes did not have much access to education in Dayanand's time. But the swami argued that this understanding of the scriptures is wrong. Women and the lower caste people should be permitted to attend school.[31] Though Dayanand attacked some of the strictures of caste as practised in his day, he did not advocate abandoning caste altogether. On the contrary, he condemned the Brahmos and other reformers who indiscriminately interdined with others regardless of caste status.

In the fourth chapter of *Satyārth Prakāś* Swami Dayanand presents at great length an alternative to the caste system which he criticizes. The swami allows that caste is a natural way to organize society, but he rejects caste based upon birth. Rather Dayanand maintains that each individual should be assigned to a caste according to his or her qualities, deeds, and nature (guna, karma, and *svabhāva*). For example, the person who is given to studying, performing religious rituals, and so forth, should be regarded as a Brahman. The swami wrote that a government commission should be set up to determine the caste of young people at the end of their education on a case by case basis. Once a caste had been assigned, then the young person would be expected to marry within that caste.[32]

This theory is a startlingly radical departure from caste as it is ordinarily practiced in the contemporary Hindu world. What practical program could members of the Arya Samaj adopt that would help to bring about Dayanand's type of caste system? The swami's writings are largely silent on this point. In this situation, where Dayanand's works provide little guidance, Arya Samajists were forced to gradually develop mechanisms for caste reform experimentally. The pressures of the times did much to influence the growth of the Samaj's program on caste. The main tool that was developed in the early history of the Arya Samaj was *śuddhi*. Eventually *śuddhi* would become the center of ideological conflicts that divided Arya Samajists among themselves, and that separated the Samaj from other religious communities.

The word *śuddhi* simply means purification. At first the term was used to apply to efforts by Arya Samajists and others to reconvert Hindus who had become Christians or Muslims. Traditionally a Hindu who converts to Christianity or Islam becomes an outcaste, and there is no mechanism whereby that individual might be restored to caste upon reconverting. Arya Samajists were among the first reformers to try to change this situation, to develop a system through which Hindu converts to other religions could become Hindu again. The motivation behind this initiative was not just sympathy for individual outcastes. Arya Samajists understood Hinduism to be hobbled by its own exclusiveness. While Christianity and Islam were able to proselytize and draw others into their community, Hinduism could not even take back reconverted Hindus, much less accept converts. From 1884 to 1894 at least eighteen local Arya Samaj chapters sponsored *śuddhi* ceremonies, whereby Hindus who had converted to other religions were accepted back into the Hindu fold.[33]

Restoration to caste depended upon the acceptance of the reconverted individual's caste fellows, many of whom were liable to be non-Arya. In this situation Arya Samajists attempted to enlist the cooperation of the orthodox in the early years. For example, the form of the *śuddhi* ceremony was based upon traditional penances (which might even include a pilgrimage to Hardwar), derived from *The Laws of Manu* and other widely accepted works. This accommodation was not acceptable to all Arya Samajists, and as early as 1888 protests against the traditional ceremonies began to appear in the Arya press.

Do Aryas hold the *Praschit* ceremony of Hindus? Do they insist

> on the eating of cow-dung, paying of visits to the Ganges, and feeding of the Brahmans?
>
> Such Praschit is degrading and a true Arya would never bow down to such unmeaning ceremonies and their selfish advocates the Brahmans.[34]

In 1893 a simple *śuddhi* ceremony was promulgated which was consistent with Arya teachings, and which became standard throughout the Arya Samaj.[35]

Winning the acceptance by the orthodox of reconversion remained problematic. Even members of the Arya Samaj sometimes refused to dine or otherwise mix with the reconverted. The problem here lay with the all powerful *birādrī*s or caste brotherhoods. It is the *birādrī* which decides when an individual should be outcasted, and when that outcaste might be taken back. If the *birādrī* determined that a *śuddhi* ceremony in a given case was not adequate to readmit someone to the caste, then that individual would remain an outcaste. And if another member of the caste—who also happened to be an Arya Samajist—decided to ignore the *birādrī*'s decision and mix with the outcaste, that second individual could become outcaste as well. In this situation the power of caste *birādrī*s came to be seen as a major obstacle to reform by Arya Samajists.

From 1895 some began to propose a *birādrī* for members of the Arya Samaj. If Arya Samajists set up their own caste brotherhood, they would no longer have to be afraid of the censure of their original *birādrī*s. Members of the Arya Samaj could then dine and marry with each other, just as if they were a caste group. Their behavior in these areas would be judged by the reformed standards of their fellow Aryas, and not by *birādrī*s often dominated by traditional Hindus. Others warned that this could lead to an isolation which would make it impossible to reform the whole of Hindu society. From 1895 to 1900 and perhaps later the Ārya Bhrātrī Sabhā ("Arya Caste Brotherhood Assembly") sponsored annual conferences in which bold proposals for caste reform in the Arya Samaj were adopted. Nonetheless, by 1902 interest in the Ārya Bhrātrī Sabhā had begun to wane, and the organization passed out of existence without being able to realize the dream of a separate *birādrī* for Arya Samajists.[36]

Despite the problems involved in acceptance of the reconverted, the applicability of *śuddhi* was being widened by an internal dynamic. The real expansion of *śuddhi* came when it was used to make untouchables into caste Hindus. On 3 June 1900 a large number of low caste

Rahtias from the Jalandhar area were declared to be no longer untouchable through a *śuddhi* ceremony sponsored by the Lahore Arya Samaj. By the 1911 census three to four thousand Rahtias had become "purified" caste Hindus. From 1903 the Sialkot Arya Samaj worked with the untouchable Meghs. By 1911 there were thirty thousand Arya Meghs.[37] The program with the Meghs was not limited to the *śuddhi* ceremony. The Sialkot Samaj also supported the establishment of an industrial training school and grammar schools for the "purified" Meghs, who were called Arya *bhagats*. This work was probably patterned at least partially on Christian missionary efforts among untouchables.[38]

In fact, a strong encouragement to *śuddhi* in the untouchable community came from the Christian activity in this area. With the decennial census, the success of different religions in India came to be seen more and more as a question of numbers. And the Christian and Muslim communities in Punjab consistently grew faster than the Hindu community. The most spectacular growth by Christians came among untouchables. The Christian missionary offered not only freedom from the scourge of untouchability, but also education and other benefits. Arya Samajists attempted to stem the flow of untouchables to Christianity with a similar program.

The limits of *śuddhi* for untouchables became clear in Hoshiarpur. Here the Arya Samaj "purified" large numbers of Kabīrpanthīs who were also Chamars. Traditionally Chamars are leather workers, an occupation that is perceived as particularly defiling by most Hindus. The attempt to make these very lowliest untouchables into caste Hindus was not greeted with enthusiasm by the orthodox. Some Arya Samajists were actually outcasted for their involvement in this project. After this row, *śuddhi* was seldom attempted for the most "unclean" untouchable groups. Aryas continued to effect the "purification" of some untouchables, however.[39]

In 1921 an event occurred which softened the attitude of the orthodox to reconversion. In that year the Moplahs, a Muslim group of the Malabar coast, rose up in revolt against the British. In the mayhem attendant on the rebellion large numbers of Hindus were forcibly converted to Islam under pain of death. Arya Samajists were among the first to rush to the aid of the Hindu victims, offering them not only material support but also the opportunity to reconvert to Hinduism. Many Hindus were shocked by the accounts of forcible conversions that they read in the newspapers, and were glad that the Arya Samaj held out to these people the chance of returning to their former religious community. Even Pandit Madan Mohan Malaviya and the Hindu Mahasabha were willing to accept the justice of reconversion under these conditions.[40]

Śuddhi was not seen as an adequate attempt at caste reform by some Arya Samajists. In 1922 Bhai Parmanand gave a speech at the anniversary celebrations of the Lahore Arya Samaj bitterly denouncing caste and its continued existence in the Samaj. In that same year he took part in the establishment of the Jāt Pāt Toṛak Maṇḍal ("Association for Breaking Caste"). The program of the Maṇḍal included: "Establishing an Inter-Caste Marriage Department in order to encourage and help in arranging inter-caste marriages amongst all sections of the Hindu Society inside or outside the various Provinces of India," and "Encouraging and arranging Inter-caste dinners and adopting such other means of social intercourse as would be conducive to the removal of untouchability."[41]

Although the Jāt Pāt Toṛak Maṇḍal enjoyed the support of some prominent Arya Samajists, its program was more radical than Swami Dayanand's in many ways. As has been noted, the swami did not support interdining as a caste reform activity, but intercaste meals were often sponsored by the Maṇḍal. Some of the leaders of the Jāt Pāt Toṛak Maṇḍal even went so far as to attack Dayanand's basic position on caste. Swami Dayanand criticized caste practices of his time, but he supported the basic notion that society should be divided into castes. In the Maṇḍal it was argued that this theory instead of leading to caste reform was being used by some to defend the status quo. The Jāt Pāt Toṛak Maṇḍal stood for nothing short of the abolition of caste.[42]

Even so, there were limits to how far the Jāt Pāt Toṛak Maṇḍal was prepared to go. This was underscored by a clash with Dr. B.R. Ambedkar, the leader of the untouchables who became the father of India's constitution. Ambedkar was invited to give the presidential address at the annual conference of the Maṇḍal in 1936. But after a copy of his address was circulated amongst leaders of the organization, they asked him to alter his remarks or to withdraw as a speaker at the conference altogether. In his speech Ambedkar said that caste would never disappear until the scriptures that support it are repudiated. The leader of the untouchables planned to announce that this would be his last speech as a Hindu. Ambedkar was abandoning Hinduism because of its support for objectionable caste practices. Such a wholesale condemnation of the Hindu scriptures and of Hinduism itself could not be countenanced by the Jāt Pāt Toṛak Maṇḍal.[43]

In the 1920s and 1930s the Jāt Pāt Toṛak Maṇḍal was relatively successful in winning adherents to its cause. Conferences were held, and journals published. Intercaste marriages and meals were conducted. The membership grew. Leaders of the movement attributed its success partially to a general liberalizing of attitudes about caste. And the Maṇḍal proceeded prudently. J. Reid Graham notes that most of the intercaste marriages sponsored by the Maṇḍal were between Hindus and many were between Arya Samajists. The Maṇḍal was careful not to support marriages that would arouse very violent criticism. Yet the Maṇḍal was not just an Arya organization. V.D. Savarkar, President of the Hindu Mahasabha, was a supporter of the Maṇḍal.[44]

Caste reform served to define differences within the Arya Samaj and between the Samaj and others. The conflict over the Ārya Bhrātrī Sabhā is an example of how reform led to intense debate in the Samaj. The clashes between Arya Samajists and traditional Hindus over the acceptance of "purified" individuals also often became quite bitter. Finally *śuddhi* became a bone of contention between the Arya Samaj and Christians, Sikhs, and Muslims. The Arya effort to counteract Christian proselytizing among untouchables has been noted. Originally Sikhs cooperated with Arya Samajists in Śuddhi Sabhās, but eventually competition between the two groups led to acrimony.[45] *Śuddhi* was also a cause of the growing animosity between Arya Samajists and Muslims in the early years of the Samaj's history, an animosity that has sometimes erupted in violence. Through these conflicts over caste reform and *śuddhi* the identity of the Arya Samaj was forged.

In the struggle over caste the Arya Samaj sought to avoid an exclusiveness that would limit its ability to effect change in the Hindu community as a whole. At the same time, Arya Samajists strived to be true to Swami Dayanand's radical teachings. In the first half century of the history of the Arya Samaj the result of the pursuit of these two ends seems to have been an oscillation between an uneasy acceptance of the status quo and bold but short-lived experiments with radical change (like the Arya Bhrātrī Sabhā and the Jāt Pāt Toṛak Maṇḍal). The struggle of the Arya Samaj to maintain a distinct identity on the issue of caste, without falling into a rigid separatism, has still not reached any lasting resolution.

FUNDAMENTALISM AS OPPOSITIONAL

From the outset the Arya Samaj has defined itself through its opposition to non-Aryas. Though the conflict with Hindus was probably most important in defining the movement, Arya Samajists also have engaged in public dispute with Christians, Muslims, Sikhs, and others. It is the struggle with Muslims that was the most acrimonious and the most significant in the years before the partition of India and Pakistan in 1947. It is not feasible here to cover all the details of this protracted and complicated feud. Nonetheless it should be possible to demonstrate that some of the most important events in the history of the Arya Samaj, and some of the greatest leaders were involved in the confrontation with Islam.

The pattern for Arya attacks on Islam was set by the founder of the movement, Swami Dayanand. Even before the birth of the Samaj Dayanand had become well known for his *śāstrārthas* with Muslims. A *śāstrārtha* is a public debate on a religious topic. Dayanand was a master of *śāstrārtha*, meeting Muslims in argument as well as Hindus, Christians, and others.[46] Most of these debates were not recorded.[47] Fortunately we have a more complete version of the swami's arguments in his book *Satyārth Prakāś*.

The fourteenth and final chapter of *Satyārth Prakāś* is about Islam. In this chapter Swami Dayanand concentrates on the Qur'an, without discussing Islamic history or current Muslim practice.[48] In his criticism of the Qur'an Dayanand quotes and then comments upon individual verses or groups of verses. He does not treat all of the text, but he does deal with the verses that he quotes in the order that they occur in the Qur'an. Hence the swami's argument is not organized by topic. Even so, some objections are repeated so often that they can be said to represent general themes in Dayanand's criticism of the Qur'an.

The Allah of the Qur'an is criticized by Dayanand as arbitrary in his judgments. The Qur'an affirms repeatedly that Allah condemns and saves whom he wills. The swami argues that individuals should only be judged on the basis of their deeds.[49] In contrast with the promises of divine mercy in the Qur'an, Swami Dayanand insists that God does not forgive sins. Every individual must suffer the consequences of his or her actions.[50] Dayanand quotes several verses from the Qur'an which admonish Muslims to struggle relentlessly with non-Muslims. Some passages do not stop short of urging a jihad to the death against kafirs. The swami criticizes these injunctions as leading to discord. Surely there is some good and bad in every sect, Dayanand writes. A blanket condemnation of kafirs can only lead to greater strife between religious communities.[51] In each of these cases Swami Dayanand begins with a passage from the Qur'an, which he interprets literally, and then attempts to expose as wrong. The tone of Dayanand's criticism is sometimes bitingly sarcastic.

After Dayanand the individual most important in the Arya criticism of Islam was Pandit Lekh Ram. The pandit was the leader of a group of Arya Samaj polemicists, some Muslim converts, who studied Islam in order to attack it. Lekh Ram focused particularly on Mirza Ghulam Ahmad of Qadian in Punjab. The Mirza was a visionary who proclaimed himself the Muslim Mahdi, the Christian messiah, and the tenth incarnation of the Hindu god Vishnu. These extravagant claims made Mirza Ghulam Ahmad an easy target for rationalist Arya Samajists. In 1887 Lekh Ram published a pamphlet criticizing a work by Mirza Ghulam Ahmad, which according to a Muslim newspaper contained "the most offensive (*lit.* heart-rending) and insulting language towards Islam, its leaders, its followers, including the Prophets, and things held sacred by the Muhammadans."[52] The Mirza responded to Lekh Ram's charges with a tract of his own, which led to an interchange of polemic literature of increasing acrimony. In a pattern that would appear again in the criticism of other religions by Arya Samajists, a debate over general principles was reduced to a personal struggle between two noted controversialists. During the course of this exchange Mirza Ghulam Ahmad prophesied that Pandit Lekh Ram would come to a violent end. Sure enough, in 1897 Lekh Ram was murdered by a Muslim who was living with him under the pretext of preparing to convert to Hinduism. Lekh Ram's murder was a traumatic event for the Arya Samaj. An estimated twenty thousand people attended his funeral.[53]

In 1898 a newspaper was founded in memory of the slain pandit under the supervision of Lala Munshi Ram, who was later known as Swami Shraddhanand (Śraddhānand), called *Ārya Musāfir* ("Arya Traveler"). *Ārya musāfir* was an epithet Lekh Ram had acquired in connection with his work on a biography of Swami Dayanand, because the pandit spent several years moving from city to city interviewing everyone who had known the swami. Another paper called simply *Musāfir* was started in 1905 in Agra in memory of Lekh Ram. The power behind this periodical was Pandit Bhoj Datt, who also established the Arya Musafir School and Mission to educate and support Arya Samaj *updeśaks* (missionary preachers). Bhoj Datt's missionaries were trained to carry on the martyred Lekh Ram's work against Islam. Thus Bhoj Datt became the center of a group of anti-Muslim activists in the way that Lekh Ram himself had been a decade before.[54]

During M.K. Gandhi's first mass noncooperation movement in India in 1920 the fires of communal debate died down somewhat. Gandhi had forged an agreement with the Ali brothers which included

Congress support for the *khilafat* movement and Muslim participation in the noncooperation drive. But in February 1922 Gandhi called off the protests because of concern about violence that had broken out around the demonstrations. The general support for Hindu-Muslim unity faded quickly after the noncooperation movement was halted. In the disappointment that followed the sudden death of the movement polemic literature of striking viciousness was published.

The images and arguments that appear in this literature are various, but one theme may be mentioned as an indication of the tenor of these works. Much of the lowest literature relied heavily on sexual innuendo. The Arya Samaj was particularly vulnerable to charges of sexual impropriety because of *niyoga*. In the fourth chapter of *Satyārth Prakāś* for the individual unable to have children (because his or her spouse was sterile or deceased, or for other reasons) Swami Dayanand recommends a temporary sexual liaison with a third person, which is known as *niyoga*.[55] *Niyoga* was certainly never widely practiced by Arya Samajists, but most were not prepared to publicly abandon the idea out of reverence for Dayanand. *Niyoga* was frequently mentioned in the more base attacks on the Arya Samaj.[56]

Arya Samajists responded in kind by portraying Muhammad as a man of dubious sexual ethics. In the 1920s the British Indian government brought suit against the authors or publishers of three works by Arya Samajists critical of the Prophet Muhammad—a book by Pandit Kalicharan Sharma, *Vicitra Jīvan*; a pamphlet published by Mahashay Raj Pal, *Raṅgīlā Rasūl*; and an article by Devi Sharan Sharma entitled "Sair-i-Dozakh" which appeared in the periodical *Risala-i-Vartman*.[57] The government charged that these writings were in violation of section 153A of the Indian Penal Code which reads: "Whoever by words, either spoken or written, or by signs, or by visible representations, or otherwise, promotes or attempts to promote feelings of enmity or hatred between different classes of Her Majesty's subjects, shall be punished with imprisonment which may extend to two years, or with fine or with both."[58] Although not all of the accused were convicted (Mahashay Raj Pal was acquitted), the fact that these suits were filed was an indication of the communal tension of the times.[59]

By the end of the 1920s communal debate had led to violence in Punjab and elsewhere in the South Asian subcontinent. It is often difficult to identify the protagonists in riots. Still, it is clear that Arya Samajists contributed to the general atmosphere of conflict of which the riots were an outgrowth. The assassination of Swami Shraddhanand by a Muslim at the end of 1926 disturbed many Arya Samajists, who became fearful that they were not being adequately protected by the police. In 1927 meetings were held throughout north India to condemn violence against Hindus and particularly the perceived indifference of the authorities. In November of that year the first Ārya Mahāsammelan (or great conference) was held in Delhi to consider the situation. This gathering was patterned on the centenary celebration of Dayanand's birth which had taken place in Mathura in 1925.[60] Like the Mathura meeting, the Mahāsammelan had the support of all factions of the Arya Samaj. One of the most important results of the first Mahāsammelan was the creation of the Ārya Vīr Dal (literally "Party of Courageous Aryas"). Local chapters of the Vīr Dal were established where Arya Samajists would meet to exercise and train in the martial arts. In an atmosphere where police protection was thought of as unreliable, the Arya Samaj organized to protect itself. A second Ārya Mahāsammelan was held in Bareilly in 1931, at which communal competition remained the focus of concern.[61]

In Hyderabad and Sind satyagraha became a weapon in the Arya Samaj's conflict with Muslims. Satyagraha (which literally means "force of truth") is a word that M.K. Gandhi coined for his methods of political protest, usually involving nonviolent noncooperation or passive resistance. In 1939 Arya Samajists adopted satyagraha against the Nizam of Hyderabad. The Muslim Nizam had placed restrictions on Arya missionary activity as a part of a desperate attempt to stem the rising tide of Hindu-Muslim antagonism in his Hindu-majority domain. Arya Samajists came from throughout north India to court arrest as a protest against the Nizam's actions, with particularly large contingents from the Ārya Vīr Dal and the *gurukuls*.[62] After jailing over eight thousand demonstrators, the Nizam was forced to capitulate, instituting political reforms.[63]

Arya Samajists used the ultimate weapon of satyagraha again in Sind against government attempts to censor *Satyārth Prakāś*. Muslims had long been critical of Swami Dayanand's book, especially of the fourteenth chapter which so unsparingly attacks Islam. In August and December of 1943 the Muslim League passed resolutions demanding that the government of India proscribe Dayanand's book. To counteract these demands the Arya Samaj held the fourth Mahāsammelan in Delhi in February of 1944, which was attended by fifty thousand people including many non-Arya Hindus.[64] In spite of the Arya protest, on 26 October 1944 the Muslim-dominated elected government of the province of Sind announced that it was "pleased to direct that no copies of the book entitled "Satyarthaprakash" written by Swami Dayanand

Saraswati shall be printed or published unless chapter XIV (chapter fourteen) thereof is omitted."[65] When further protests fell on deaf ears, Arya Samajists began a satyagraha on 14 January 1947, inviting arrest by publishing the complete *Satyārth Prakāś*. But the government chose to ignore their activities. The protesters proclaimed this a surrender by the government and called off the satyagraha after only a few days.

In the details of this narrative it is easy to lose perspective about the significance of opposition to Muslims for the Arya Samaj. Swami Dayanand himself debated with Muslims, and devoted some of *Satyārth Prakāś* to attacking Islam. Two of the most important leaders of the Arya Samaj after Dayanand, Lekh Ram and Shraddhanand, continued the tradition of anti-Islamic polemics and ultimately gave up their lives in this struggle. With the conference in Mathura in 1925 a new mechanism was invented to build up the Arya Samaj, the Mahāsammelan. Although the Mathura meeting was not focused on communal issues, the majority of the later Mahāsammelans which were held before 1947 were. The Hyderabad satyagraha, which is remembered by Arya Samajists as one of the greatest victories of the Samaj, was a protest with a communal element. In the years before partition conflict with Muslims was one of the main foci of the Arya Samaj, and that conflict has continued in a more subdued form to the present.

Many non-Aryas regard the Samaj as primarily a controversialist movement, an organization which feeds on conflict. This is not an entirely true picture of the Arya Samaj, which has positive programs independent of communal dispute. Nevertheless, the Arya Samaj can be largely understood by what it opposes. This is especially true for the Arya opposition to other Hindus, and it is also the case for the ongoing battle with Islam.

FUNDAMENTALISM AS ABSOLUTIST

The absolutism of the Arya Samaj might be illustrated through a story in Swami Dayanand's work *Satyārth Prakāś*. The passage in question occurs near the end of the eleventh chapter of the book, after the swami has criticized a great number of Hindu traditionalist and modernist sects. It is meant to illustrate a way that the truth might be found even amidst so much falsehood. A king has gathered a thousand preachers, one from every religion, and an inquirer asks each about his beliefs. Dayanand begins the questioning with a *vāmmārgī*, a practitioner of left-handed tantra. The inquirer says, "O great one, till today I have not accepted any guru or any dharma. Tell me, from all the dharmas whose dharma is highest, which I should accept?"

> *Vāmmārgī*—Ours is.
> Inquirer—How are these 999?
> *Vāmmārgī*—They are all liars and bound for hell. Because, "There is nothing better than a tantric," on the authority of this sentence there is no dharma better than our dharma.[66]

In spite of the tantric's insistence that he convert, the inquirer refuses until he has had a chance to talk to the representatives of the other religions. He asks each which is better, and each gives the same reply, that his own dharma is best and that all the others are worthless. The Shaiva, the adherent of Vedanta, the Jain, the Christian, the Muslim, the Vaishnava—each claims that his religion is exclusively true. At this point the confused questioner goes to a truly wise man, to ask him what he should make of all this. The inquirer maintains that it would be difficult to accept any of these thousand faiths. "Because if I become the disciple of any one among these, then I will have to become the opponent of 999. For the man who has 999 enemies and one friend there can never be happiness."

The wise man suggests that the inquirer might find the true dharma in that upon which the preachers agree. "Look, that Vedic doctrine ["Vedmat"] on which these thousand are unanimous is worth accepting. And that fabricated, false irreligion ["adharm"] on which they are opposed to each other is not worth accepting." The true dharma, which the inquirer finds that all affirm, includes speaking the truth, "acquiring knowledge, practicing brahmacharya, marriage after childhood, the company of the good, striving, true behavior, and so forth."[67]

Even though he has succeeded in finding the one true religion, our inquisitive protagonist still questions.

> Then the inquirer asked all of them, "Why don't you all advance the true dharma and hurt the false way after becoming unanimous in this fashion?" They all said, "If we did that, who would concern themselves with us? Our disciples would not remain in our power, our livelihood would be destroyed. Then the ease that we enjoy now would slip from our hands. For this reason, even though we know [that there is only one true dharma], even so we continue to preach and insist each upon his own doctrine."[68]

Finally the inquirer returns to the wise man, admitting to him that all of these thousand religions is false. "Now I also will publicly denounce these imposters and proclaim the true doctrine which is set forth in the Vedas."[69]

This story is an allegory for the task which Swami Dayanand undertook in his public work, and especially in *Satyārth Prakāś*. Dayanand finds himself in a world where there are many religions, and much sectarian discord. This is a situation which the swami laments, "from mutual opposition among the learned opposition among the ignorant grows, and there is an increase of suffering and a decrease in happiness in many ways."[70] Just as the thousand preachers in the story fight among themselves, so the religions make mutually exclusive claims to being right.

Dayanand maintains that sectarianism will be overcome when everyone agrees to the truth. It is his conviction that this truth can be arrived at by distilling from the various religions the beliefs that they hold in common. Of course, the elements peculiar to each religion would have to be abandoned. This is the intention with which the swami wrote *Satyārth Prakāś*, "to publicly refute those false things in each doctrine, after accepting whatever true thing is in all doctrines, because there is not opposition among them all about it."[71] Dayanand assigns himself the task of analyzing the various religions to arrive at their common truth as does the inquirer in the story.

Swami Dayanand acknowledges that debate will be necessary to determine what is true and what is false. And some might refuse to accept the results of this debate because of moral flaws like selfishness. "The human atman is a knower of truth and untruth, yet to achieve one's own purposes with faults like stubbornness, contumacy, ignorance, and so forth, a person rejects truth and inclines to untruth."[72] The priests in any given community, for example, may be unwilling to admit that their religion is wrong because they fear that their livelihood might be undermined by such an admission. Like the inquirer in the story Dayanand finds that self-interest may keep individuals from embracing the truth.

In fact, in the story quoted above the inquirer finds that all the thousand preachers whom he questions are motivated by self-interest. From *Satyārth Prakāś* as a whole it seems that Dayanand has come to a similar conclusion. The second part of *Satyārth Prakāś*, the last four chapters, is dedicated to the criticism of other religions. In the eleventh chapter Dayanand exposes the errors of orthodox Hindu sects. Unorthodox sects of Indian origin are dealt with in the twelfth chapter, specifically Buddhism, Jainism, and the Cārvākas (a materialist philosophical school which has not survived till the modern period).

Christianity is refuted in the thirteenth chapter. Islam is criticized in the fourteenth.

Since Dayanand maintains that he wants to identify the truth which is common to all religions, it might be expected that he would have much that is positive to say in the final four chapters of *Satyārth Prakāś*, but that is not the case. Rather each chapter is given over to a merciless, hammering attack against the faith in question. There seems to be some divergence here between what the swami says that he has done, and what he has actually done.[73] Dayanand does not go about building up his position by bringing together the truths of the religions which he analyzes. Instead the swami first presents his own beliefs based on the authority of the Vedas, and then he goes on to demolish existing religious sects. Dayanand might well have made the same statement as the truth seeker in the story. "Now I also will publicly denounce these imposters and proclaim the true dharma which is set forth in the Vedas." Every contemporary religion is false: each should be attacked. The true Vedic faith, which is separate from all of them, must be propagated.

The modern world is a witness to the spectacle of a number of different religions making mutually contradictory claims. Despairing of ever sorting out these competing assertions, some argue that the only proper response to religious pluralism is relativism. Perhaps we can never know which religion is true. This is certainly not Swami Dayanand's position. Dayanand holds that it is possible to work through the conflicting creeds of the various religions and to come to some common faith. There is nothing tentative about the way that the swami presents his own position. Clearly he regards it as demonstrably true. One need not give way to relativism, because the absolute truth is to be found in the Vedas as interpreted by the Arya Samaj.

AUTHORITATIVENESS OR AUTHORITARIANISM IN FUNDAMENTALISM

The Arya Samaj is based on the authority of a text, the Vedas, and the authority of an individual, Swami Dayanand. The centrality of the Vedas is repeatedly affirmed by Arya Samajists, while Dayanand's role is more ambiguous. Ultimately the authority of the text and the founder are bound up together. We will begin with the Vedas.

According to Dayanand the Vedas were imparted by God to humans at the beginning of creation. They are wholly reliable because they are absolutely free of error. There are other texts which are largely trustworthy, but not perfectly so. These generally true works are known as *ārṣa*, because they were composed by the rishis, ancient, divinely inspired sages (*ārṣa* is an adjective based on the same root as rishi). Because the *ārṣa* literature contains some error, it must be rejected when it conflicts with the Vedas. Theoretically the authority of the *ārṣa* works is grounded in the Vedas. So it is the Vedas that are the source of all truth.[74]

The authority of the Vedas is attested to in many ways in Swami Dayanand's writings. In terms of volume, Swami Dayanand's greatest work is his commentaries on the Vedas. Although the swami was not able to finish commentaries on all four Vedas as he planned, a complete commentary is available for the Yajur Veda, along with a partial one for the Ṛg Veda. The standard edition of the swami's work on the Yajur Veda is four volumes long,[75] while the commentary on the Ṛg Veda stretches to nine volumes.[76] Swami Dayanand also wrote one other work that is exclusively concerned with the Vedas, *Āryābhivinay*.[77] This short book is composed of meditative commentaries on just over a hundred mantras drawn from the Ṛg and Yajur Vedas. In addition to these works which are dedicated solely to the Vedas, Dayanand frequently quoted the Vedas in his other writings. So the Vedas are an important text in Dayanand's oeuvre.

According to the third *niyam* of the Arya Samaj, the propagation of the Vedas is the highest dharma of all the members of the Samaj. And the Vedas do occupy an important place in the life of the Arya Samaj. During the *havan*, a fire sacrifice which is the most basic Arya ritual, Vedic mantras are chanted. In the sermons delivered at Arya Samaj services the Vedas are one of the most frequently quoted sources. If the mantra cited is a common one, the congregation will spontaneously join the speaker in his or her recitation of it. The Vedas are even invoked to support the social reform program of the Samaj (by methods of interpretation which are the bane of non-Arya scholars). The Vedas are the authority in all areas of the faith and practice of the Arya Samaj.

With regard to the importance of authoritarian individuals, the position of the Arya Samaj is ambiguous. Swami Dayanand was certainly a commanding figure. A powerful polemicist, he was imperious towards those with whom he did not agree. Even so, Dayanand criticized the gurudom that is characteristic of some Hindu sects, and he resisted becoming captive to the sycophantic loyalty of his followers. The swami was invited to become the guru of various Arya Samaj chapters, but he always refused.[78] Dayanand intended that each Samaj be run by its local leadership. He was ready with advice when asked, but he was not interested in issuing orders.

Swami Dayanand was, nonetheless, not only the founder of the Arya Samaj, but also the author of its philosophy. The teachings of the swami have never been publicly repudiated by the Samaj as a body on any issue. And Swami Dayanand has been a source of inspiration and an object of devotion for Arya Samajists throughout the Samaj's history. His picture (often from calendars) adorns most Arya Samaj temples and many Arya homes, devotional songs about him are sung in Arya services, and his life is the source of endless comment in sermons. In this way Dayanand continues to be a living force in the Arya Samaj over a century after his death.[79]

There is a powerful link between the authority of the Vedas and that of Swami Dayanand. Arya Samajists accept that the swami's teaching is consistent with the Vedas, which would guarantee its truth. Beyond this, Dayanand has restored the authority of the Vedas to the extent that he has saved them from the neglect to which they have been consigned by Hindus in recent centuries. It is the Vedas as interpreted by Swami Dayanand which are the basis of the life of the Arya Samaj. The interpretation of Dayanand makes it possible to understand the Vedas, which are the ultimate authority.

FUNDAMENTALISM AS ANTIEVOLUTIONARY

There is no passage in Dayanand's works which deals with Charles Darwin's theory on the origin of species. Dayanand died in 1883 just a year after Darwin, and the English naturalist's thinking had not yet made an impact in India during the swami's lifetime. So Dayanand's works are silent on evolution in the narrow sense. Swami Dayanand did have very specific ideas about history, but they were based on a pattern of degeneration not development.

According to Swami Dayanand the world in which we live was created by God almost two billion years ago.[80] "From creation until a time five thousand years ago throughout the world there was only one universal imperial kingdom of the Aryas over all," Dayanand wrote.[81] As evidence for this assertion Dayanand cites the *rājasūya* ritual of Yudhiṣṭhira which is recounted in the *Mahābhārata*. Various minor kings attended this coronation ceremony, swearing their fealty to Yudhiṣṭhira. It is Dayanand's interpretation of the *Mahābhārata* that kings came from China, America, Europe, Iran and so forth to affirm their loyalty to the king.[82] Thus, according to Swami Dayanand, the kings of India (or of *Āryāvarta*, which includes most of north India and some other territory as well) enjoyed universal sovereignty up to five thousand years ago.

The period when the Aryas dominated the world was a golden age in the view of Swami Dayanand. It was a time of great learning and righteousness. Dayanand also believed that this was a period of some technological advancement. The swami maintained, for example, that there are weapons described in the *Mahābhārata*, the epic written at the end of the golden age, that were as powerful as the guns and cannons of his day. Some of the devices in the *Mahābhārata*, Dayanand said, were of even greater destructive force that the weapons that were available in his time.[83] Hence, according to Swami Dayanand, the ancient texts reveal that the era when the Aryas ruled the world was an age advanced in technology as well as virtue.

Swami Dayanand believed that this golden age was ended by the war described in the *Mahābhārata*. India had been great, "but the Mahābhārata war gave this crest-jewel nation such a shock that even to the present it has not returned to its former state."[84] Many great kings and sages were killed in the war, Dayanand wrote, and the propagation of knowledge and Vedic religion was ended. "The preaching of the study of the Vedas and other scriptures [*Vedādiśāstra*] along with their meanings, which had come down in the tradition, was also interrupted."[85] Since this great war, Dayanand observed, Brahmans have only memorized the ancient texts to make a living, without understanding their meaning. The golden age ended in a cataclysm, according to Swami Dayanand, and the present age was begun, an epoch not equal to the ancient times in any field of human endeavor.

Swami Dayanand did have a general theory of history, but it is hardly evolutionary. History has not been marked by progress, but by degeneration. The present age is one of vice, the age of virtue having ended five thousand years ago. More will be said about history, and especially about the future, in the section below on teleology.

FUNDAMENTALISM AS ANTIPERMISSIVE

To a degree Arya Samajists are perceived as puritanical by others. This judgment has been made not only in the context of questions of generally accepted morality, but also in that of things which are peculiarly proscribed for Arya Samajists because of the Samaj's doctrines. Frequently non-Aryas criticize Arya Samajists for their unwillingness to participate in traditional Hindu festivals, for example. Arya Samajists themselves readily admit that it is difficult for them to keep their lives free of popular practices and beliefs which are inconsistent with the teachings of the Samaj.[86] It is in this area that Arya Samajists scrupulously struggle to be antipermissive.

An important example of the Arya Samaj's attempt to hold itself aloof from the non-Arya world is the diverse network of educational institutions which the Samaj sustains. The Arya Samaj is best known for its D.A.V. schools and colleges, but it also supports a network of *gurukuls* as well. These two different systems reflect the diversity of ways that Arya Samajists conceive of themselves, but they are both equally an indication of the need of the Arya Samaj to maintain itself against non-Aryas.

Arya Samajists developed educational institutions to protect their children from non-Arya influences. In 1886 the Dayanand Anglo-Vedic (or D.A.V.) High School (later College) in Lahore, a memorial to the recently deceased founder of the Arya Samaj, began to hold classes. As the name indicates, it was decided that this institution should be a purveyor of English and practical Western knowledge as well as Sanskrit and ancient Vedic lore. Previous experiments in education in Punjab had failed to gain widespread support. There were some Christian missionary schools in the province, for example, but Hindu parents were reluctant to send their children to them for fear they would be converted to Christianity. With its emphasis on English education in a Hindu context, the D.A.V. school was able to win the hearts of the Hindu populace of Lahore, and soon other schools were opened. The Dayanand Anglo-Vedic schools would eventually grow to become the largest nongovernmental educational system in India.[87]

From its early years, some Arya Samajists criticized the D.A.V. movement for not adopting a sufficiently radical Arya curriculum, and a schism developed in the Samaj over this issue. Actually the split was sparked by a fracas about vegetarianism. Citing Swami Dayanand's own advocacy of it, radicals demanded that vegetarianism be imposed as a condition for holding office in Arya organizations. Moderates argued that vegetarianism should not be required, because the ten principles and bylaws of the Arya Samaj adopted in Lahore say nothing about it, and because from the outset the membership of the Samaj included meat eaters as well as vegetarians. This contest was indicative of two very different ideas of what it means to be a member of the Arya Samaj. The vegetarians believed that the Arya Samajist should be a new person, radically changing his or her life-style in accordance with the ideals of Swami Dayanand. The nonvegetarians held that it was sufficient to accept the ten principles of the Samaj—the Arya Samajist need not alter every aspect of his or her life.

In 1893 when the leadership of the Arya Samaj chapter in the Wachhowali area of Lahore fell into the hands of the vegetarians, the nonvegetarians founded a new chapter in Anarkali in the same city. Over the next few years the two Lahore Samajes competed vigorously for the loyalty of other Arya Samaj chapters. Attempts by the vegetarians to get control of the D.A.V. school failed in 1894, when the Managing Committee decided that for its purposes the Anarkali Samaj was the only legitimate Lahore Arya Samaj. The vegetarian faction then withdrew its support from the College. Cut off from many of the Arya Samaj chapters which had sustained it, the D.A.V. College was forced to search for sources of revenue beyond the Arya Samaj, and donations were forthcoming. The College was an institution that appealed to many Hindu families looking for a safe place to educate their children. The elimination of the more militant vegetarian faction from the Managing Committee ensured that the College would continue to speak to the needs of a broad spectrum of moderates in Punjab, rather than conforming to a more narrowly Arya agenda.[88]

The vegetarians were freed by the split from having to concentrate on the D.A.V. College, and they naturally turned their attention to other matters. In 1902 a new experiment in education was undertaken by Swami Shraddhanand, the vegetarian leader who had previously been known as Lala Munshi Ram. This was the Gurukul Kangri, founded outside Hardwar near the village of Kangri.[89] The Gurukul was intended as a radical departure from existing schools. It was modeled on the *gurukuls* (the forest hermitage schools) of classical Hinduism. The students would live together with their teachers in a remote area, where full attention could be given to the development of each youngster. The Gurukul would not ignore modern knowledge, science and the English language were to be a part of the curriculum, but there would be a strong emphasis on classical learning in Hindi and Sanskrit. Only male students and teachers were permitted at the Gurukul Kangri.

Brahmacharya or celibacy, which was thought to be essential to the proper moral growth of a child, could only be safeguarded in a single sex institution. Separate *gurukuls* would be established for girls.[90]

The Gurukul Kangri was the laboratory in which the ideal Arya Samajist of the militants was to be created. Students who went to the Gurukul were allowed only very minimal contact with their families and with the outside world in general. In the Gurukul no difference of caste or class was observed. The regimen was the same for rich and poor students, and all the boys dined together regardless of caste background. Of course religious events were celebrated according to the reformed rites of Swami Dayanand in the Gurukul. In this way a new generation of leaders for the Arya Samaj emerged from the Gurukul, the products of an exclusively Arya world. Other *gurukuls* were started on the pattern of the Gurukul Kangri, many of which maintained formal ties with the first *gurukul*. The *gurukul* system has never enjoyed the great popularity of the D.A.V. schools. Nevertheless the *gurukuls* remained a significant focus of activity for the militant vegetarian wing of the Arya Samaj. Frequently the two factions of the Arya Samaj would cooperate in later years, especially in times of crisis, and yet parallel organizations continue to exist in the present.

The antipermissiveness of the Arya Samaj is even more obvious in the *gurukuls* than in the D.A.V. schools. The D.A.V. system was begun partially to counteract the influence of Christian missionary schools by providing a good education in a Hindu environment. Yet aside from the fact that the D.A.V. schools are run by Hindus, there is little that separates them from Christian or government ones. The curriculum of the D.A.V. schools is quite similar to that of other institutions. For some Arya Samajists this situation was intolerable. Militants argued that Arya education demanded not only new management, but an entirely new system of moral and academic training. The *gurukuls* were started in order to realize the militants' vision of purely Arya Samajist schools. Both the D.A.V. schools and the *gurukul* system reflect an antipermissive attempt on the part of Arya Samajists to raise their children independent of non-Arya communities.

FUNDAMENTALISM AS ANTIHERMENEUTICAL

Swami Dayanand maintained that his teachings in every area are based on the Vedas. In conformity with this argument Dayanand tended to read the Vedas as unambiguously consistent with his own views, and in this

his interpretation of the Vedas is antihermeneutic. That is not to say that there can be only one reading of every Vedic mantra in the swami's system. On the contrary, the Swami Dayanand argued explicitly that some mantras can be understood on at least two levels. Mantras which mention *agni*, for example, often can be taken to refer either to the ordinary fire or to God. These verses have both a *vyāvahārika* (practical) sense and a *pāramārthika* (spiritual) one.[91] So theoretically more than one interpretation of some Vedic mantras is possible.

Dayanand himself offers an allegorical interpretation of several traditional Hindu myths. For example, in the Ṛg Veda there is a hymn which is traditionally understood to describe the defeat in battle of a powerful serpent demon Vṛtra by the great warrior god Indra. In his reinterpretation Dayanand identifies Indra with the sun and Vṛtra with the clouds. For the swami this hymn is not about a fight between a warrior god and a serpent demon, rather it is an allegorical (*ālaṃkārika*) description of the clouds releasing the rains under the heat of the sun.[92] There is no room in Dayanand's cosmology for warrior gods or serpent demons. So the swami's reinterpretation of the story serves to bring it into line with his own teachings.

Although Swami Dayanand does allow that some mantras might be interpreted in more than one way, this does not mean that the basic sense of the Vedic text is at all unclear. On the contrary Dayanand has no trouble identifying perspectives on the Vedas that are wrong, and he strongly denounces them.

> As for the commentaries which were written by Rāvaṇa, Uvaṭa, Sāyaṇa, Mahīdhara, and so forth, that are opposed to the meaning of the Vedas, and the limited expositions based on them written by Europeans from England and Germany in their own languages, and the expositions based on them which have been written or are being written in the modern vernaculars by some in India, these glosses will be abandoned as their many faults become known, when there is real light in the hearts of good people that all of them are filled with nonsense.[93]

Here Swami Dayanand condemns three groups of commentators on the Vedas. The first group (Rāvaṇa, Uvaṭa, Sāyaṇa, Mahīdhara, and so forth) includes the great medieval Vedic interpreters, the scholiasts who are regarded as authoritative by traditional Hindus. Then Dayanand attacks the European scholars of his day, especially the English and Germans. And the last group condemned are those who were writing

Vedic commentaries in the modern Indian languages. The swami says that the work of the modern Indian scholars is based on that of the Western Vedicists, which is in turn derived from the commentaries of the great medieval thinkers.

Because he claims that all the interpretations which he condemns are ultimately based on the medieval commentaries, Dayanand can dispose of them all by proving the medieval scholiasts wrong, which is just what he sets out to do in *Ṛgvedādibhāṣyabhūmikā*. Dayanand first deals with Sāyaṇa, who is probably the most important Vedic commentator. At the outset Dayanand notes that Sāyaṇa takes the highest meaning of the Vedas to be concerned with ritual (with the *kriyākāṇḍa*).[94] Dayanand believed that all knowledge had its roots in the Vedas, and so he could not accept Sāyaṇa's limited formulation of their thrust. Dayanand also points out a few errors in detail in Sāyaṇa's commentary. Next Swami Dayanand takes up the Vedic interpretation of Mahīdhara. Although the swami devotes several pages to criticizing Mahīdhara, he is concerned throughout with only one hymn from the Yajur Veda, the twenty-third *adhyāya*. Some of the verses of this hymn have been understood as describing a fertility rite which is conducted within the context of the great royal sacrifice the *aśvamedha*. Specifically Mahīdhara says that the queen, the wife of the sponsor of the ritual, should copulate with the sacrificial horse. Swami Dayanand interprets these mantras allegorically as describing the proper relationship of the king to his subjects, and he condemns Mahīdhara's reading as "exceedingly corrupt" ("atīvaduṣṭa").[95] It is not hard to imagine that Dayanand's readers, many of whom were not familiar with this elaborate Vedic ritual, would have found Mahīdhara's bestial reading repugnant. This is the only hymn that Dayanand quotes, taking the most extreme example to expose the defective nature of Mahīdhara's commentary.

Apparently the swami regards this refutation of Sāyaṇa and Mahīdhara to be a sufficient expose of all the medieval commentators. And as they have been found false, so must be the modern interpretations of the Vedas which are based on them. "If the methods of the expositions of Sāyaṇa, Mahīdhara, and so forth, who lived in India are false in this way, what can be said about the nonsensical methods of the expositions of the meaning of the Vedas which are based on them of Europeans in their own languages?"[96] By exposing the errors of the great medieval commentators, Dayanand presumes to do away with the Vedic interpretation of modern European and Indian scholars as well.

It is not the case that Swami Dayanand does not rely on any secondary sources in his own work. Rather the swami argues that the assistance of some commentary is necessary to understand the Vedas. But for this purpose he only accepts the most ancient sources, in one context he mentions the Brahmanas, the Vedangas, the Upāṅgas, and the Śākhās.[97] The works Dayanand takes as authoritative will be described in detail in the next chapter of this study. For now it is sufficient to note that the element that these ancient sources have in common is that they are all *ārṣa*, books composed by the rishis in the golden age at the beginning of history. The *ārṣa* literature includes works that enjoy a limited authority in Dayanand's system, an authority which is ultimately based on the Vedas.

There is a significant sense in which Swami Dayanand's interpretation of the Vedas is circular. In order to understand the Vedas some commentary is needed. The only reliable guide in this area is the *ārṣa* literature. According to Swami Dayanand the Vedas are infallible, they contain nothing but the truth. And the *ārṣa* books are only true to the extent that they are consistent with the Vedas. Anything in any *ārṣa* work which is not in conformity with the Vedas must be discarded. So one must simultaneously use the *ārṣa* literature to understand the Vedas while using the Vedas to judge the *ārṣa* literature.

From the perspective of non-Arya students of the Vedas this is a vicious circle. Swami Dayanand admits that some explanation is needed to understand the Vedas, but he rejects most commentaries out of hand. Even in the case of those works which have some limited authority, Dayanand reserves for himself the right to determine which parts are consistent with the Vedas and which are inconsistent. In this situation it is Dayanand's own interpretation that becomes the arbiter for what is Vedic. Dayanand is thus free to read his own philosophy into the Vedas, according to his critics. But from within this circular argument the perspective is very different. For Arya Samajists this is a powerful system where their own teachings are supported by the Vedas and the most ancient and authoritative commentaries on the Vedas.

FUNDAMENTALISTS AS AGENTS IN HISTORY

The Arya Samaj's role in history according to its adherents is expressed by the oft quoted Vedic phrase, "kṛṇvanto viśvam āryam," "making the world Arya."[98] Although the truth of the organization's teachings guarantees for Arya Samajists that this goal is attainable, it is not something that they hope to achieve automatically. Rather the Arya Samaj is run according to definite bureaucratic procedures. In this section we will look at the structures which the Samaj developed to realize its goal of converting the world to the Vedic religion.

The local chapter, which is the basic building block of the Arya Samaj, spreads the message of the Samaj through regular (usually weekly) services. Such a service is sometimes called the *sāptahik adhiveśan* ("the weekly meeting"), but it is much more commonly referred to as the *sāptahik satsaṅg*. *Satsaṅg*, a term which has a long history in Hindu devotionalism, simply means association (*saṅg*) with the good (*sant*). Although there is no fixed form for the service, so there may be some local variations, an Arya *satsaṅg* usually consists of three major parts: a *havan*, a *bhajan* (or several *bhajans*), and an *updeś* (or several *updeśes*).

The Arya *havan* is a fire "sacrifice," in which clarified butter and aromatic herbs are oblated in a fire to the accompaniment of mantras, most of which are from the Vedas. Although animal sacrifice is practiced in some Hindu communities, it is not popular in the area of north India where the Arya Samaj has won most of its adherents. Arya Samajists have actively opposed the killing of animals in ritual. Scholars claim that the life of the ancient Aryans included animal sacrifice, but the Arya Samaj denies this. Another thing that distinguishes this *havan* from the rituals of traditional Hindus is that the Arya service is quite simple. On special occasions an Arya *havan* may be more elaborate, but the basic ritual can be completed in less than a half an hour. The *havan* of the Arya Samaj is also distinguished from traditional sacrifices in who is permitted to participate. Everyone at an Arya Samaj service is invited to chant the *havan* mantras—pamphlets with the text of the ritual are often distributed for those who can read but do not know the ritual by heart. Anyone who wishes can take part in the ritual, including women and members of the lower castes.[99]

The second part of the *satsaṅg* is made up of *bhajans* or religious songs. An individual may sing a hymn solo, but usually the congregation is urged to join in repeating each line after the song leader. This song might be an original composition, but a gifted singer will also be familiar with a number of hymns commonly sung at Arya Samaj services. Often poems are recited during this part of the *satsaṅg* as well, which are much more likely to be original. There are some *bhajans* sung in Arya *satsaṅgs* which are also popular with traditional Hindus, but this is not usually the case. Frequently the Arya hymns and poems make reference to the peculiar beliefs of the Samaj. Many popular *bhajans* are about the life of Swami Dayanand, for example.

The last major part of the Arya Samaj *satsaṅg* is usually an *updeś* (also called a *pravacan* or *vyākhyān*). Theoretically these talks can be on any topic, but they are most often concerned with religion and might properly be called sermons. On special occasions there can be several sermons at an Arya Samaj *satsaṅg*, but frequently there is just one *updeś*. The length of a speaker's remarks will also vary with the situation, so an *updeś* might be over in a few minutes or it might last for an hour or more. It is possible that a learned individual who is not an Arya Samajist may be invited to speak at a *satsaṅg*, but this is not common. Often the *updeś* at an Arya *satsaṅg* is dedicated to explaining some basic point of Swami Dayanand's teachings. It is unlikely that a direct contradiction of Arya doctrine in a Samaj service would be allowed to go unchallenged.

Though it is in the *updeś* at an Arya *satsaṅg* that the teachings of the Samaj are most directly promoted, the whole service reflects those teachings. The use of Vedic mantras in the *havan* is a reminder of the importance of the Vedas in the Arya Samaj's philosophy. The participation of women and those of lower caste in the ritual is an expression of the Samaj's support for social reform. In the *bhajans* points of Arya doctrine are reaffirmed, and incidents from the life of the founder of the Samaj are often illustrated. The entire Arya *satsaṅg* is a public celebration of the distinctive beliefs of the Arya Samaj. It is significant that there are no limitations on who may attend the weekly services. Nonmembers are welcome. It is the *satsaṅg* that is the primary instrument of proselytizing.

When an individual becomes further involved, there are regular provisions for membership in the Arya Samaj which are more or less the same throughout the world. According to the constitution for local Samajes promulgated by the Arya Samaj's international governing body, the conditions for membership are simple. To become a member (an "Arya" in the language of the constitution) an individual must be at least eighteen years of age. He or she (there are no gender restrictions on membership or eligibility for office) must accept "the aims and objects of the Arya Samaj (as stated in its Principles) and its doctrines (as they are written in the works of Rishi Dayanand on the basis of the Vedas)" and act in accordance with them. Even if this affirmation is forthcoming the constitution provides that the aspirant may be denied membership by the executive committee (*antaraṅg sabhā*) of the Arya Samaj "for any special reason."[100]

In order to become a voting member of the Arya Samaj (which the constitution calls an "Arya Sabhasada," a "member of the Arya assembly") the following conditions are imposed: (1) One must have been a member of the Samaj for one year. (2) During that time one's conduct must have been righteous. (3) One must have contributed 1 per cent of one's income to the Samaj during that year or Rs. 250.[101] And (4) one must have attended 25 per cent of the Arya Samaj's weekly meetings. Under normal circumstances only the voting members of the Arya Samaj may cast their ballot in elections, though the executive committee may consult non-voting members on some issues. Also to hold any office in the Samaj one must be a voting member.[102]

It is noteworthy that these provisions of the constitution serve to limit power in the organization to committed Arya Samajists. One must attest one's acceptance of the principles and doctrines of the Samaj before joining. In order for the member to take part in decision making in the Arya Samaj, a year's probation is required. During this period the individual will be indoctrinated in the Samaj's teachings through the weekly services, attending one-fourth of them. Throughout this year the member must also give evidence of commitment to the Samaj by donating 1 per cent of his or her income.[103] Having become thoroughly familiar with and committed to the teachings of the Arya Samaj, the full voting member is in a position to contribute to spreading its message as a leader in the organization.

To carry on the work of the Arya Samaj there are administrative structures beyond the local chapter. Though the original bylaws of the Lahore Arya Samaj do not contain any provision for larger administrative units, the need for concerted action prompted innovation. In October 1886 in Lahore a central organization was established called the Ārya Pratinidhi Sabhā ("Arya Representative Assembly").[104] Arya Samaj preachers traveled throughout north India. Following their successes umbrella organizations like the Ārya Pratinidhi Sabhā, Punjab were set up in other areas: in the United Provinces in 1886, in Rajasthan in 1888, in Bengal and Bihar in 1889, in Madhya Pradesh and Vidarbha also in 1889, and in Bombay province in 1902.[105] Structures of proselytization and administration expanded.

In 1909 the Sārvadeśik Ārya Pratinidhi Sabhā ("International Arya Representative Assembly," often called the International Aryan League in official Arya publications in English) was established. All the provincial bodies associated themselves with the Sārvadeśik Sabhā except for the Prādeśik Ārya Pratinidhi Sabhā.[106] Sārvadeśik helped to sponsor Arya Samaj missionary efforts overseas, especially in emigrant Indian communities. Eventually organizations in other countries came to affiliate themselves with Sārvadeśik: in British East Africa (1922), South Africa (1927), Fiji (1928), Mauritius (1930), and Dutch Guyana

(1937).[107] Thus the Sārvadeśik Ārya Pratinidhi Sabhā has become the center of an international network of regional Arya Samaj agencies. These bodies are the administrative expression of the Arya Samaj's worldwide outreach.

From time to time, following successful proselytization and a large number of conversions, there has arisen a fervent hope that the Arya Samaj might fulfil its mission to convert the world in the very near future, but this has not been common. More frequently Arya Samajists have sought to contribute to the movement's work by unrelenting but unspectacular efforts to bring in individuals one by one. The Arya Samaj's regular organizational structures are a reflection of this undramatic attempt to advance the Arya Samaj's grand mission.

FUNDAMENTALISM AS TELEOLOGICAL

As a background to the Arya Samaj's understanding of future history, a basic presentation of the traditional Hindu view is helpful. Most Hindu sects agree that we are living in the kali yuga. The kali yuga is an age of vice that will be characterized by ever greater degeneration for hundreds of thousands of years, culminating in a catastrophe (pralaya). After the pralaya the world will be recreated, and virtue will reign for some time in the pristine period before degeneration sets in again. The history of re-creation and degeneration is divided into four ages (the krita or *satya* yuga, the treta yuga, the dvapara yuga, and finally the kali yuga). The cycle of four yugas is collective known as a great yuga (a *mahāyuga*). The *mahāyugas* are embedded in manvantaras, which are in turn combined to make up days of Brahma. This vast cosmic history repeats itself, with the cycle of the four yugas occurring again and again throughout the endless days of Brahma.

Traditionally in the Hindu world-view the movement of history is understood to be inexorable. In the kali yuga individuals might with difficulty keep themselves virtuous, but they cannot hope to check the spread of vice. Of course eventually as the cycle of rebirths and redeaths rolls on, the soul will be reborn in a virtuous world after the coming of pralaya. But then there would be degeneration again. The only escape from the unending experience of death and birth, vice and virtue is mukti, liberation from the world of rebirth and redeath. The cycle must continue unabated, but the individual can save himself or herself through achieving mukti.

Swami Dayanand's ideas about history agree with traditional notions as presented above on many points, but there are also significant differences. When Dayanand discusses the history of the world, it is clear enough that he accepts the usual periodization more or less. He does reckon history in yugas, and *mahāyugas*, and manvantaras. And for Dayanand these ages have repeated themselves without end in the past and they will continue to do so endlessly in the future. From Dayanand's account of the predominance of virtue and learning at the beginning of the current *mahāyuga*, it seems that he accepts the notion that the yugas have been growing progressively worse. Nonetheless, Dayanand rejects the idea that the current age is necessarily one of increasing vice.

In *Satyārth Prakāś* Dayanand's hypothetical interlocutor argues, "This is the kali yuga. Don't wish for the things of the *satya yuga*." Dayanand responds:

> Kali yuga is the name of an age. Because an age is not capable of action, it can be neither an aid nor an obstacle in religion or irreligion. You yourselves [the wrongheaded interlocutors] are becoming the embodiment of the kali yuga. If the kali yuga and the *satya* yuga were not just human, no one in the world would be religious. All this is based on the virtues and faults of one's company, it is not natural.[108]

Dayanand begins by asserting emphatically that the kali yuga is just a period of time, and as such is incapable of hindering the practice of virtue or promoting the spread of vice. If vice and virtue were determined by the age, Dayanand argues, then it would be impossible to call anyone religious. Goodness or evil would be out of the hands of the person. The purport of the last sentence in this paragraph is not clear. Perhaps Dayanand's point here is simply that the company of the good encourages virtue, while the company of the bad is liable to lead to vice. In addition to this Dayanand might be allowing that it is indeed difficult to be virtuous in this age, not because of anything inherent in the age, but because of the prevalence of bad people. Despite this ambiguity, the general point is obvious. If anyone wishes to make the world better, there is nothing about the current age which necessarily would prevent it.

There is another important point in this area where Dayanand's ideas depart from the tradition. Generally mukti or liberation is thought of as a permanent state, but Dayanand disagrees. Dayanand argues that limited deeds, the virtuous acts of the aspirant for liberation, could not produce an unlimited result. Dayanand does accept that there is a blissful state called mukti, but he maintains that the soul can only remain in this state for a limited time, and then it must return to the mundane world.[109]

On these two points Dayanand's philosophy seems consistently activist. Unlike other Hindus, Dayanand argues that the current age is not doomed to ever greater decay. Presumably it would be possible to reverse the downward spiral of history by earnestly striving for good. Traditionally the ultimate goal of the individual in Hinduism is not to affect history, but to opt out of it through mukti. This solution is not so attractive in Dayanand's thought, where it does not lead to a permanent state. The bliss of mukti lasts for an extraordinarily long time by Dayanand's reckoning, and it is something to be hoped for, but it is not endless.[110] In contrast to prevailing notions, for Dayanand it is possible to change history, while one cannot escape permanently from it.

On one level Dayanand's philosophy demands action in history. The current age is a part of larger cycles, however, which will be marked by re-creation and degeneration. The ebb and flow of history is parallel to the rise and fall of the individual soul. Dayanand writes that mukti is bound to end eventually, that the good person is destined to backslide into evil. Dayanand does not offer any vision that would lead one to hope for any sustained advance in the future for individuals or for the world. Unlike fundamentalist Christian ideas, where history is leading to a definite and glorious end, Dayanand's history is endless with alternating periods of glory and despair.

A COMPARISON OF THE ARYA SAMAJ WITH BOB JONES UNIVERSITY AND THE JAMA'AT-I ISLAMI

Having presented a basic analysis of the Arya Samaj in light of Martin Marty's definition of fundamentalism, it is now possible to compare it with the movements which were the subject of the last chapter. This comparison is divided into two parts. We have already noted that there is a significant difference between Bob Jones University and the Jama'at-i Islami in the area of politics. In the first part of this section we will investigate the role of the Arya Samaj in politics and compare it with Christian and Islamic fundamentalism. The second part will be devoted to other comparisons of the three movements. This discussion will not be directly organized around Marty's twelve aspects of fundamentalism. Rather a series of observations will be offered centered on history, scripture, and universalism and particularism. It will not be possible in this section to bring to light all of the similarities and differences between the Arya Samaj and Bob Jones University and the Jama'at-i Islami. Instead we will focus on those points which produce significant insights into the nature of fundamentalism itself.

THE ARYA SAMAJ AND POLITICS

As we discussed in the conclusion to the last chapter, there is some difference between Bob Jones University and the Jama'at-i Islami with regard to politics. The Jama'at-i Islami has been directly involved in political life throughout its history, including taking part in elections in Pakistan as a separate party. While officials at Bob Jones have also occasionally spoken out on political issues, their involvement in politics has not been as intensive or as consistent as that of their Muslim counterparts. The relationship of the Arya Samaj to politics has been more like that of Bob Jones University than that of the Jama'at-i Islami.

The Arya Samaj is not a political party. The Samaj as a group has never endorsed any political party. From early in its history members affirmed that the Arya Samaj is a religious and social organization, not a political one. In the face of oppressive police measures following the disturbances of 1907, for example, the Ārya Prādeśik Pratinidhi Sabhā (the governing body of the Arya Samaj chapters affiliated with the College faction) reaffirmed:

> Resolved that the Arya Samaj has always been and is now a non-political body and this fact the Arya Samaj has publicly declared and expressed in writings, but as some mischievous people have now here and there spread rumours to the contrary, this meeting of the Executive Committee of the Arya Pradeshik Pratinidhi Sabha, takes this opportunity to reiterate its old creed and declares that it has no connection of any kind with any political body or with political agitation in any shape.[111]

Disclaimers of this type were common in an era when political organizations in India were bound to be subject to British government scrutiny. This is not to say that Arya Samajists have not been involved in politics—they most certainly have been. And the Arya Samaj has consistently supported some positions in the political arena. In this section we will briefly describe the Arya Samaj's role in politics in India.

It is appropriate to begin this discussion with the political activities of Swami Dayanand. After founding the Arya Samaj Dayanand spent a great deal of his time in Rajasthan. The swami continued with his public preaching, but he especially looked for opportunities to instruct India's native princes in right living and proper governance. The swami's teaching in this context was probably similar to that contained in the sixth chapter of *Satyārth Prakāś*, in which the classical code *The Laws of Manu* is used heavily in an explication of *rājadharma*, the duties of kings.[112] J.T.F. Jordens interprets this mission to Rajasthan on Dayanand's part as an attempt to widen his appeal. The swami did not want his influence to be confined to the membership of the Arya Samaj. Through the native princes he saw the opportunity to reform whole states.[113] Later history would largely nullify Swami Dayanand's work in this area. After India became independent these principalities were made a part of the Indian union, and the princes lost most of their power.

As for the struggle against the British, which has been the major movement in Indian history over the past century, Swami Dayanand did criticize foreign rule. In *Satyārth Prakāś* he wrote:

> No matter how much someone else does, self-government is best of all. Though a foreign government be devoid of religious prejudice, and free of partiality towards its own or others, and possessed of kindness, justice, and mercy towards its subjects like a father and mother, still it cannot completely satisfy them. It is very difficult to be free of the opposition that arises from different languages, separate educations, and distinct customs. Without being free of it, it is hard to accomplish completely the good of all and to fulfil the hopes of all. For this reason it is the task of good people to believe in the system and history written in the Vedas and other scriptures.[114]

Nowadays this paragraph is quoted by some Arya Samajists to prove that Dayanand supported independence, but it does not appear that the swami was directly involved in anti-British activity.[115] Nonetheless, the vision of ancient glory that Dayanand presented in his writings and the hope for a brighter future provided a spark for practical political action.

The dominant force in Indian politics throughout the twentieth century has been the Indian National Congress. In the early years of the organization around the turn of the century there was a heavy note of skepticism in the attitude in Punjab toward the Congress. Punjabis tended to criticize the Congress as all talk and no action. Aside from its annual session, the Congress could boast of little in terms of ongoing work. Participation in the Congress by Punjabis tended to increase when there were attempts to make the the party more activist, and decrease when these efforts failed. When the Congress's meeting was held in Lahore in 1900, for example, Punjabis succeeded in adding committees on self-help in education and industry to the Congress structure. But this trend was not supported by the more conservative Bengali Congressmen at the next annual session in Calcutta in 1901, and enthusiasm in Punjab dropped as a consequence thereafter.

It should be noted that not every Congressman in Punjab was an Arya Samajist, nor was every member of the Samaj active in the Congress. Nonetheless, members of the Arya Samaj made a significant contribution to Punjabi involvement with the Congress. N.G. Barrier has concluded that Arya Samajists made up around 50 per cent of the Punjabi delegates to the annual sessions of the Congress in the first few years of this century, and they were consistently in the majority among Punjabis on the important Subjects Committee of the Congress during the same period.[116] The names of Arya Samajists appear time and again in the early history of the Congress in Punjab as leaders of the movement in that province.

Of the Arya Samajists who were involved in Congress the best known is Lala Lajpat Rai (1865-1928). Lajpat Rai joined the Arya Samaj in his teens and was active in the organization throughout his life. He was a particularly important figure during the split of 1893. Siding with the meat eaters, Lajpat Rai became the president of the new Anarkali Arya Samaj and the secretary of the D.A.V. College's managing committee. Lajpat Rai first attended a Congress annual meeting in 1888, but his involvement with that party would remain irregular for several years thereafter. He emerged as a major force in the Congress in 1905. Angry at the partition of Bengal, young radicals led by Bal Gangadhar Tilak demanded that the Congress confront the British more directly, and Lajpat Rai was an important supporter of this movement. In 1920 Lajpat Rai took part in M.K. Gandhi's noncooperation campaign. That year Lajpat Rai was president of the Congress's annual session in Calcutta. For the rest of his life Lajpat Rai remained active in politics.

After 1922 Lajpat Rai's interests began to shift from the Congress to an emerging Hindu politics. Although Lajpat Rai had supported the *khilafat* movement from 1920 to 1922, he came to disagree with Gandhi over Hindu-Muslim unity and noncooperation in later years. Lajpat Rai believed that Muslims were taking advantage of the noncooperation of the Congress, advancing their interests at the expense of those of the Hindu community. In 1926 Lajpat Rai founded the Independent Congress Party (or the Nationalist Party) with Pandit Madan Mohan Malaviya, which was a Hindu party working with the Hindu Mahasabha.[117] He explained his position as follows:

> The Hindus have so far followed a National policy and, I think, they must stick to that. They will be stultifyiug [*sic*] themselves if they replace their nationalism by communalism. Yet we cannot ignore the fact that there are some communities in India who want to take undue advantage of our nationalism and are pushing forward their communalism to such an extent as is injurious to the interests of the whole nation and certainly disastrous to those of the Hindu Community. Such communalism we are bound to oppose as, in our judgement, it can only lead to permanent slavery, permanent disunity and a state of perpetual dependence.[118]

Ultimately Lajpat Rai saw the communalism of "some communities in India," and he is undoubtedly referring to Muslims here primarily, as a threat to Indian nationalism. Lajpat Rai supported organizations like the Hindu Mahasabha not to foment Hindu communalism, but to counteract the Muslim activities which he understood to be undermining the Indian struggle for freedom.[119]

Another Arya Samajist who was an important figure in the history of the Congress is Swami Shraddhanand (1857-1926). Shraddhanand was the leader of the vegetarian faction who founded the Gurukul Kangri. For most of his life Shraddhanand was uninterested in the Congress, but the peculiar combination of activism and saintliness in Gandhi's approach proved irresistible to the dynamic swami. During 1919 Shraddhanand was one of the leaders of the satyagraha against the Rowlatt Act in Delhi, a position which thrust him to national prominence. Then, because of disagreements with Gandhi especially over untouchability and Hindu-Muslim unity, Shraddhanand withdrew all support from the Congress by 1922. The swami accused the Mahatma of having abandoned his commitment to the uplift of untouchables for political reasons, and he criticized Gandhi for ignoring the concerns of the Hindu community in reaching out to Muslim leaders.

To pursue his own agenda on both these issues Swami Shraddhanand turned to the Hindu Mahasabha. In 1923 he toured north India, supporting Hindu *saṅgaṭhan* (or consolidation) and urging his listeners to take part in the Mahasabha's meeting in Benares in that year. Because the Mahasabha supported Hindu interests it was free of the weakness towards Muslims which afflicted the Congress in Shraddhanand's view. On the other hand, since the Mahasabha aspired to represent the whole Hindu community, including traditional Hindus, Shraddhanand's program for the abolition of untouchability was not endorsed by the organization. After the rejection of his radical caste reform proposals, Shraddhanand's involvement with the Mahasabha decreased until he finally severed ties with it in 1926. Because he could not find consistent support for untouchable uplift in the Congress or the Hindu Mahasabha, Swami Shraddhanand was forced to establish more radical organizations to that end.[120]

It is clear from the political careers of Lajpat Rai and Shraddhanand that Arya Samajists were involved not only with the Congress but also with the Hindu Mahasabha. The Akhil Bhārat Hindū Mahāsabhā (the "All-India Hindu Society") was founded in Hardwar during the Kumbh Mela of 1915.[121] The Mahasabha was the result of a proposal made at the Punjab Hindu Conference in 1913. The latter organization was founded by the Arya leader Lala Lal Chand after a series of articles by him on the situation of the Hindu community appeared in the *Panjabee* entitled "Self-Abnegation in Politics." Lal Chand argued that there was a consistent pattern of favoritism towards the Muslims in India by the British government which Hindus were not effectively opposing. The commitment of Hindu leaders in the Congress to Hindu-Muslim collaboration restrained them from advancing the interests of their own community.

> *If there is one thing which is strictly forbidden within the precincts of the Congress it is the term "Hindu". Resolution may be passed to favour purely Mohammadan interests but the Hindu is tabooed there.*[122]

To counteract this Lal Chand supported the development of organizations which would defend the rights of Hindus, like the Punjab Hindu Conference and eventually the Hindu Mahasabha.

The Subjects Committee of the Hindu Mahasabha defined its goals as follows:

a. To promote greater union and solidarity amongst all sections of the Hindu Community and to unite them more closely as parts of one organic whole.

b. To promote education among members of the Hindu Community.
c. To ameliorate and improve the condition of all classes of the Hindu Community.
d. To protect and promote Hindu interests whenever and wherever it may be necessary.
e. To promote good feelings between the Hindus and other Communities in India and to act in a friendly way with them, and in loyal Co-operattion [*sic*] with the Government.
f. Generally to take steps for promoting religious, moral, educational, social and political interests of the community.[123]

This statement of purpose is necessarily general since the membership of the Mahasabha included not only Arya Samajists but also traditional Hindus of every stripe. At the 1923 meeting of the Mahasabha in Benares, for example, a major clash between Hindu reformers and conservatives was only narrowly averted when M.M. Malaviya convinced Shraddhanand to water down his planned motions against untouchability. Despite these internal problems, the Hindu Mahasabha increased in popularity as a consequence of rising communalism in the 1920s.

Another major internal dispute surfaced at the annual session of the Hindu Mahasabha in Delhi in 1926 when Bhai Parmanand proposed that the organization field candidates in the elections to legislative councils to be held in that year. Parmanand was an Arya Samajist who was involved with the College Party. His initiative was defeated, in favor of a compromise that the Mahasabha would not run its own candidates, but it would oppose those candidates judged to be against the interests of the Hindu community. Moderates like Lajpat Rai and Malaviya believed that the Mahasabha should concentrate on consolidating the Hindu community through supporting cultural unity and social improvement, rather than directly entering politics.[124] But the moderates lost out, and from 1937, when Bhai Parmanand became its president, the Mahasabha became more openly political.[125]

Consistent with the general shift to communal concerns in the political activities of Arya Samajists prior to 1947, the issues with which the Samaj has been identified in post-independence India have had a communal character. Perhaps the most important of these is the advocacy of Hindi. The Arya Samaj's support for Hindi became a part of the contention surrounding the linguistic reorganization of the state of

Punjab in 1966. Before that year Punjab, which had a Hindi-speaking Hindu majority, included a sizable population of persons whose mother tongue was Punjabi.[126] These Punjabi speakers, many of them Sikhs, were concentrated in the prosperous northwestern region of the state. After decades of agitation by Sikh political bodies the government of India agreed to divide Punjab into three states, Punjab, Haryana, and Himachal Pradesh. The Arya Samaj fought this decision.

The Arya Samaj first became identified with Hindi in the nineteenth century, when members of the organization supported a drive to have that language replace Urdu as the official vernacular in Punjab. At a time when there was vigorous competition between Hindus and Muslims for positions in the British government of India, Arya Samajists believed that the recognition of Urdu gave Muslims a natural advantage. They demanded that Hindi be substituted so that Hindus might gain greater access to government jobs. This agitation was opposed by Muslims, and the supporters of Hindi were not able to convince the British to accept their claims.

With the partition of the India and Pakistan in 1947 the Urdu-speaking population of Punjab in India dropped precipitously as large numbers of Muslims migrated across the border. With their departure the debate over Urdu in Punjab died, but this did not mark the end of linguistic dispute. Even before partition some Sikh leaders had begun to call for a separate Sikh state to be carved out of Punjab. The attempt in independent India to satisfy the separatists through various regional formulas was unsuccessful. The demand for a Punjabi-speaking state persisted until the division of Punjab in 1966.

Some of the same practical considerations which motivated Arya Samajists' advocacy of Hindi over Urdu were behind the opposition to the creation of a Punjabi state. This is obvious from a division that arose among members of the Arya Samaj over the issue. On the one hand, the leaders of the Arya Samaj in Punjab, who were concentrated in the urban centers of the northwest in areas dominated by Punjabi, consistently opposed the reorganization of the state. They had no interest in becoming a linguistic and religious minority in an overwhelmingly Punjabi-speaking Sikh state. On the other hand, some Arya Samajists in the rural areas to the southeast eventually came to support the division of Punjab. They would then become a part of Haryana, a state with a great preponderance of Hindi-speaking Hindus. They would no longer have to concern themselves with a politically powerful Sikh minority, as they did in undivided Punjab.[127]

Yet in these linguistic wrangles Arya Samajists were motivated not only by self-interest, but also by a peculiar view of the interests of the Hindu community and of India as a nation. Underlying the arguments against Punjabi and Urdu in Punjab was a powerful conflation of language, religion, and culture in the mind of some members of the Arya Samaj. Punjabi was identified by Arya Samajists (and others) as the language of Sikhs, and Urdu as the language of Muslims. Many Arya Samajists believed that in Punjab the mother tongue of Hindus is Hindi. Not only in Punjab but for the whole country, the Arya Samaj's affirmation that Hindi should be the language of India was implicitly linked to a belief that the nation's culture and religion should be Hindu.

It might seem paradoxical that Arya Samajists have struggled to defend the interests of the Hindu community in public life at the same time that they have been bitterly critical of the beliefs and practices of most Hindus. Yet their behavior is consistent with the Samaj's perception of itself as the guardian of the true Hindu tradition in our age. Although Arya Samajists attack other Hindus, they do so in the interests of purifying and strengthening Hinduism. In the political arena as well Arya Samajists have attempted to make the Hindu community strong by awakening it from its quiescence.

Though the Arya Samaj is not a political party, its members have taken part in politics, and they have tended to embrace a certain set of issues in the public realm. In recounting what fundamentalism is not Marty has asserted that "fundamentalists are not always activists, militants, belligerents, or terrorists."[128] It is true that fundamentalist groups across cultures have played different roles in political life. Even in the case of a single movement the level of political involvement of fundamentalists may vary over time. North American Protestant fundamentalists, for example, spoke out as a group in the 1920s on certain political issues and they have been active again in politics in recent decades, but between the 1920s and the 1970s they were more quiescent. Despite these variations, it is possible to say that there is a tendency for political engagement in fundamentalist movements. The American constitutional separation of church and state notwithstanding, it is inevitable that some religious issues have public policy implications. It should hardly be surprising that groups which see themselves as the sole defenders of the true religion might attempt to impose their version of that truth on others in politics.

OTHER COMPARISONS

As the evidence presented in this chapter makes clear, most of the aspects of fundamentalism which have been identified by Martin Marty are present in the Arya Samaj. The Samaj did arise as a reaction against the penetration of Western ideas into India. It engaged in a selective retrieval of certain fundamentals from the Hindu tradition which are scandalous to non-Aryas. The Samaj has been separatist, though only to a limited extent. The Arya Samaj has been defined by the groups to which it is opposed, and it also tends to an absolutist understanding of the truth. Arya Samajists base their movement on an authoritative scripture. In the theory of the Arya Samaj the history leading up to present has been characterized by degeneration and not progress, but an attack on evolution has not occupied a prominent place in the Samaj's program. Arya Samajists have been antipermissive, but this has been the case more for the rules that separate them from non-Aryas than for more general moral principles. The Samaj's reading of the Vedas certainly has been antihermeneutical, undercutting the authority of interpretations which compete with Swami Dayanand's. For the members of the Arya Samaj that organization does have a role to play in history, though radical change does not appear imminent. Lastly the Arya Samaj has a view of future history which supports activism, but this view could not be dubbed teleological. It is only this final element of Marty's definition which is clearly not applicable to the Arya Samaj.

Beyond the specific contents of our definition there are some characteristics of the Arya Samaj which are also manifest in either Bob Jones University or the Jama'at-i Islami or both, which will be highlighted in this section. But before going on with that, it is important to acknowledge one significant difference between the Arya Samaj and the two fundamentalist movements analyzed in the last chapter. In the previous chapter we saw that Bob Jones and the Jama'at-i Islami developed as a reaction against the modernization and Westernization that were rapidly gaining adherents in their traditions. In contrast to this, the Arya Samaj's main fight has been against traditionalists, though it has also debated Westernizing modernists in India.

The position of the Arya Samaj here casts a strong light on an aspect of many fundamentalist movements which is sometimes overlooked. While the primary conflict of the Christian fundamentalist has been with theological liberals, divisions with conservatives have also developed. Since the 1920s, when the coalition against modernism in the denominations came unglued, fundamentalists have condemned not only the liberals but also the orthodox, those conservatives who would not join them in their crusade against the new theology. By the same token the Jama'at-i Islami has criticized the traditionalist ulama on the right as well as Westernized Muslims on the left. In both these cases when the fundamentalists have engaged the modernists in conflict, they have found that they must do battle with traditionalists also. Nonetheless it is true that the orientation of the Arya Samaj is different from the other fundamentalist movements which we have discussed, because its chief opponents have been traditionalists and not modernists.

For the remainder of this chapter we will discuss the complex dynamics related to history, scripture, and universalism and particularism in these fundamentalist movements. There are significant similarities and differences between the Arya Samaj and Bob Jones University and the Jama'at-i Islami with regard to perceptions of their role in history. In the conclusion to our first chapter we saw that there are problems with describing non-Western fundamentalist movements as antievolutionary. Here it need only be added that the evidence on the Arya Samaj supports this general point. Polemics against evolutionary theories of history have not been a central concern of Arya Samajists. In the last chapter we noted that in contrast to the North American Protestant case there has not been such a furious debate over Darwinian evolution in Islamic cultures. This is true for Hindu India as well. Progressive theories of history, whether based on Darwin or others, have not been a major bone of contention in India.

Despite the problems with the term "antievolutionary," there is a similar pattern to past history according to all of the three fundamentalist movements under consideration here. Christian fundamentalists look upon the New Testament period as a golden age, with later history characterized by increasing degeneracy. For the Jama'at-i Islami as well there is a stark contrast between the ideal time of Muhammad and the rightly guided caliphs and the corrupt present. And in the Arya Samaj's understanding there is a world of difference between the virtuous Vedic age and our own vicious time. For each of these three movements there is a strong contrast between a perfect past and a corrupt present. The North American Protestant fundamentalist's rejection of Darwinian evolution can be seen as just one example of the more general fundamentalist tendency to understand the history that leads up to the present as degenerative and not progressive.

In relation to their role as divine agents in the present, it should be understood that the histories of these fundamentalist movements themselves are significant. In the first decade after its founding it must have seemed that the Arya Samaj was on the cutting edge of a historic change. Swami Dayanand was directly confronting traditionalists and modernists and besting them in debate. New Arya Samaj chapters were being established at a rapid rate. Social reform was in the air as caste barriers, for example, were being weakened in some ways as a by-product of the activities of the British in India. In contrast to this ferment a century ago, now there is a sense among Arya Samajists that their organization is no longer such a powerful agent for change.[129] On the one hand the Arya Samaj has been undone by its own success as social reforms have robbed the Samaj's appeals of their urgency. Women and members of the lower castes enjoy greater legal protection in contemporary India than they did in the nineteenth century, for instance. On the other hand some of these issues have been intractable in a way that may not have been appreciated fully by the early leaders of the Arya Samaj. To take the same example again, in spite of legal reforms it has proven difficult to remove the barriers against the equality of women and lower caste people even within the Samaj itself. Whatever may be the explanation for the current state of the Arya Samaj, it must be acknowledged that an anticipation of rapid change has largely been replaced by a resolve to work steadily for the unspectacular growth of the Samaj one convert at a time.

There is some tension not only in the Arya Samaj but also in the other fundamentalist movements surveyed here on the issue of their role in history. The great plans of the Jama'at-i Islami to convert Pakistan to its Islamic ideology were dashed by the poor showing of the party when it first fielded candidates for election in 1951.[130] Since then the members of the Jama'at have learned to hold out more modest hopes. They work to increase the following of the organization, prepared for a long struggle to win power. Even Christian fundamentalists must strive to maintain their millenarian expectations while living in the world. Fundamentalists in all three cases have had to accept that history has sometimes refused to bend to their will.

Contrary to Marty's definition there does not seem to be anything distinctively teleological in the theories about the future of the Jama'at-i Islami and the Arya Samaj. The Arya Samaj does have ideas about history which distinguish it from traditional Hinduism, but they do not add up to a teleology. The Samaj's doctrine tends to impel its members to activism, since it allows that improvement of the present degenerate age is possible while permanent escape from it is not. Like most Muslims Maulana Maududi accepted that history has an end, but his understanding of this end militated against the anticipation of any imminent apocalyptic event. Maududi placed an emphasis on practical attempts to reform the Islamic world, rather that on mystical figures who might achieve revitalization through divine intervention. The theories about the future which distinguish the Arya Samaj and the Jama'at-i Islami motivate those groups to be more active in trying to change history, but they are not directed towards any distinctive end.

On this point there is a strong contrast between the Arya Samaj and the Jama'at-i Islami on the one hand and Bob Jones University on the other. The Samaj and the Jama'at are focused on the present and not the future. They emphasize activism now rather than a myth of the end of history. Christian fundamentalism is focused on the future and not the present. Although there have been some groups which have been activist, dispensational premillennialism provides support for quietism in the present in anticipation of Christ's saving action at the end of days. Perhaps a distinction must be made between activist fundamentalist groups which are not teleological and quietist ones which are.

Now we will turn from history to scripturalism. Beyond the original revelation it must be admitted that the Arya Samaj has an explicit theory about the authority of other religious literature which is echoed in the Jama'at-i Islami but not in North American Protestant fundamentalism. According to Maulana Maududi in addition to the Qur'an which is absolutely reliable, there are other texts that must be accepted, most notably from Hadith. Though a good proportion of these traditions are spurious, some can be proven authentic and should be understood as binding upon Muslims. In the Arya Samaj alongside the Vedas there is the *ārṣa* literature as well, which is authoritative to a limited extent.

There is an interesting parallel between the Arya Samaj's theories about the Vedas and the *ārṣa* literature and Jama'at's ideas about Qur'an and Hadith. The absolute inerrancy of the Qur'an for the Jama'at-i Islami (and for other Muslims) follows from its divine authorship, and Swami Dayanand made the same argument about the Vedas. The position of Hadith for the Jama'at-i Islami is more ambiguous, in that there are some traditions which are reliable and some which are not. The touchstone for this reliability is the relationship of a given tradition to the Prophet Muhammad and his companions. Theoretically those Hadith must be followed which date back to the time of the Prophet, and are thus an accurate reflection of his judgments. Later Hadith which have been inaccurately attributed to the Prophet are not binding. Similarly, other than the Vedas those religious texts are binding upon the Arya Samaj which were written by the ancient sages known as the rishis. Later works falsely said to have been written by the rishis are to be disregarded. So for both the Jama'at-i Islami and the Arya Samaj the absolute authority of their inerrant scripture derives from the belief that it was written by God, while the relative authority of other texts depends upon their having been written by religious leaders in the ancient golden age.

Having noted a parallel between the Arya Samaj and the Jama'at-i Islami in the area of scripture, let us address a similarity in this area shared by the Arya Samaj and Bob Jones University. Arya Samajists maintain that the Vedas are inerrant. In classical Indian philosophy reverence towards the Vedas is the defining characteristic of Hindu orthodoxy. So the Arya emphasis on the Vedas comes out of a hoary tradition. Yet even in the classical period the use of the Vedas (especially the Vedic hymns or Samhitas) was largely confined to ritual contexts. When Arya Samajists proclaim that the Vedas must be accepted not only as a text for ritual recitation but also as a guide for social behavior and even as an introduction to scientific knowledge, they are extending the authority of the Vedas into new areas.

By the same token when Christian fundamentalists claim that the Bible is inerrant in matters of history and science, they are departing from the traditional understanding of the nature of the Bible itself. Down through the centuries the historical veracity of the Bible has not been a central concern of Christians. It is only in the modern period that history and science have come to be understood as separate disciplines which provide knowledge independent of that derived from theology and the Bible. In claiming that the Bible is inerrant in these areas fundamentalists turn from the religious concerns which are at the heart of the traditional understanding of scripture to a new set of categories of thought which are distinctly modern. In both the Christian and Hindu traditions it is the extension of the authority of scripture to new categories which is the real innovation in the assertion of inerrancy.

Having dealt with inerrancy, it is appropriate to take up the question of literalism. Like the two other movements examined in the last chapter the Arya Samaj, too, is antihermeneutical in its interpretation of scripture. This is not to say that fundamentalists always understand their sacred texts literally. Even among North American Protestant fundamentalists, who are generally known for their literal reading of the Bible, some admit that there are passages which must be taken figuratively.[131] From the evidence presented for all three movements it is clear that the issue is not whether one should read sacred texts literally, but who has the right to determine what is an acceptable reading.[132] Maulana Maududi does allow that some interpretation of the Qur'an is called for, but he seems to reserve for himself the office of determining what counts as an appropriate interpretation. Rejecting all medieval and modern Vedic commentaries Swami Dayanand does admit that the most ancient texts on the Vedas are reliable to a certain extent, but he arrogates to himself the responsibility for discriminating which passages from those texts must be disregarded as inconsistent with the Vedas. A plurality of interpretations would undercut the very certainty that fundamentalists are driving at when they retrieve sacred texts. So they save for themselves the right to interpret their scriptures.

The previous paragraph makes clear that for the Arya Samaj as for Bob Jones University and the Jama'at-i Islami there is a link between the authority of the elements retrieved from the tradition and the authoritativeness of the founders and leaders of those movements. Theoretically the authority of Swami Dayanand's teaching is dependent on the Vedas, but there is also a subtle sense in which the Vedas rely upon the work of the swami. At the basis of a fundamentalist movement there must be some authoritative individual who selects the elements of the tradition that will define the movement.

In the case of all three movements considered here the importance of their founders and leaders for understanding the authorities from the tradition on which they are based is not fully acknowledged. Though the evangelist is their guide in interpreting the Bible, Christian fundamentalists affirm a Common Sense faith in the ability of the common person to understand scripture. Maulana Maududi does not explicitly adumbrate any theory about his uniquely authentic insight into the interpretation of the Qur'an, though his commentary seems to assume such an insight. In the case of the Arya Samaj Dayanand only claimed that the ancient commentaries and reason were the basis of his reading of the Vedas. He was not a pretender to any singular status in understanding those texts. In each of these cases there is a commitment to demonstrating that it is the authorities from the tradition which are the basis of the movement. For this reason the contribution of the founders and leaders of the group to understanding those traditional authorities are de-emphasized.

Finally let us take up the question of the universalism and particularism of fundamentalist movements. In the conclusion to the first chapter we discussed the paradoxical combination of universalism and particularism which is characteristic of Bob Jones and the Jama'at-i Islami. Here we must add that this paradox is very much a part of the Arya Samaj as well. Both the Arya Samaj and the Jama'at-i Islami denounce the dividedness of their communities, for example, even while their exclusive claims to the truth are condemned as divisive by others. Swami Dayanand criticized "sectarian people opposed to each other" in the Hindu tradition.[133] About Maulana Maududi a Western scholar has written, "Distressed as he was by the divisive effects of sectarianism, he has always emphasized heavily that the doctrine he expounds is not a new interpretation of Islam, indeed, not an interpretation at all, but on the contrary only a reiteration of pure, original Islam without embellishment or change."[134] This quote points to a resolution of the apparent contradiction in these movements between their condemnation of sectarianism and their exacerbation of it. A sect puts forth some new understanding of its tradition which is peculiar to that group and marks it off from others. But the Jama'at-i Islami does not see itself as advocating a novel and different religion, rather it maintains the same truth that was expressed by Muhammad centuries ago. By this logic the Jama'at does not seek to establish a sect, but to return to the original Islam. This claim is made by Arya Samajists as well: what they defend is the true *sanātana dharma*, the eternal religion.

As in the case of other fundamentalist movements the Arya Samaj engages in a selective retrieval of the fundamentals of its tradition by reaching back to a golden age. This retrieval is another reflection of the simultaneous universalism and particularism which marks fundamentalism. In all three of our examples the golden age of the fundamentalists is also a normative period for their nonfundamentalist coreligionists. The Vedic era is an ideal time for traditional Hindus as well as Arya Samajists. All Muslims aspire to live up to the standards of the age of the Prophet Muhammad and the first four caliphs, not just the Jama'at-i Islami. And it is certainly the case that the New Testament period is an idyllic one for all Christians. Yet each of these movements uses the golden age to criticize the present practices of nonfundamentalists. Fundamentalists hark back to an age which is generally revered by their coreligionists in order to attack them.

The combined universalism and particularism of fundamentalism is reflected in its limited separatism. On the basis of the evidence considered here fundamentalist movements are separatist, but they are not absolutely so. Members of the Arya Samaj certainly have a group identity which distinguishes them from other Hindus, for example, and yet they have resisted becoming totally cut off from the traditional Hindu community. And the Jama'at-i Islami has displayed a remarkable ability to compromise with other opposition parties, even while demanding a rigorous ideological purity from its members. Fundamentalists have a mission to convert others which militates against any unambiguous separatism. They must remain separate enough to protect their version of the truth, while maintaining sufficient communication with other groups to permit proselytization.

We see further evidence of the tension between universalism and particularism in the antipermissiveness of the Arya Samaj. The scrupulosity of Arya Samajists has been directed much more at those ideas and actions which separate them from other Hindus than at general moral questions. The things which Arya Samajists strive to eliminate from their lives are not even recognized as immoral by traditionalists. This is true to a certain extent for other fundamentalist movements as well. When Bob Jones III condemns rock music because it glorifies immoral behavior, for example, he elicits the sympathy of many nonfundamentalists. But when he goes on to criticize even Christian rock music because the beat inspires sensuality, he leaves others behind. In this area he is taking an ethical stand against something that most other Americans regard as innocuous. Fundamentalists are distinguished from others not only by their moral earnestness, but by their peculiar judgment about what constitutes morality and immorality.

In this section we have presented a few of the salient insights that emerge from a comparison of the Arya Samaj with Bob Jones University and the Jama'at-i Islami. Some of these insights were concerned with scripturalism. In the final two chapters of this book the scripturalism of the Arya Samaj will be considered in greater depth. This is not a move away from the characterization of the Arya Samaj as a fundamentalist movement offered in this chapter. Rather it represents an attempt to better comprehend the nature of fundamentalism through an intensive analysis of one movement.

NOTES

1. Daniel Gold has analyzed the Arya Samaj as a fundamentalist movement at some length. Daniel Gold, "Organized Hinduisms: From Vedic Truth to Hindu Nation," Paper presented at the Fundamentalism Observed conference of the Fundamentalism Project of the American Academy of Arts and Sciences, Chicago, 17 November 1988. Others have made passing references to the fundamentalist character of the Arya Samaj. For example, Donald Taylor, "Incipient Fundamentalism: Religion and Politics among Sri Lankan Hindus in Britain," in *Studies in Religious Fundamentalism*, ed. Lionel Caplan (Albany: State University of New York Press, 1987), 140. Apparently Taylor is no student of the Arya Samaj, since he gives the name of the founder as Ananda rather than Dayanand.
2. Martin E. Marty, "Fundamentalism as a Social Phenomenon,"

Bulletin of the American Academy of Arts and Sciences 42, no. 2 (November 1988): 15-29.

3. Kenneth W. Jones, *Arya Dharm: Hindu Consciousness in 19th-Century Punjab* (Berkeley: University of California Press, 1976), 13-18 and passim.
4. Arya Samajists have debated not only with Hindus, but also with Christians, Muslims, Sikhs, and others. In the section below on the oppositional nature of Arya fundamentalism we will have more to say about the confrontation with Islam. In this section it is appropriate to focus on the distinctive position which separates the Arya Samaj from other Hindu groups.
5. Swami Dayanand Sarasvati, *Satyārtha-Prakāśaḥ* [Light for truth], ed. Yudhiṣṭhir Mīmāṃsak, 2d ed., Āryasamāj-Śatābdī-Saṃskaraṇ (Bahalgarh [Sonipat]: Ram Lal Kapoor Trust, 1975), 591-601. Perhaps the best English edition of this work is *The Light of Truth: English Translation of Svami Dayananda's "Satyārtha Prakāśa,"* trans. Ganga Prasad Upadhyaya, 2d ed., Ganga Prasad Upadhyaya Centenary Edition (Allahabad: Dr. Ratna Kumari Svadhyaya Sansthana, 1981). The references here are to the Hindi edition.
6. The Brahmo Samaj had held to the infallibility of the Vedas, but had turned away from that position from around 1847. Sivanath Sastri, *History of the Brahmo Samaj*, 2d ed. (Calcutta: Sadharan Brahmo Samaj, 1974), 63-68.
7. Dayanand, *Satyārth Prakāś*, 596-597. All quotes from Dayanand's works are my own translation.
8. Ibid., 488-496.
9. Ibid., 511.
10. Ibid., 521.
11. Ibid., 514-530.
12. This observation is my own, based on fieldwork with Arya Samajists from 1985 to 1987.
13. Kenneth Jones has noted that in the early history of the Arya Samaj it is sometimes difficult to sort out organizations advocating the *sanātana dharma* since the term was adopted by Arya Samajists and their opponents. But by the end of the 1880s the convention had been fairly well established that *sanātana* would be used to characterize the defenders of traditional Hinduism. Jones, *Arya Dharm*, 111.
14. This account of the work of Śraddhā Rām is based upon Kenneth W. Jones, *Socio-Religious Reform Movements in British India*, New Cambridge History of India, part 3, vol. 1 (Cambridge: Cambridge University Press, 1989), 106-109. I am grateful to

Professor Jones for sharing a prepublication manuscript of this text with me.

15. Jones, *Arya Dharm*, 108-112. For more on the Bhārat Dharma Mahāmaṇḍal see Jones, *Socio-Religious Reform Movements in British India*, 77-82.
16. Although it is the opinion of many Arya Samajists that Swami Dayanand himself actually wrote the *niyams*, Western scholars do not concur. J.T.F. Jordens, *Dayānanda Sarasvatī: His Life and Ideas* (Delhi: Oxford University Press, 1978), 174-175; Jones, *Arya Dharm*, 37. In any event it is certain that Dayanand accepted the ten principles.
17. In many versions of the *niyams*, including the one quoted here, the word "all" (*sab*, in Hindi) is inserted before "true knowledge." "The Veda is the book of all true knowledge." Dr. Bhārtīy has established that the word "sab" is not to be found in the oldest versions of the *niyams*. Bhavānīlāl Bhārtīy, *Navjāgaraṇ ke Purodhā: Dayānand Sarasvatī* (Ajmer: Paropkāriṇī Sabhā, 1983), 326-327. Still, it should be noted that "knowledge" is plural, so that more than just one type of knowledge is intended here.
18. Lekh Rām, *Jīvancaritra: Maharṣi Swāmī Dayānand Sarasvatī*, ed. Bhavānīlāl Bhārtīy, trans. Raghunandansiṃh, 2d printing (Delhi: Ārṣ Sāhitya Pracār Trust, Vikram Saṃvat 2041), 329-330. The translation is my own.
19. Jordens, *Dayānanda Sarasvatī*, 175-176.
20. Jones, *Arya Dharm*, 168-174.
21. Dayanand, *Satyārth Prakāś*, 951-961.
22. Ibid., 953-954.
23. Ibid., 956.
24. Ibid., 953.
25. Ibid., 956.
26. Charles H. Heimsath, *Indian Nationalism and Hindu Social Reform* (Princeton: Princeton University Press, 1964), 113-130.
27. Dayanand, *Satyārth Prakāś*, 955.
28. On the interaction of Unitarians and Brahmos see Spencer Lavan, *Unitarians and India: A Study in Encounter and Response* (Boston: Beacon Press, 1977), especially 32-40 (for Rammohun Roy) and 104-130 (for Keshub Chandra Sen).
29. Dayanand, *Satyārth Prakāś*, 741-837.
30. David Kopf, *The Brahmo Samaj and the Shaping of the Modern Indian Mind* (Princeton: Princeton University Press, 1979), 132-136.

31. Dayanand, *Satyārth Prakāś*, 124-128.
32. Ibid., 140-150.
33. Jones, *Arya Dharm*, 132.
34. *Arya Patrika* (Lahore), 21 August 1888, n. p., quoted in J. Reid Graham, *The Arya Samaj as a Reformation in Hinduism with Special Reference to Caste* (Ann Arbor: University Microfilms, 1965), 464. This is a photomechanical reproduction of a Ph.D. dissertation, Yale University, 1942. *Praschit* is a corruption of *prāyaścitta*, the Sanskrit word for the traditional purification rituals. The actions condemned in the first paragraph (eating cow dung, pilgrimage to the Ganges, feeding Brahmans) are all penances prescribed as a part of *prāyaścittas*.
35. Graham sees a move away from traditional rituals of purification in the 1890s through the 1910s, then a return to those rituals again in the 1920s. Graham, 511.
36. Graham, 475-487.
37. This is on the basis of a report by Rambhaj Datta, the president of the All-India Shuddhi Sabha, in the 1911 census. *Census of India, 1911*, vol. 14, *Punjab*, part I, *Report*, by Harikishan Kaul (Lahore: Government of India, 1912), 149.
38. Jones, *Arya Dharm*, 202-215.
39. Ibid., 308-309.
40. Graham, 511.
41. Jāt Pāt Toṛak Maṇḍal, *General Review of the Jat Pat Todak Mandal* (Lahore: n. p., 1939), 1-2, quoted in Graham, 538-539.
42. Graham, 542.
43. For not only the text of his address, but also the correspondence between him and the Maṇḍal see B.R. Ambedkar, *Annihilation of Caste*, 3d ed. (Jalandhar: Bheem Patrika Publications, 1968), 17-97 (for the address) and 1-15 (for the correspondence).
44. Graham, 542.
45. Jones, *Arya Dharm*, 205-212.
46. There is a list of the important *śāstrārthas* in which Dayanand took part in Harbilas Sarda, *Life of Dayanand Saraswati: World Teacher*, 2d ed. (Ajmer: Paropkāriṇī Sabhā, 1968), 345-346.
47. The material that is available on the *śāstrārthas* has been published in Bhavānīlāl Bhārtīy and Yudhiṣṭhir Mīmāṃsak, eds., *Ṛṣi Dayānand Sarasvatī ke Śāstrārtha aur Pravacan* (Bahalgarh [Sonipat]: Ram Lal Kapoor Trust, 1988), 1-240. There is an English translation of one encounter with a Christian and Muslim, Ratan Lal, trans., *Chandapur Fair* (Ajmer: Paropkāriṇī Sabhā, 1974).
48. There is a very brief excursus at the end of the chapter on another

text, the *Allopaniṣad*. This is a work in Sanskrit cast as one of the Upanishads which praises Allah. Dayanand demonstrates that this work is modern and not ancient, and thus dismisses it. Dayanand, *Satyārth Prakāś*, 948-950.

49. For example, Dayanand, *Satyārth Prakāś*, 843, commenting on Qur'an 1.6-7.
50. For example, Dayanand, *Satyārth Prakāś*, 852, commenting on Qur'an 2.58.
51. For example, Dayanand, *Satyārth Prakāś*, 856, commenting on Qur'an 2.88.
52. *Paisā Akhbār* (Lahore), 29 August 1896, n.p., summarized in *Selections from the Vernacular Newspapers Published in the Punjab* 9 (1896): 517.
53. Jones, *Arya Dharm*, 193-202.
54. G.R. Thursby, *Hindu-Muslim Relations in British India: A Study of Controversy, Conflict, and Communal Movements in Northern India, 1923-1928*, Studies in the History of Religions (Supplements to *Numen*), vol. 35 (Leiden: E.J. Brill, 1975), 15-16.
55. Dayanand, *Satyārth Prakāś*, 182-193.
56. Attacks on the Arya Samaj through *niyoga* have not been limited to the South Asian subcontinent. John Kelly has documented that this was an issue in debates between "Sanatanists" and Arya Samajists among Indian emigrants in Fiji. John Dunham Kelly, "*Bhakti* and the Spirit of Capitalism in Fiji: The Ontology of the Fiji Indians" (Ph.D. diss., University of Chicago, 1988), 2: 544-558. The same was true in Trinidad. Richard Huntington Forbes, *Arya Samaj in Trinidad: An Historical Study of Hindu Organizational Process in Acculturative Conditions* (Ann Arbor: University Microfilms, 1985), 109-112. This is a reprint of a Ph. D. dissertation, University of Miami, Coral Gables, Florida, 1984.
57. Thursby was not able to find original edition of all of these works, and had to reconstruct the publication information from government files. This is what he found: Pandit Kalicharan Sharma, *Vicitra Jīvan* (Agra: published by the author, 1923); [Pandit Camūpati], *Raṅgīlā Rasūl* (Lahore: Mahashay Raj Pal, 1924); and Devi Sharan Sharma, "Sair-i-Dozakh," *Risala-i-Vartman* (Amritsar), May 1927, no page number given; cited in Thursby, 40. *Raṅgīlā Rasūl* was published anonymously. Thursby discusses the evidence that Camūpati was the author on p. 43.
58. Government of India, *The Indian Penal Code* (*Act XLV of 1860*) (Calcutta: Government of India, 1929), 72.

59. Thursby, 40-62.
60. Indra Vidyāvācaspati, *Āryasamāj kā Itihās* (Delhi: Sārvadeśik Ārya Pratinidhi Sabhā, 1957), 2: 132-142.
61. Kenneth W. Jones, "The Arya Samaj in British India, 1875-1947," in *Religion in Modern India*, ed. Robert D. Baird (Delhi: Manohar, 1981), 44-46.
62. Because there was a broad movement against the Nizam, the protest was supported not only by Arya organizations, but also by the banned Hyderabad State Congress, the Hindu Mahasabha, and other non-Arya groups. Jones, "The Arya Samaj in British India, 1875-1947," 46-51. In recent years Arya Samajists have lobbied the Government of India with some success to make the Hyderabad protesters and their families eligible for pensions and other privileges which have been granted to participants in the Indian freedom struggle.
63. Carolyn M. Elliot, "Decline of a Patrimonial Regime: The Telengana Rebellion in India, 1946-1951," *Journal of Asian Studies* 34 (1974-1975): 36.
64. The number fifty thousand is from Jones, "The Arya Samaj in British India, 1875-1947," 50. Indra Vidyāvācaspati describes the conference at greater length, *Āryasamāj kā Itihās*, 2: 340-345.
65. Indra Vidyāvācaspati, *Āryasamāj kā Itihās*, 2: 346.
66. Dayanand, *Satyārth Prakāś*, 602-603.
67. Ibid., 606.
68. Ibid., 607.
69. Ibid., 612.
70. Ibid., 6.
71. Ibid., 7.
72. Ibid., 6.
73. H.G. Coward has also drawn attention to this divergence in his "The Response of the Arya Samaj," in *Modern Indian Responses to Religious Pluralism*, ed. Howard G. Coward (Albany: State University of New York Press, 1987), 50.
74. Swami Dayanand Sarasvati, *Ṛgvedādibhāṣyabhūmikā* [Introduction to the commentaries on the Ṛg and other Vedas], in *Ṛgveda-Bhāṣyam*, ed. Yudhiṣṭhir Mīmāṃsak, Āryasamāja-Śatābdī-Saṃskaraṇam (Bahalgarh [Sonipat]: Ram Lal Kapoor Trust, 1973), vol. 1, 316. Here and throughout references to the *Ṛgvedādibhāṣyabhūmikā* will be to the Sanskrit rather than to the Hindi, unless otherwise stated. The Sanskrit text of the *Ṛgvedādibhāṣyabhūmikā* was written by Dayanand himself, while the Hindi is a translation of the Sanskrit written by pandits in Dayanand's employ. Thus the Sanskrit text should be regarded as more

authoritative, as it represents Dayanand's views without mediation. The *Ṛgvedādibhāṣyabhūmikā* has been translated into English: ***Introduction to the Commentry** [sic] **on the Vedas by Maharshi Dayanand Saraswati***, trans. Ghasi Ram, 2d ed., Maharshi Dayanand Nirvan Centenary Publication (Delhi: Sārvadeśik Ārya Pratinidhi Sabhā, 1984).

75. Swami Dayanand Sarasvati, *Yajurveda-Bhāṣyam*, 4 vols., 4th impression (Ajmer: Vaidik Pustakālay, Vikram Saṃvat 2029-2031).

76. The best edition of Dayanand's commentary on the Ṛg Veda is unfortunately very incomplete: Swami Dayanand Sarasvati, *Ṛgveda-Bhāṣyam*, ed. Yudhiṣṭhir Mīmāṃsak, Āryasamāja-Śatābdī-Saṃskaraṇam, 3 vols. to date (Bahalgarh [Sonipat]: Ram Lal Kapoor Trust, 1973-1974). For a complete edition that is not as well edited: Swami Dayanand Sarasvati, *Ṛgvedabhāṣyam*, 9 vols. (Ajmer: Vaidik Pustakālay). The Paropkāriṇī Sabhā (which oversees the Vaidik Pustakālay) reprints volumes of the commentary as they run out of stock, so the version that is available has various dates and edition numbers. Including the entirety of Dayanand's incomplete commentary on the Ṛg Veda, the Paropkāriṇī Sabhā's edition stretches through the second mantra of the seventy-first *sūkta* of the seventh *maṇḍala* (Ṛg Veda 7.61.2). The better Ram Lal Kapoor Trust version has only been published through Ṛg Veda 1.105.

77. Swami Dayanand Sarasvati, *Āryābhivinay* [Arya devotions], in *Dayānandīya-Laghugrantha-Saṃgrahaḥ* [Collected minor works by Dayanand], ed. Yudhiṣṭhir Mīmāṃsak, Āryasamāja-Śatābdī-Saṃskaraṇam (Bahalgarh [Sonipat]: Ram Lal Kapoor Trust, 1975), 39-133. In English, *Aryabhivinaya*, trans. Swami Bhumananda Saraswati, 2d ed. (Bahalgarh [Sonipat]: Ram Lal Kapoor Trust, 1986).

78. See Jordens, *Dayānanda Sarasvatī*, 196-200 on Dayanand's relationship to the Arya Samaj.

79. The terms that Arya Samajists use to refer to Dayanand are an indication of their understanding of his extraordinary character. In my survey of Arya Samaj services the most common title for the swami was rishi or some variation of rishi (*ṛṣi, ṛṣivar*, or *maharṣi*). If this appellation is used self-consciously, it is literally epochal, since according to the Arya Samaj's theory of history the tradition of the rishis died out around five thousand years ago. My enumeration of the titles used for Dayanand is based upon transcriptions of audio tape recordings of the speakers at Arya Samaj services conducted by the Arya Samaj Mandir, Hardwar from 20 April 1986 to 20 July 1986.

80. Dayanand, *Ṛgvedādibhāśyabhūmikā*, in *Ṛgveda-Bhāṣyam*, vol. 1, 24.
81. Idem, *Satyārth Prakāś*, 428.
82. Ibid.
83. Ibid., 430-431.
84. Ibid., 434.
85. Ibid., 435.
86. For example, this admission was made to the congregation at a weekly service by a leader of the local Arya Samaj chapter in Hardwar after a sermon condemning compromises with traditional Hinduism. Arya Samaj Mandir, Hardwar; 24 November 1985.
87. Darbari Lal and D.P. Seth, "Centenary Celebrations," not paginated. A pamphlet soliciting funds on behalf of the D.A.V. College Managing Committee on the centenary of the D.A.V. College movement in 1986. This pamphlet states that in 1986 there were three hundred D.A.V. educational institutions.
88. Jones, *Arya Dharm*, pp. 168-174.
89. In the 1920s because of repeated flooding the Gurukul Kangri was moved from near Kangri village to its present site near Kankhal outside Hardwar.
90. Most of this account of the *gurukuls* and their history is based on my fieldwork at the Gurukul Kangri.
91. Dayanand, *Ṛgvedādibhāśyabhūmikā* in *Ṛgveda-Bhāṣyam*, vol. 1, 399-400.
92. Ibid., 329-333, commenting on Ṛg Veda 1.32.
93. Dayanand, *Ṛgvedādibhāśyabhūmikā*, in *Ṛgveda-Bhāṣyam*, vol. 1, 370.
94. Ibid., 370-371.
95. Ibid., 380.
96. Ibid., 386-387.
97. Ibid., 370.
98. This is a part of Ṛg Veda 9.63.5.
99. Usually there is one individual who is more or less responsible for conducting the ritual, leading others in the recitation of the mantras and instructing them in the required actions. It is not uncommon to see a woman in this role.
100. *The Constitution of the Arya Samaj: Principles & Bye-Laws* (Delhi: Sārvadeśik Ārya Pratinidhi Sabhā, 1958), n.p., quoted in Forbes, 402. Forbes gives the whole text of the model constitution provided to local chapters by the Sārvadeśik Ārya Pratinidhi Sabhā in an appendix, pp. 402-411.
101. A woman who is not of independent means must pay only one quarter of 1 per cent of her guardian's income.

102. The current constitution is based on the bylaws of the Lahore Arya Samaj which were written upon its founding in 1877. But there are two significant differences between the original bylaws and the constitution that is being promulgated now, which are a reflection of the split between the College Party and the Gurukul Party in 1893. The most obvious is that the later constitution specifically mentions that meat eating is considered "unrighteous conduct" and can thus be grounds for denying an individual membership in the Samaj. The second addition is more subtle, but potentially has much more wide-ranging significance. In the statement that an individual must sign to join the Samaj, the aspirant must affirm belief not only in "the aims and objects of the Arya Samaj (as stated in its Principles)" but also in "its doctrines (as they are written in the works of Rishi Dayanand on the basis of the Vedas)." While the militant Gurukul Party demanded that Swami Dayanand's teachings be taken as binding in all areas (particularly but not exclusively with regard to vegetarianism), the moderate members of the College Party understood the ten principles of the Arya Samaj to constitute a sufficient condition for membership. After the vegetarians took over provincial representative bodies, they wrote their understanding of the nature of the Arya Samaj into the constitution. Compare the constitution in Forbes with the Lahore bylaws: Ganeshi Lal, *The Arya Samaj or 'The New Light of Asia'* (Lahore: n.p., 1889), n.p., quoted in Jordens, *Dayānanda Sarasvatī*, 340-344.

103. The constitution allows that the requirements for voting membership might be relaxed by the executive committee of the Samaj under extraordinary circumstances. That is, in a special case an individual might be allowed to vote who has been a member for less than a year, or contributed less than 1 per cent of his or her income, or attended less that 25 per cent of the weekly meetings.

104. Jones, *Arya Dharm*, 122.

105. Raghuvir Singh Shastri, *Sārvadeśik Ārya Pratinidhi Sabhā kā Saṃkṣipt Itihās* (Delhi: Sārvadeśik Ārya Pratinidhi Sabhā, Vikram Saṃvat 2018), 1, cited in Jones, "The Arya Samaj in British India, 1875-1947," 36. Jones gives the author's first name as Radhuvir, but Jordens has Raghuvir, which seems the more likely reading. J. T.F. Jordens, *Swāmī Shraddhānanda: His Life and Causes* (Delhi: Oxford University Press, 1981), 202.

106. After 1895 the nonvegetarian faction of the Arya Samaj withdrew from the Ārya Pratinidhi Sabhā. In 1903 a central organization for the local Samajes that had aligned with the nonvegetarians in the split was set up, called the Prādeśik Ārya Pratinidhi Sabhā

("Provincial Arya Representative Assembly"). The Prādeśik Ārya Pratinidhi Sabhā remains a separate body to this day.

107. Raghuvir Singh Shastri, 5, in Jones, "The Arya Samaj in British India, 1875-1947," 38.
108. Dayanand, *Satyārth Prakāś*, 611.
109. Ibid., 369-386.
110. The length of mukti is held to be 3.1104 x 10^{14} years. Dayanand, *Satyārth Prakāś*, 377.
111. *Panjabee* (Lahore), 29 May 1907, 4, quoted in Jones, *Arya Dharm*, 275.
112. Dayanand, *Satyārth Prakāś*, 220-273.
113. Jordens, *Dayānanda Sarasvatī*, 227-241.
114. Dayanand, *Satyārth Prakāś*, 354.
115. Many Arya Samajists believe that Swami Dayanand took part in the Anglo-Indian War of 1857. J. T. F. Jordens has discussed the published attempts to document the swami's involvement, which he finds unconvincing. Jordens, *Dayānanda Sarasvatī*, 335-337.
116. Norman G. Barrier, "The Arya Samaj and Congress Politics in the Punjab, 1894-1908," *Journal of Asian Studies* 26 (1966-1967): 367.
117. Purushottam Nagar, *Lala Lajpat Rai: The Man and His Ideas* (Delhi: Manohar, 1977), 138.
118. Indra Prakash, *A Review of the History & Work of the Hindu Mahasabha and Hindu Sanghatan Movement* (Delhi: Akhil Bharatiya Hindu Mahasabha, 1938), 93. This is an excerpt from Lajpat Rai's address as president of the 1925 annual meeting of the Hindu Mahasabha. Of course the "*Sanghatan*" in the title above would usually be transliterated *saṅgaṭhan*.
119. Nonetheless, as a member of the Central Legislative Assembly Lajpat Rai did support efforts to restrict communalist literature. Particularly he advocated an amendment to the Indian Penal Code which made it illegal to engage in activities designed to increase hatred between religious communities. He explicitly condemned the pamphlet *Raṅgīlā Rasūl*, a book mentioned above which attacks Muhammad for his alleged sensualism. Nagar, 141-142.
120. Jordens, *Swāmī Shraddhānand*, 103-167.
121. Jones indicates that original name of the organization was the "Sarvadeshak Hindu Sabha." It was changed to the Akhil Bharat Hindu Mahasabha in 1921. Kenneth W. Jones, "Politicized Hinduism: The Ideology and Program of the Hindu Mahasabha," in *Religion in Modern India*, ed. Robert D. Baird (Delhi: Manohar, 1981), 451, 453. According to Shraddhanand the first part of the name is "Sarvadeshik," which seems the more likely reading.

Swami Shraddhanand, *Hindu Sangathan: Saviour of the Dying Race* (Delhi: Arjun Press, 1926), 109.

122. Lal Chand, *Self-Abnegation in Politics*, with a Foreword by Bhai Parmanand, 2d ed. (Lahore: Central Hindu Yuvak Sabha, 1938), 2. The italics are in the original.

123. Swami Shraddhanand, 109-110.

124. Jones, "Politicized Hinduism," 458-459.

125. After Indian independence the Hindu Mahasabha formally entered politics as a separate party, producing a slate of candidates for the first general election in 1952.

126. See the tables in Paul R. Brass, "Sikhs and Hindus in the Punjab: The Development of Social and Political Differentiation," chap. in *Language, Religion and Politics in North India* (London: Cambridge University Press, 1974), 277-336.

127. Ibid., 331-333.

128. Martin E. Marty, "Fundamentalism as a Social Phenomenon," *Bulletin of the American Academy of Arts and Sciences* 42, no. 2 (November 1988): 19.

129. Several Arya intellectuals and leaders admitted this in interviews conducted in India from 1985 to 1987.

130. Only one of fifty-three candidates from the Jama'at was successful. Kalim Bahadur, *The Jama'at-i Islami of Pakistan: Political Thought and Political Action* (Delhi: Chetana Publications, 1977), 64.

131. "The Literalist (so called) is not one who denies that *figurative* language, that *symbols*, are used in prophecy, nor does he deny that great *spiritual* truths are set forth therein; his position is, simply, that the prophecies are to be *normally* interpreted (i.e. according to the received laws of language) as any other utterances are interpreted—that which is manifestly literal being regarded as literal, that which is manifestly figurative being so regarded." John Peter Lange, *A Commentary on the Holy Scriptures*, vol. 10 of the New Testament, *The Revelation of John*, ed. E.R. Craven, trans. Evelina Moore (New York: Scribner, Armstrong & Co., 1874), 98. The passage quoted is from a footnote written by the editor Craven.

132. James Chancellor expresses a similar point when he argues that the real concern in fundamentalism is not with literalism but authority. James Darrell Chancellor, "A Comparative Approach to Religious Fundamentalism: Egyptian Sunni Islam and American Protestant Christianity" (Ph.D. diss., Duke University, 1988), 56.

133. This phrase is used to describe the authors of the Puranas. Dayanand, *Satyārth Prakāś*, 515.

134. Charles J. Adams, "The Ideology of Mawlana Mawdudi," in *South Asian Politics and Religion*, ed. Donald Eugene Smith (Princeton: Princeton University Press, 1966), 394.

PART II

THE ARYA SAMAJ AND HINDU SCRIPTURE

3

HINDU SCRIPTURE IN THE WRITINGS OF SWAMI DAYANAND

Given the prominence of the study of myth and sacred story in the history of religions, it is appropriate to begin this chapter with a tale that Swami Dayanand Sarasvati, the founder of the Arya Samaj, told about a turning point in his own life. The incident occurred in 1855 or 1856 at a time when Dayanand was wandering in the Himalayas along the River Ganges seeking higher truth.

> Besides other religious works, I had with me the "Sibsanda," "Hat-pradipika," "Yog-Bij" and "Keberanda Sangata," which I used to study during my travels. Some of these books treated on the Narichakant, and Narichakars (nervous system) giving very exhaustive descriptions of the same, which I could never grasp, and which finally made me doubt as to the correctness of these works. I had been for some time trying to remove my doubts, but had found as yet no opportunity. One day, I chanced to meet a corpse floating down the river. There was the opportunity and it remained with me to satisfy myself as to the correctness of the statements contained in the books about anatomy and man's inner organs. Ridding myself of the books which I laid near by, and, taking off my clothes, I resolutely entered the river and soon brought the dead body out and laid him on the shore. I then proceeded to cut him open with a large knife in the best manner I could. I took out and examined the *Kamal* (the heart) and cutting him from the navel to the ribs, and a portion of the head and neck, I carefully examined and compared him with the descriptions in the books. Finding they did not tally at all, I tore the

> books to pieces and threw them into the river after the corpse. From that time I gradually came to the conclusion that with the exception of the Vedas, Upanishads, Patanjali and Sankhya, all other works upon science and Yog *were false.*[1]

A couple of the texts that Swami Dayanand mentions at the outset of his story are obscure, but at least one is well known. *Haṭhayoga-pradīpikā* is an important work on hatha-yoga, a system of meditation focused on strenuous exercises. The effects of this discipline are explained with reference to an elaborate physiology. Within the body there are various channels or *nāḍīs* which run to centers of energy known as chakras.[2] Apparently it was this system of internal organs which Dayanand searched for, but failed to find, in the corpse in the story. It has been argued that hatha-yoga describes a subtle physiology, one which cannot be seen by the naked eye but which is manifest to the individual with spiritual vision. But if Dayanand was familiar with this argument he does not entertain it here. Rather he insists on operating on a more literal level. Either the body is as the texts describe it, or it is not. If it is not, then they are false. The Arya Samaj propagates the practice of yoga, but following the swami it does not have much use for hatha-yoga.

This story is not only interesting for the evidence which it provides of the development of Dayanand's beliefs about yoga, however. It is much more important for the insight that it suggests into Swami Dayanand's approach to Hindu scripture.[3] From this story it is clear that the swami believed that it was incumbent upon him not only to study religious works, but also to try to understand them, and ultimately come to some judgment about their truth or falsity. In this chapter we will review the conclusions which Dayanand reached through this process.

At the end of the last chapter we noted that the position of the Arya Samaj with respect to scripture (like the Jama'at-i Islami) is more complicated than that of Bob Jones University. Just as Christian fundamentalism is based upon an inerrant sacred text, so is the Arya Samaj. Yet for the Samaj there are works which are basically reliable other than the infallible Vedas. This secondary group of books which are basically authoritative, but not perfectly so, is known as the *ārṣa* literature. Finally there is a third body of writings that are absolutely devoid of authority, the *anārṣa* works.

This chapter will be devoted to analyzing Swami Dayanand Sarasvati's theories about Hindu religious texts and his use of them. It is appropriate for us to limit our attention here to the writings of Swami Dayanand, since he was not only the founder of the Arya Samaj, but also the source of its views on religious books. His theories about scripture have been accepted by later generations of Arya Samajists without criticism. We will only concern ourselves with Hindu writings, because that is where discrimination of authoritative religious literature must begin and end according to Swami Dayanand. As has already been noted, the scriptures of other traditions are systematically attacked by Dayanand in the last three chapters of his most popular work *Satyārth Prakāś*. There is no instance in Swami Dayanand's major writings where he quotes a non-Hindu religious text approvingly.

Our discussion of Swami Dayanand's position with respect to Hindu scripture will be divided into three sections. In the first we will outline the swami's tripartite classification of Hindu religious texts. Armed with this introduction, in the second section we will analyze in detail those works which were regarded as authoritative by Dayanand, and those which lack any authority. Finally we will scrutinize the texts from the Hindu tradition which Dayanand actually quoted in his major works.

In the previous chapter it was pointed out that the Arya Samaj's doctrines have been expressed in ten principles, which every member of the organization must accept. The third of these principles states, "The Veda is the book of true knowledge. To study the Veda and to teach it, to hear and expound it is the highest dharma of all Arya Samajists."[4] Consistent with this principle Arya missionaries have preached the Vedas wherever they have gone. This may have created the impression that the Vedas are the only scripture in the Arya Samaj. In this chapter we will dispel that impression. In theory the Vedas do enjoy a unique status in Swami Dayanand's mature thought, but many other works are also granted some limited authority. And in practice Dayanand quotes other texts as much as the Vedas in his major writings. As we will discuss in the conclusion, it is characteristic of the Arya Samaj as a fundamentalist movement that an effort is made to derive all of its program from an unimpeachable source. To the extent that Swami Dayanand had to base some of his ideas not upon the inerrant Vedas but upon the fallible *ārṣa* literature, this effort was not entirely successful. Still, in the case of the Arya Samaj as in other fundamentalist movements this failure goes unacknowledged.

DAYANAND'S CLASSIFICATION OF HINDU SCRIPTURE

In order to understand Swami Dayanand's perspective on Hindu scripture it is necessary to reiterate his account of the history of the world.[5] The world in which we presently live was created almost two billion years ago, Dayanand believed. For many generations after creation the entire planet was dominated by the Aryans. The period of Aryan rule was a golden age, marked by learning and righteousness. This all came to an end around five thousand years ago with the war described in the *Mahābhārata*. So many great rulers and august sages died as a result of this conflict that justice and wisdom everywhere declined. With this event the current, degenerate age was begun. On the basis of this version of history Swami Dayanand divided all texts into three classes: the Vedas, the *ārṣa* literature (works written by the ancient sages or rishis), and *anārṣa* literature (works written by those who were not rishis). Now we will briefly describe these three classes.

Dayanand taught that at the beginning of history God imparted the Vedas to humans. He enlightened the rishi Agni with the Ṛg Veda, Vāyu with the Yajur Veda, Āditya with the Sāma Veda, and Aṅgirā with the Atharva Veda. God did not convey the Vedas orally or in written form, Dayanand explained, but imparted them directly to the souls (*jīvas*) of these four sages as their pervader (*antaryāmī*).[6] It should not be understood from this that God gave these rishis knowledge, and then they wrote the Vedas.[7] Such works could have only been produced by one who is omniscient, that is, by God himself.[8] Swami Dayanand does not allow the rishis any role in the composition of the Vedas, they only served to transmit those texts from God to the human community. Dayanand argued that as God's knowledge is free from error, so the Vedas that he composed are inerrant.[9] The Vedas are the only texts that have been composed by God, and they alone are devoid of error. The Vedas are to be taken as independently authoritative (*svataḥ pramāṇa*) according to Dayanand.[10]

Along with the Vedas the *ārṣa* literature enjoys a certain limited authority in Swami Dayanand's system.[11] The *ārṣa* texts are worthy of study as they were composed by rishis, sages who were religious, learned, and conversant with all the *śāstras*.[12] There are some errors in *ārṣa* books, but they are mostly reliable, and they are to be believed to the extent that they are consistent with the Vedas.[13] The *ārṣa* literature is *parataḥ pramāṇa* or dependently authoritative, that is, the authority of the *ārṣa* corpus is dependent on the Vedas. The teachings of *ārṣa* works should only be adopted, Dayanand argued, to the extent that they do not conflict with the Vedas.[14]

Finally the third class of scripture according to Swami Dayanand's system is the *anārṣa* literature, works written by those who were not rishis. Dayanand argues that this literature is like its authors, who knew little of the *śāstras* and who were partial in their judgments.[15] These books, Dayanand believed, are not at all worthy of study. Dayanand wrote that in the *anārṣa* literature there may be some modicum of truth, but there is also much falsehood. The truth in the *anārṣa* books can be gleaned from a study of the Vedas and the *ārṣa* literature Dayanand believed. So Dayanand concluded that by studying the *anārṣa* corpus nothing is to be gained, but much might be lost.[16] The *anārṣa* texts are designated by Dayanand *apramāṇa*, completely unauthoritative.[17]

It should be noted that the tradition of the rishis only continued up until soon after the cataclysmic *Mahābhārata* war, according to Swami Dayanand. So all the *ārṣa* literature was written before that event, in the ancient golden age. The *anārṣa* corpus, Dayanand explained, has been written since the *Mahābhārata* in the degenerate age which continues to the present.

So there are three classes of literature in Swami Dayanand's system. The Vedas were produced by God at the beginning of creation. They are absolutely free of error and are independently authoritative (*svataḥ pramāṇa*). The *ārṣa* literature was written by rishis or sages in the period up to the great *Mahābhārata* war. These texts are not totally without error, but they are generally reliable. The authoritativeness of the *ārṣa* works is dependent upon the Vedas (that is, the *ārṣa* texts are *parataḥ pramāṇa*). Finally there is the *anārṣa* literature which has been written by those who were not rishis in the present period of vice. The *anārṣa* works contain little truth and they are not at all authoritative (*apramāṇa*). These are the three classes of literature according to Swami Dayanand.[18]

Before going on to discuss in detail the works that Swami Dayanand identified as worthy of study, a few words should be said about the division of texts outlined above. Some attention must be paid to the limits that Dayanand set down for the three classes of books. By "Vedas" Swami Dayanand was referring in this context only to the Vedic hymns or Samhitas.[19] In traditional usage, "Veda" refers to a vast body of texts. In this library the original Vedic Samhitas were included, along with several layers of commentaries on the hymns (the Brahmanas, Aranyakas, and Upanishads), and other types of literature related to the application of the hymns in ritual (the Gṛhya, Kalpa, Śrauta, and Dharma Sutras). Swami Dayanand used the word "Veda" only to refer to the Samhitas or hymns. He allowed that the other Vedic literature should be studied, but he maintained that it does not share equal authority with the Vedic hymns. Only the hymns were composed by God, Dayanand believed. The rest of the Vedic literature was composed by rishis. Only the Vedic hymns are *svataḥ pramāṇa*, all the other Vedic works are included with the *ārṣa* literature as *parataḥ pramāṇa*. So the boundary between the Vedas and the *ārṣa* works is drawn between the Vedic Samhitas and the rest of Vedic literature.

The boundary between the works that were written by the sages (the *ārṣa* literature) and the works that were written by others (the *anārṣa* literature) is much more difficult to delineate. The problem here is that many works that have been attributed to the ancient rishis were not in fact written by those sages, but are recent compositions according to Dayanand.[20] The primary method for distinguishing the spurious works for Dayanand was to analyze their content. Only the books which are basically consistent with the Vedas as Dayanand understood them are to be taken as *ārṣa* literature. Works which are sectarian, for example, cannot be understood to be compositions of the rishis. So the first test for determining if a work is *ārṣa* or *anārṣa* is to evaluate its content.

There is another formal test that Swami Dayanand notes to distinguish *ārṣa* and *anārṣa* books. *Ārṣa* works generally begin with the words *om* or *atha*, Dayanand wrote. *Anārṣa* works usually commence with a *maṅgalācaraṇa* or invocation to one of the gods or goddesses of traditional Hinduism. In place of *om* or *atha* an *anārṣa* work might have a phrase like "Śrīgaṇeśāya namaḥ" ("Salutation to Lord Gaṇeśa.").[21] Since Dayanand did not believe in the gods and goddesses of traditional Hinduism, it is not surprising that he was not willing to accord any authority to works beginning with the praise of one of these divinities. This formal test is thus closely related to the test of the content of the text mentioned in the previous paragraph.

The distinction between *ārṣa* and *anārṣa* literature is obviously a very subtle matter. This is an area in which some dispute might be possible. Generally the Arya Samaj has accepted the judgments of Swami Dayanand about what works are *ārṣa* and what works are *anārṣa*. Hence no significant disagreement has arisen in the Arya Samaj over this issue.

A further word should be said about the relationship of the Vedas and the *ārṣa* literature. The authority of the *ārṣa* corpus is dependent on the Vedas such that if there is a conflict between the two bodies of texts the Vedas must be accepted and the *ārṣa* literature must be rejected. But the relationship of the *ārṣa* literature to the Vedas is stronger than just noncontradiction. The *ārṣa* works are said to be consistent with the Vedas (*Vedānukūla*). Dayanand writes that the Vedas and the *ārṣa* literature are like the sun and an object illumined by it. The sun shines by its own light; the object is bright only because it reflects the light of the sun.[22] The Vedas are true in their own right, as they are the knowledge promulgated by God. The *ārṣa* literature is true only to the extent that it reflects some of God's knowledge, which is fully manifest solely in the Vedas.

From the metaphor in the last paragraph it may seem that the *ārṣa* literature enjoys no independent authority. The reader might expect that Dayanand would rely heavily on the Vedas and only grant some minimal consideration to *ārṣa* works, but that is not the case. In the next section we will see that there is a large body of *ārṣa* literature that Swami Dayanand believed was worthy of study, and in the third section it will be noted that Dayanand quoted heavily from *ārṣa* books. Practically speaking it would be difficult to take the Vedas as the sole authority in every area of human life. In the chapter on statecraft in Dayanand's book *Satyārth Prakāś*, for example, the author relies heavily on the law code of Manu. In this area the few references to kings and battles in the Vedas are not sufficient to develop a full theory of polity, so another source is quoted extensively. Although Swami Dayanand does rely practically exclusively on *ārṣa* texts in areas where the Vedas do not offer much material, the significance of this practice is never openly acknowledged. Swami Dayanand maintains throughout his works that the source for his philosophy is the Vedas and the *ārṣa* literature as based upon the Vedas. The *ārṣa* literature is not recognized as an independent authority in any area.

AUTHORITATIVE AND UNAUTHORITATIVE WORKS ACCORDING TO DAYANAND

In this section we will consider the Hindu scriptural works that are authoritative and those that are not authoritative according to Swami Dayanand. The discussion will be divided into three subsections: (1) the works that Dayanand designates as authoritative in his major works; (2) the works that Dayanand rejects as unauthoritative; and in conclusion (3) a general discussion of the lists of authoritative and unauthoritative works. After presenting Swami Dayanand's lists of what books are authoritative and what books are not authoritative in this section, we will go on in the next section to analyze the texts which Dayanand actually quotes.

AUTHORITATIVE WORKS

Swami Dayanand's three most important books are his *Satyārth Prakāś*, *Ṛgvedādibhāṣyabhūmikā*, and *Saṃskār Vidhi*. *Satyārth Prakāś* is a very broadly based explanation of Swami Dayanand's philosophy. In *Ṛgvedādibhāṣyabhūmikā* Dayanand explains his teaching especially in relation to the Vedas. *Saṃskār Vidhi* is a work that explains how the life-cycle rituals should be conducted, but there are also passages of more general interest.[23] In each of these books there is a section in which Swami Dayanand lists the texts that he regards as authoritative. These lists in *Satyārth Prakāś*, *Ṛgvedādibhāṣyabhūmikā*, and *Saṃskār Vidhi* are the point of departure for our analysis.[24]

The purpose of the lists is not the same in these three works. In *Ṛgvedādibhāṣyabhūmikā* Swami Dayanand states very broadly that his subject is the authoritativeness and unauthoritativeness of books.[25] In *Satyārth Prakāś* and *Saṃskār Vidhi* the lists are presented under the rubric of education. In these two books the works listed are those that are to be studied by the student—each list is a sort of curriculum. Nevertheless the contents of the lists in all three books are very similar, as the reader will see. Swami Dayanand clearly did not see any difference between the works that are authoritative and those that are to be studied by the student.

The content of Swami Dayanand's lists of authoritative works are presented in Table 1. Before we review the items in the table in detail, a few general points should be made. The order of works in Swami Dayanand's lists is not the same in *Satyārth Prakāś*, *Ṛgvedādibhāṣya-bhūmikā*, and *Saṃskār Vidhi*. The largest difference is that in *Ṛgvedādibhāṣyabhūmikā* the Vedas are mentioned first, while they only appear late in the curricula in *Satyārth Prakāś* and *Saṃskār Vidhi*. This variation is based on the difference in the purposes of the list in *Ṛgvedādibhāṣyabhūmikā* on the one hand and those in *Satyārth Prakāś* and *Saṃskār Vidhi* on the other. As curricula the lists in *Satyārth Prakāś* and *Saṃskār Vidhi* begin with the most elementary discipline, *Śikṣā*. The Vedas, which are difficult texts, only come late in the program. The discussion in *Ṛgvedādibhāṣyabhūmikā* is concerned

TABLE 1

AUTHORITATIVE WORKS ACCORDING TO DAYANAND

Group	Discipline	Texts in *Satyārth Prakāś*	Texts in *Ṛgvedādibhāṣyabhūmikā*	Texts in *Saṃskār Vidhi*
Vedangas	Śikṣā	Pāṇini's Śikṣā	Pāṇini's Śikṣā, etc.	Pāṇini's Śikṣā
	Kalpa	General reference[1]	Mānavakalpa Sūtra, etc.[2]	Āśvalāyana Kalpa, Śrauta, and Gṛhya Sūtras[3]

1. Dayanand mentions this discipline, but he does not recommend a specific text.
2. Here the Hindi also has the *Āśvalāyana Śrauta Sūtra*. *Ṛgvedādibhāṣyabhūmikā*, in *Ṛgveda-Bhāṣyam*, vol. 1, 319.
3. Dayanand's list in *Saṃskār Vidhi* at this point is not as detailed as one might like it to be. Dayanand says that the Āśvalāyana sutra texts should be studied along with the Ṛg Veda, and he implies that the other sutras should be studied with the other Vedas. But since he doesn't give the names of the other sutras, they have not been included here. *Saṃskār Vidhi*, 131-132.

Table 1—*Continued*

Group	Discipline	Texts in *Satyārth Prakāś*	Texts in *Ṛgvedādibhāṣyabhūmikā*	Texts in *Saṃskār Vidhi*
Vedangas—contin-ued	Vyākaraṇa	Aṣṭādhyāyī, Dhātu-pāṭha, Mahābhāṣya	Aṣṭādhyāyī, Dhātu-pāṭha, Gaṇapāṭha, Mahābhāṣya	Aṣṭādhyāyī, Dhātu-pāṭha, Gaṇapāṭha, Liṅgānuśāsana, Mahābhāṣya
	Nirukta	Yāska Nighaṇṭu and Nirukta[1]	Yāska Nighaṇṭu and Nirukta	Yāska Nighaṇṭu and Nirukta; the Kośas of Kātyāyana, etc.; Aptamuni's Avyayārtha[2]

1. The attribution of the *Nighaṇṭu* to Yāska is debatable, but Dayanand believed that it is the work of Yāska.
2. Mīmāṃsak points out that there are some references to a dictionary by Kātyāyana in grammatical manuscripts. He indicates that he is not familiar with any other references to a work on *avyaya* by Āptamuni. *Saṃskār Vidhi*, 130, nn. 1, 2.

Table 1—*Continued*

Group	Discipline	Texts in *Satyārth Prakāś*	Texts in *Ṛgvedādibhāṣyabhūmikā*	Texts in *Saṃskār Vidhi*
Vedangas--continued	Chandas	Piṅgala's Chandaḥ-sūtras[1]	Piṅgala's Chandaḥ-sūtras and commentary	Piṅgala's Chandaḥ-sūtras and commentary
	Jyotis	Sūryasiddhānta, etc.	Works of Vaśiṣṭa, etc.	Sūryasiddhānta, etc.
Kavya	--	Manu, Rāmāyaṇa, Viduranīti and other edifying passages of the Mahābhārata	--	Manu, any 10 sargas of the Rāmāyaṇa, Viduranīti, Yāska's Kāvyālaṅkārasūtra and Vātsyāyana's commentary

1. In both *Satyārth Prakāś* and *Saṃskār Vidhi* the works listed under Kavya directly follow *Chandas*. This order could not be maintained here without breaking up the Vedangas. *Satyārth Prakāś*, 115; *Saṃskār Vidhi*, 130-131.

Table 1—*Continued*

Group	Discipline	Texts in *Satyārth Prakāś*	Texts in *Ṛgvedādibhāṣyabhūmikā*	Texts in *Saṃskār Vidhi*
Upāṅgas	Mimamsa	Sutras and Vyāsa's commentary	Jaimini's Sutras and Vyāsa's commentary	Jaimini's Sutras and Vyāsa's commentary
	Vaisheshika	Sutras and Gotama's Praśastapāda commentary[1]	Kaṇāda's Sutras and Praśastapāda's commentary[2]	Kaṇāda's Sutras and Gotama's Praśastapāda commentary

1. In this context the edition of Yudhiṣṭhir Mīmāṃsak reads: "Vaiśeṣik par Gautammuni kṛt, Nyāysūtra par Vātsyāyanmunikṛt bhāṣya." *Satyārth Prakāś*, 119. Another standard edition reads (note the differences in italics): "Vaiśeṣik par Gotammunikṛt *Praśastpādbhāṣya, Gotammunikṛt* Nyāysūtra par Vāstyāyanmunikṛt bhāṣya." Swami Dayanand Sarasvati, *Dayānand-Granthmālā*, Nirvāṇ-Śatābdī-Saṃskaraṇ, 2d printing (Ajmer: Paropkāriṇī Sabhā, 1983), vol. 1, 65. Mīmāṃsak usually notes were his text differs from that of the Paropkāriṇī Sabhā, but there is no note here. So I assume that Mīmāṃsak's reading is an error. The list in this chart corresponds on this point to the text of the Paropkāriṇī Sabhā.
2. There seems to be some confusion here over whether ***Praśastapāda*** is the name of an author or of a work.

Table 1—*Continued*

Group	Discipline	Texts in *Satyārth Prakāś*	Texts in *Ṛgvedādibhāṣyabhūmikā*	Texts in *Saṃskār Vidhi*
Upāṅgas—continued	Nyaya	Gotama's Sutras and Vātsyāyana's commentary	Gotama's Sutras and Vātsyāyana's commentary	Gotama's Sutras and Vātsyāyana's commentary
	Yoga	Patañjali's Sutras and Vyāsa's commentary	Patañjali's Sutras and Vyāsa's commentary	Patañjali's Sutras and Vyāsa's commentary
	Sankhya	Kapila's Sutras and Bhāguri's commentary	Kapila's Sutras and Bhāguri's commentary	Kapila's Sutras and Bhāguri's commentary
	Vedanta	Vyāsa's Sutras and Vātsyāyana's and Baudhāyana's commentaries	Vyāsa's Sutras and Baudhāyana's commentary, etc.	Vyāsa's Sutras and Jaimini's and Bauddhāyana's commentaries

Table 1—*Continued*

Group	Discipline	Texts in *Satyārth Prakāś*	Texts in *Ṛgvedādibhāṣyabhūmikā*	Texts in *Saṃskār Vidhi*
Upanishads	--	Īśa, Kena, Kaṭha, Praśna, Muṇḍaka, Māṇḍūkya, Aitare-ya, Taittirīya, Chāndogya, Bṛhad-āraṇyaka	Īśa, Kena, Kaṭha, Praśna, Muṇḍaka, Māṇḍūkya, Aitare-ya, Taittirīya, Chāndogya, Bṛhad-āraṇyaka	Īśa, Kena, Kaṭha, Praśna, Muṇḍaka, Māṇḍūkya, Aitare-ya, Taittirīya, Chāndogya, Bṛhad-āraṇyaka
Vedas	–	Ṛg, Yajur, Sāma, Atharva	Ṛg, Yajur, Sāma, Atharva, Vedic Śākhās[1]	Ṛg, Yajur, Sāma, Atharva, Padakrama of all four Vedas, Gāna of the Sāma Veda[2]

1. Dayanand does not say that the Vedic *Śākhās* are a part of the Veda. They have only been included here to keep the chart as brief as possible.
2. Dayanand enjoins that the *Padakramas* of all four Vedas should be studied with the Vedas and the *Gāna* of the Sāma Veda should be studied with that Veda, but that does not mean that these auxiliary texts are actually to be taken as a part of the Veda.

Table 1—*Continued*

Group	Discipline	Texts in *Satyārth Prakāś*	Texts in *Ṛgvedādibhāṣyabhūmikā*	Texts in *Saṃskār Vidhi*
Brahmanas	–	Aitareya, Śatapatha, Sāma, Gopatha[1]	Aitareya, Śatapatha, Sāma, Gopatha[2]	Aitareya, Śatapatha, Sāma, Gopatha
Upavedas	Ayur Veda	Caraka, Suśruta, etc.	Caraka, Suśruta, Nighaṇṭu, etc.[3]	Caraka, Suśruta, Nighaṇṭu, etc.

1. There is no text called *Sāma Brāhmaṇa*. This is apparently a general reference to the Brahmanas that are associated with the Sāma Vedic tradition.
2. In the immediate context in the Sanskrit text of *Ṛgvedādibhāṣyabhūmikā* the Brahmanas are mentioned, but no specific text is identified. In the Hindi translation the *Aitareya* and *Śatapatha Brāhmaṇas* are listed. In another context in *Ṛgvedādibhāṣyabhūmikā* all four Brahmanas are mentioned in the Sanskrit text. *Ṛgvedādibhāṣyabhūmikā*, in *Ṛgveda-Bhāṣyam*, vol. 1, 316, 318, 368.
3. This is not the *Nighaṇṭu* listed in the chart under *Nirukta*, but is another text on medicine by Dhanvantari.

Table 1—*Continued*

Group	Discipline	Texts in *Satyārth Prakāś*	Texts in *Ṛgveādibhāṣyabhūmikā*	Texts in *Saṃskār Vidhi*
Upavedas—continued	Dhanur Veda	General reference	Works by Aṅgiras, etc.[1]	Aṅgirā, etc.[2]
	Gāndharva Veda	Narada's Samhita, etc.	General reference[3]	Narada's Samhita, etc.

1. The Hindi also includes the Samhita of Bharadvāja. Dayanand confesses in *Ṛgvedādibhāṣyabhūmikā* that these texts are not extant in our time. *Ṛgvedādibhāṣyabhūmikā*, in *Ṛgveda-Bhāṣyam*, vol. 1, 317, 318.
2. Dayanand admits that the texts in this discipline have been almost entirely forgotten.
3. The Sanskrit text mentions the discipline, but no text. The Hindi has Narada's Samhita, etc. *Ṛgvedādibhāṣyabhūmikā*, in *Ṛgveda-Bhāṣyam*, vol. 1, 317, 318.

Table 1—*Continued*

Group	Discipline	Texts in *Satyārth Prakāś*	Texts in *Ṛgvedādibhāṣyabhūmikā*	Texts in *Saṃskār Vidhi*
Upavedas—contin-ued	Artha Veda	General reference	Viśvakarman's, Tvastṛ's, and Maya's Samhitas[1]	Works by Viśva-karmā, Tvastṛ, and Maya

Sources: Dayanand, *Satyārth Prakāś*, 110-119; idem, *Ṛgvedādibhāṣyabhūmikā*, in *Ṛgveda-Bhāṣyam*, vol. 1, 316-319; idem, *Saṃskār Vidhi*, 129-132. In Yudhiṣṭhir Mīmāṃsak's editions of Swami Dayanand's works, which are the texts used throughout this chapter, there are appendixes which contain information similar to that in this table, though there are some errors in his work. *Satyārth Prakāś*, 986-990; *Ṛgvedādibhāṣyabhūmikā*, in *Ṛgveda-Bhāṣyam*, vol. 1, 730-732; *Saṃskār Vidhi*, 361-364.

1. The Hindi adds another Samhita by Devajña. *Ṛgvedādibhāṣyabhūmikā*, in *Ṛgveda-Bhāṣyam*, vol. 1, 318.

only with what works are authoritative and what works are not authoritative. In this context Dayanand begins with the Vedas, which are the basis of the authority of all the other works which he recommends. In Table 1 the order of *Satyārth Prakāś* and *Saṃskār Vidhi* has generally been followed. Variations will be noted in the discussions of the relevant discipline.

The grouping of the disciplines here is a traditional one. Swami Dayanand in *Ṛgvedādibhāṣyabhūmikā* follows this system rather closely. In *Satyārth Prakāś* and *Saṃskār Vidhi* some parts of the system are not found in their expected order. This is natural as these two works are presenting curricula. Still, the traditional arrangement of the disciplines is generally followed by Swami Dayanand.

It is significant that this traditional system subordinates all disciplines to the Vedas. The Vedangas, or "limbs or parts of the Vedas," are arguably important for understanding the Vedas. Obviously one must know something about *Vyākaraṇa* or grammar, for example, to be able to read the Vedas. Still, under the rubric of *Vyākaraṇa* classical Sanskrit is taught as well as the Vedic dialect. So the material covered by *Vyākaraṇa* and the other Vedangas is not by any means limited to the Vedas.

The *Upāṅgas* ("secondary parts of the Vedas") are even less closely related to the Vedic Samhitas or hymns. Among the *Upāṅgas* Mimamsa is particularly concerned with the problem of Vedic exegesis especially in ritual contexts. The other five philosophical systems are by and large independent of the Vedas. So most of the *Upāṅgas* do not bear any obvious close relation to the Vedas.

Each of the *Upavedas*, "secondary Vedas," is traditionally grouped with one of the Vedic Samhitas (Ayur Veda with the Ṛg Veda [sometimes also with the Atharva Veda], *Dhanur Veda* with the Yajur Veda, *Gāndharva Veda* with the Sāma Veda, and *Artha Veda* with the Atharva Veda). There is admittedly a special relationship between the Sāma Veda, a text which is to be sung, and the *Gāndharva Veda*, which is the discipline concerned with music. Otherwise any substantive connection between the *Upavedas* and the Vedic Samhitas is difficult to discern.

Most of the disciplines in Table 1 are not closely related to the Vedic Samhitas. Still, the nomenclature of the grouping of the disciplines seems to indicate that they are all subordinate to the Vedas. This nomenclature is quite appropriate for Swami Dayanand, who placed such an emphasis on the Vedas in his philosophy.

It is worth noting that the contents of some of the disciplines are greatly expanded by Swami Dayanand. For example, under *Jyotis*, the discipline traditionally concerned with astronomy and astrology, Dayanand recommends that the student take up mathematics and other sciences. Hence the curriculum that Dayanand outlines is not as traditional as it might appear at first glance. It will be noted below in individual cases where Dayanand has expanded the traditional disciplines.

Now we begin a detailed study of the lists of books to be read. The first group is the Vedangas. The first of the Vedangas that Dayanand presents is *Śikṣā* or pronunciation. This is the most elementary discipline which the student must master. In this discipline Dayanand recommends only one text, the work on *Śikṣā* by Pāṇini. As we will see, in *Vyākaraṇa* also Pāṇini is important.

In *Ṛgvedādibhāṣyabhūmikā Kalpa* or ritual follows *Śikṣā*. In *Satyārth Prakāś Kalpa* is mentioned only perfunctorily in a list of the Vedangas, without any discussion of the place that it should occupy in the curriculum being set forth. In *Saṃskār Vidhi* Swami Dayanand says that this discipline should be studied along with the Vedas. This seems natural since the Vedas are important in Brahmanic ritual. As is pointed out in the footnotes to Table 1, in *Saṃskār Vidhi* Swami Dayanand may intend that other works in addition to the ones that he specifically indicates should be studied in *Kalpa*.

Vyākaraṇa or grammar directly follows *Śikṣā* in Swami Dayanand's curricula in *Satyārth Prakāś* and *Saṃskār Vidhi*. Hence it is the second discipline to be studied by the student. The two important texts in this discipline are the *Aṣṭādhyāyī* of Pāṇini, which is a comprehensive work on Sanskrit grammar, and Patañjali's commentary on it, the *Mahābhāṣya*. The other texts that Swami Dayanand recommends all cover some minor aspect of grammar, and all of them have been attributed to Pāṇini. It is noteworthy that no other general grammatical work is recommended.

Swami Dayanand's perspective on language was taught to him by his guru Swami Virjānand Sarasvatī (1779-1868). Virjānand was a master of grammar, and it was in this discipline that he worked with Dayanand. Virjānand's teaching was based only on the *Aṣṭādhyāyī* and the *Mahābhāṣya*. Virjānand rejected all other grammatical works. Virjānand believed that the *Aṣṭādhyāyī* and *Mahābhāṣya* are the work of rishis or sages, and are fully authoritative. Other works on grammar are *anārṣa*, that is, they are not the work of rishis, and are vastly inferior to these two great works. True to the teaching of his guru, Dayanand also regarded the *Aṣṭādhyāyī* with its commentary the *Mahābhāṣya* to be uniquely authoritative.[26]

In Swami Dayanand's curricula after *Vyākaraṇa* comes *Nirukta* or etymology. In this discipline Dayanand recommends the *Nirukta* of Yāska, which is a commentary on the *Nighaṇṭu*. It is Yāska's etymological explanation which is the key to understanding the meaning of Sanskrit words according to Swami Dayanand. The *Nirukta* and the *Nighaṇṭu* are particularly heavily quoted in Dayanand's Vedic commentaries. Other works having to do with Sanskrit vocabulary are also mentioned in this context by Dayanand in *Saṃskār Vidhi*. Dayanand recommends the dictionaries of Kātyāyana and others, and the *Avyayārtha* of Āptamuni. As indicated in the footnotes to the table, the last two references are obscure.[27]

After *Nirukta* comes *Chandas* or meter in Swami Dayanand's curricula in *Satyārth Prakāś* and *Saṃskār Vidhi*. One text is recommended in this discipline in all three of Dayanand's books under consideration here, the *Chandaḥsūtras* of Piṅgala. The commentary on this text is also mentioned in *Ṛgvedādibhāṣyabhūmikā* and *Saṃskār Vidhi*.

The *Chandaḥsūtras* includes meters used in classical Sanskrit as well as the Vedas. Perhaps it is because the classical meters are already being studied that Swami Dayanand introduces Kavya or poetic literature at this point. In *Satyārth Prakāś Manu*, the *Rāmāyaṇa* of Vālmīki, and the *Mahābhārata* are mentioned. In the *Mahābhārata* Dayanand enjoins that "Viduranīti" and other morally uplifting passages be studied. Dayanand did not regard all of the *Mahābhārata* as authoritative, but "Viduranīti" was one passage that he did find acceptable.[28] In *Satyārth Prakāś* Dayanand says that these works should be studied in the way that Kavya is taught ("kāvyarīti se"), with an analysis of word-division, syntax, and so forth.[29]

In *Saṃskār Vidhi* the relationship between Kavya and *Manu*, the *Rāmāyaṇa*, and the *Mahābhārata* is made even more explicit. Swami Dayanand here enjoins the study of *Manu*, "Viduranīti" (the rest of the *Mahābhārata* is not mentioned), and any ten *sargas* (or "chapters") of the *Rāmāyaṇa* along with the *Kāvyālaṅkārasūtra* of Yāska and its commentary by Vātsyāyana. *Manu*, the *Rāmāyaṇa*, and "Viduranīti" are to be used as anthologies for the study of figures of speech and other aspects of literary usage. Of course Swami Dayanand is concerned that the texts should be edifying, but they are not studied for their content as much as they are as examples of usage. This is the only provision for the study of literature in Swami Dayanand's curricula, a point to which we shall return.

No mention of Kavya is made in this context in *Ṛgvedādibhāṣya-bhūmikā*, nor are the *Mahābhārata* or the *Rāmāyaṇa* included in the discussion of authoritative texts. *Manu* is mentioned in the discussion of texts that are not authoritative, where it is said that all law codes but *Manu* are not authoritative.[30] This may be taken as an indication that *Manu* is authoritative, but it is an offhand one.

In the curriculum in *Saṃskār Vidhi Jyotis* follows directly after *Chandas* and Kavya. *Jyotis* in *Satyārth Prakāś* comes at the very end of the curriculum, being the last discipline to be studied. Traditional *Jyotis* is concerned with astronomy and astrology. In all three of the works being discussed Dayanand includes mathematics and other sciences under the heading of *Jyotis*. In *Satyārth Prakāś* in *Jyotis* are to be taught algebra (*bījagaṇita*), arithmetic (*aṅkavidyā*), geography (*bhūgolavidyā*), astronomy (*khagolavidyā*), and geology (*bhūgarbhavidyā*).[31] Algebra (*bījagaṇita*) and geometry (*rekhāgaṇita*) are listed as a part of *Jyotis* in *Ṛgvedādibhāṣyabhūmikā*.[32] *Saṃskār Vidhi* also includes algebra (*bījagaṇita*), arithmetic (*aṅkavidyā*), and geometry (*rekhāgaṇita*) under the heading of *Jyotis*.[33] This is a very good example of how Swami Dayanand used the traditional names of the disciplines in his own work, but greatly expanded the sphere that they cover.

In the curricula in *Satyārth Prakāś* and *Saṃskār Vidhi* the Vedangas are followed by the *Upāṅgas*. The *Upāṅgas* are comprised of the traditionally recognized six systems of Indian philosophy, the *darśanas*. Mimamsa is the philosophical system concerned with the exegesis of the Vedas in relation to ritual. The Vaisheshika system sets forth an atomistic metaphysics. Nyaya contains the rules for logical argument. In Yoga meditation is the central concern. The Sankhya system is known for its theory of emanation. Vedanta focuses on *brahman*, the principle which underlies the cosmos.

Only in the case of Vedanta is there some difference in the lists of works to be read in Swami Dayanand's three main books. In *Satyārth Prakāś* Dayanand recommends the commentaries on the *Vedanta Sutras* by Vātsyāyana and Baudhāyana. In *Ṛgvedādibhāṣya-bhūmikā* only Baudhāyana, and so forth are listed. Yet a third version can be found in *Saṃskār Vidhi*, where Jaimini and Bauddhāyana, and so on are spoken of as authoritative. It is worth noting that in *Ṛgvedādibhāṣyabhūmikā* and *Saṃskār Vidhi* this list of commentaries is open-ended, since Dayanand adds *ādi* or *et cetera* to the texts that he cites. The syllabus for the other five philosophical systems in all three of Dayanand's works is closed, the word "ādi" does not occur at all. In Vedanta there may be some study beyond the texts that Dayanand specifically names.

It is not surprising that Vedanta enjoys a special status here. Vedanta is the most important of the philosophical systems, to the extent that the other schools are often presented as subsidiaries of Vedanta. Also the *Vedanta Sutras* have been more frequently commented upon than any of the other *darśana* sutras, and they are the most widely studied. So it is natural that Swami Dayanand in this area has allowed for more expansive reading.

Directly following the Vedanta are listed the Upanishads that Swami Dayanand takes as authoritative in Table 1. Actually in *Ṛgvedādibhāṣyabhūmikā* the Upanishads are enumerated after Vedanta in the Sanskrit text, but they come before Vedanta in the Hindi translation. In *Saṃskār Vidhi* the *Vedanta Sutras* are mentioned, then the Upanishads are spelled out, then the *Vedanta Sutras* are mentioned again. The solution to this apparent confusion of order can be found in *Satyārth Prakāś*. There the *Upāṅgas* are mentioned together, including Vedanta. After this the Upanishads are given, but it is stated that they should be studied before Vedanta is taken up. So the actual order of study should be: the first five philosophical systems, then the Upanishads, and finally Vedanta.

Ordinarily the Upanishads are considered a part of Vedic literature, but here Swami Dayanand has separated them from the Vedas and placed them in his curriculum as a prologue to Vedanta. The relationship between the Upanishads and the Vedanta *darśana* is quite close. The very word "vedānta" or "end of the Vedas" is used to refer to the Upanishads, as they are the last layer of commentaries on the Vedas. The Upanishads are one of the *prasthānatrayī*, one of the three textual sources for Vedanta philosophy according to Śaṅkara (the other sources are the *Vedanta Sutras* themselves and the *Bhagavad Gītā*). Finally the ultimate concern of the Upanishads with *brahman* is congruent with Vedanta speculation. Thus it is natural to link the Upanishads with the study of Vedanta. The place of the Upanishads in Swami Dayanand's curricula will be discussed further in the context of the Vedas below.

In both *Satyārth Prakāś* and *Saṃskār Vidhi* the Vedas are introduced after the study of the *Upāṅgas* and the Upanishads. In *Satyārth Prakāś* Swami Dayanand says that the Vedic Samhitas are to be studied along with their Brahmanas. In *Saṃskār Vidhi* the study of the Vedas is even more dense, with the Vedic Samhitas being accompanied by the various *Padakramas* (systems of memorizing the Vedas), Brahmanas, and ritual texts which relate to the Vedas. Dayanand specifically mentions the *Āśvalāyana Śrauta*, *Gṛhya*, and *Kalpa Sutras* in connection with the Ṛg Veda. Presumably he intended that the sutras of the other

Vedas should be studied along with their respective Saṃhitas. Also in this connection it should be noted that the Vedic *Śākhās* (or Vedic schools) are listed among the authoritative works in *Ṛgvedādibhāṣyabhūmikā*. *Śākhā* is a very general term and might be taken to refer to all of the ancillary literature related to the Vedas. The Vedic *Śākhās* are not mentioned as such in the curricula in *Satyārth Prakāś* and *Saṃskār Vidhi*.

As was discussed above, Swami Dayanand regarded the Vedic Samhitas or hymns as separate from the rest of Vedic literature. The Samhitas are inerrant, while the other texts known as Vedic may contain error. Despite this distinction Swami Dayanand still recommends that the Samhitas be studied along with the other Vedic literature.

The only Vedic texts not included at this point in the curriculum are the Upanishads, which are to be read with Vedanta. It is perhaps significant that the Upanishads are distinguished from the Vedas. Of all the Vedic literature the Upanishads are probably the texts that have been most widely studied in recent centuries. In fact the Upanishads are sometimes read to the exclusion of other Vedic literature, since it is believed that they contain what is best and most exalted in the Vedic teachings.[34] In Swami Dayanand's curriculum the Upanishads are studied separately from the Vedas, which might encourage the student to develop a greater appreciation of the independent character of the Vedic Samhitas.

Finally in Swami Dayanand's curricula are the four *Upavedas*. More time is to be spent on this group than on any other in Dayanand's system.[35] Three of the four disciplines are very broad (*Ayur Veda*, *Dhanur Veda*, and *Artha Veda*). Dayanand's lists of works to be studied are generally open-ended for the disciplines in this group.

Ayur Veda covers the medical sciences. The traditional texts in this discipline are recommended by Dayanand, *Caraka*, *Suśruta*, and the *Nighaṇṭu* of Dhanvantari. Dayanand also allows the possibility of studying other books by adding *ādi* (etc.) at the end of this lists of recommended works. In this discipline Swami Dayanand introduces a very interesting innovation. He writes: "Having made instruments as described in the *Suśruta*, they [the students] should dissect all the parts of the body, so that they can establish for themselves the knowledge that is written in the medical texts."[36] In the medical sciences the student should not only memorize the classical texts in the traditional way, but he or she should also test that knowledge experimentally.[37] The emphasis on experimentation was not present in Ayur Veda as traditionally taught. So this discipline has been redefined by Swami Dayanand.

The next discipline is *Dhanur Veda*, which literally means the "Veda of the bow" or archery. Here Dayanand notes the names of one or two sages who are said to have composed works in this discipline, but he admits that the texts attributed to these sages have been lost. Still, Dayanand affirms in *Ṛgvedādibhāṣyabhūmikā* that one can write texts in this discipline in the present with the help of the knowledge of the other disciplines. In *Satyārth Prakāś* Swami Dayanand describes what the study of *Dhanur Veda* should include. He says that *Dhanur Veda* is composed of two halves, one related to kings and the other related to their subjects. In the study related to kings Dayanand places the martial sciences—weapons, drill, and so forth. The study related to subjects involves statecraft, Dayanand particularly mentions the administration of justice.[38] So *Dhanur Veda* is not just the military sciences as it has been traditionally defined, but has come to include all of statecraft in Dayanand's system.

It should be noted that this is the only place where the study of statecraft is discussed in Swami Dayanand's curricula. As has been mentioned, where Dayanand describes the ideal state in *Satyārth Prakāś* he relies heavily on *Manu*. Yet in his educational system *Manu* only appears in the study of Kavya. In general the syllabi for the *Upavedas* are vague in the extreme as compared to the syllabi in some other parts of Dayanand's curricula.

The next *Upaveda* is *Gāndharva Veda* or the musical sciences. In connection with this discipline Dayanand enjoins the study of all aspects of music and even dance. Yet in *Satyārth Prakāś* Swami Dayanand cautions that music should be studied in relation to the Sāma Veda. Students "should never engage in the pointless singing like the braying of an ass of procurers, courtesans, and mendicants who promote sensuality."[39] Music is to be studied along with the Vedas, not for sensual enjoyment.

The final *Upaveda* is *Artha Veda*, which is also called *Śilpaśāstra* by Swami Dayanand. *Śilpaśāstra* is a very broad discipline as traditionally defined, including all the manual arts and crafts. In *Satyārth Prakāś* Dayanand describes this discipline as involved with anything that leads to the increase of wealth (*artha* means "wealth"), especially the study of materials and their properties and how to make things. That this study should include modern technology is clear from *Saṃskār Vidhi*. In that work Dayanand says that "aeronautics, telegraphy, geology, etc.," should be studied as a part of *Artha Veda*.[40] The fine arts, especially sculpture, are often designated a part of *Śilpaśāstra*, but Swami Dayanand makes no mention of them. As Dayanand's name for this discipline (*Artha Veda*, the science of wealth) indicates, he is concerned with arts of a practical cast.

These are all the works which Swami Dayanand designates authoritative. We will postpone a general discussion of these works until after the next subsection, which will be on the works that Swami Dayanand indicated are not authoritative.

UNAUTHORITATIVE WORKS

In *Satyārth Prakāś* and *Ṛgvedādibhāṣyabhūmikā* Swami Dayanand gives lists of the works that he does not regard as authoritative or worth studying.[41] The contents of those lists are presented in Table 2. There is no such list in *Saṃskār Vidhi*, so that work is not included in the table. Before discussing the table in detail, a few general points are to be made.

The lists of works not regarded as authoritative are quite heterogeneous. Some works are included which are quite popular and important in the present, others are obscure. Dayanand's lists should not be regarded as comprehensive, rather only a few works are noted as examples of the types of literature that Dayanand did not accept. Presumably many other works might be added.

In the discussion that follows some attempt will be made to identify the reason why individual works are singled out for condemnation. This necessarily involves some speculation, as Dayanand does not in every case explain what he objects to in a given book. One general principle should be noted at the outset. In both *Satyārth Prakāś* and *Ṛgvedādibhāṣyabhūmikā* the lists of texts that are not authoritative directly follow the lists of those that are authoritative. In the latter enumeration Dayanand made an effort to single out the best text in a given discipline. Other works in that discipline were regarded as inferior by Dayanand, and are as such worthy of rejection. In other words, the fact that a text is not included in the list of authoritative books is in itself a reason for its censure.

We will now proceed to examine Table 2 in detail. As in Table 1 we will generally follow the order of Dayanand's curricula in *Satyārth Prakāś* and *Saṃskār Vidhi*. Hence we begin with the Vedangas and *Śikṣā*. In *Satyārth Prakāś* Swami Dayanand identifies one text on *Śikṣā* or pronunciation that he does not regard as authoritative. The editor of *Satyārth Prakāś* Yudhiṣṭhir Mīmāṃsak identifies this work as

TABLE 2

UNAUTHORITATIVE WORKS ACCORDING TO DAYANAND

Group	Discipline	Texts in *Satyārth Prakāś*	Texts in *Ṛgvedādibhāṣyabhūmikā*
Vedangas	Śikṣā	The text that begins "Atha śikṣāṃ pravakṣyāmi Pāṇinīyaṃ matam yathā"[1]	—
	Kalpa	—	Trikaṇḍika, Snānasūtra, Pariśiṣṭa, etc.
	Vyākaraṇa	Kātantra, Sārasvata, Candrikā,[2] Mughdabodha, Kaumudī,[3] Śekhara,[4] Manoramā,[5] etc.	Sārasvata, Candrikā, Kaumudī, etc.

1. The editor, Yudhiṣṭhir Mīmāṃsak, notes that this is the first line of a work on *Śikśā* that is falsely attributed to Pāṇini. *Satyārth Prakāś*, 120, n. 6.
2. Mīmāṃsak identifies the full title of this work as *Sārasvatacandrikā*. *Satyārth Prakāś*, 120, n. 2.
3. Mīmāṃsak says this is *Siddhāntakaumudī* and *Prakriyākaumudī*. *Satyārth Prakāś*, 120, n. 3.
4. Mīmāṃsak indicates that this name refers to three texts: *Laghuśabdenduśekhara*, *Bṛhacchabdenduśekhara*, and *Paribhāṣenduśekhara*. *Satyārth Prakāś*, 120, n. 4.
5. This is the *Prauḍhamanoramā* according to Mīmāṃsak. *Satyārth Prakāś*, 120, n. 5.

Table 2—*Continued*

Group	Discipline	Texts in *Satyārth Prakāś*	Texts in *Ṛgvedādibhāṣyabhūmikā*
Vedangas Continued	Nirukta	Amarakośa, etc.	—
	Chandas	Vṛttaratnākara, etc.	—
	Jyotis	Śīghrabodha, Muhūrtacintāmaṇi, etc.	Muhūrtacintāmaṇi, etc.
Kavya	—	Nāyikābheda, Kuvalayānanda, Raghuvaṃśa, Māgha, Kirātārjunīya, etc.	—[1]
Upāṅgas	Mimamsa	Dharmasindhu, Vratārka, etc.	Nirṇayasindhu, etc.
	Vaisheshika	Tarkasaṃgraha, etc.	Tarkasaṃgraha, etc.[2]
	Nyaya	Jāgadīśī, etc.	Jāgadīśī, etc.
	Yoga	Haṭhapradīpikā, etc.	Haṭhapradīpikā, etc.

1. *Manu* is listed under *Smṛti*.
2. The Hindi also mentions *Muktāvalī* here. *Ṛgvedādibhāṣyabhūmikā*, in *Ṛgveda-Bhāṣyam*, vol. 1, 321.

Table 2—*Continued*

Group	Discipline	Texts in *Satyārth Prakāś*	Texts in *Ṛgvedādibhāṣyabhūmikā*
Upāṅgas Continued	Sankhya	Sāṅkhyatattva-kaumudī, etc.	Sāṅkhyatattva-kaumudī, etc.
	Vedanta	Yogavāsiṣṭha, Pañcadaśī, etc.	Vedāntasāra, Pañcadaśī, Yoga-vāsiṣṭha, etc.
Upavedas	Ayur Veda	Śārṅgadhara, etc.	—
Smṛti	—	The interpolated verses in Manu, all works other than Manu	The interpolated verses in Manu, all works other than Manu
Tantra	—	All works	Rudrayāmala, etc.[1]
Puranas	—	All works	Brahmavaivarta, etc.[2]
Upapurāṇas	—	All works	—[3]

1. The entire group is intended here. The single text noted is just one example.
2. Again the entire group is intended: the text cited is one example.
3. The Sanskrit doesn't mention the *Upapurāṇas*, but the Hindi has "Sūryyagāthā *ādi Uppurāṇ*," that is, "the *Upapurāṇas Sūryagāthā*, etc." *Ṛgvedādibhāṣyabhūmikā*, in *Ṛgveda-Bhāṣyam*, vol. 1, 321.

Table 2—*Continued*

Group	Discipline	Texts in *Satyārth Prakāś*	Texts in *Ṛgvedādibhāṣyabhūmikā*
Māhātmyas	—	—	General reference[1]
Works of paṣaṇḍisam-pradāya	—	—	General reference[2]
Works of nāstikas	—	—	General reference[3]
Works in Hindi	—	All works	—
Individual works in Hindi	—	Rāmcaritmānas, Rukmiṇīmaṅgal	—

Sources: Dayanand, *Satyārth Prakāś*, 110-121; idem, *Ṛgvedādi-bhāṣyabhūmikā*, in *Ṛgveda-Bhāṣyam*, vol. 1, 321-322. See Mīmāṃsak's appendixes: *Satyārth Prakāś*, 989-990; *Ṛgvedādibhāṣyabhūmikā*, in *Ṛgveda-Bhāṣyam*, vol. 1, 732.

1. The group is condemned, but no specific texts are mentioned.
2. In the Sanskrit the works of the *paṣaṇḍisampradāya* (heretical sects) are condemned, but no specific work is mentioned. While no works are given in the Hindi either, the names of some of the sects in question are noted: Shaivas, Shaktas, Gāṇapatas, Vaishnavas, etc. *Ṛgvedādibhāṣyabhūmikā*, in *Ṛgveda-Bhāṣyam*, vol. 1, 322.
3. The group is condemned, but no specific texts are mentioned.

spuriously attributed to Pāṇini. Dayanand does not explain what his objection is to this book.

In *Kalpa* or ritual Swami Dayanand mentions three works which are not worthy of acceptance in *Ṛgvedādibhāṣyabhūmikā*. They are characterized as opposed to the Śrauta Sutras, but otherwise their vices are not detailed. The context of the condemnation of these books gives a clue as to their deficiency. After these works are condemned Swami Dayanand rejects all works that teach the removal of sin and the attainment of liberation by fasts, pilgrimages, worship of images, and other similar practices.[42] Dayanand taught that such ritual acts are not efficacious in the removal of sin or the attainment of liberation. The *Kalpa* works which are mentioned here support such practices, and hence are rejected by Swami Dayanand.

In *Satyārth Prakāś* there is a list of several works on *Vyākaraṇa* or grammar that are not authoritative, including those condemned in *Ṛgvedādibhāṣyabhūmikā*. The prime fault of these works according to Dayanand is that they make it difficult to learn the Sanskrit language. "And the amount of knowledge that comes from studying these [the works that Dayanand recommends] for three years, that much knowledge could not be acquired from studying even for fifty years bad books such as *Sārasvata, Candrikā, Kaumudī, Manoramā*, and so forth."[43] This is a sentiment which is echoed several times in Dayanand's writings, these grammatical works are to be rejected because they make the process of studying Sanskrit more difficult than it need be.

The grammatical texts which Dayanand condemns all differ from Pāṇini to a greater or lesser extent. *Sārasvata*, for example, is a grammar in which Vedic usage has been eliminated in order to simplify the study of classical Sanskrit. Since the Vedas are so important to Dayanand, it is not surprising that he has no use for this book. *Mugdhabodha* is an elementary work on Sanskrit grammar for the student. It was Dayanand's conviction that the most perspicuous explanation of Sanskrit grammar was offered by Pāṇini. Any attempt to simplify the discussion could not achieve the brevity and completeness of the great master's work. Hence any so-called simplification would ultimately only make the study of Sanskrit grammar more complicated, according to Dayanand. So *Mugdhabodha* is rejected. *Siddhānta Kaumudī* is often used to teach aspects of Sanskrit grammar in schools in India today, because its ordering is regarded as more simple than Pāṇini's for some purposes. Still, Dayanand might argue that Bhaṭṭoji Dīkṣita's rearrangement is not a better guide to Sanskrit as a whole, and his work is condemned. It was the belief of Dayanand's guru Virjānand that

Pāṇini's *Aṣṭādhyāyī* and its commentary the *Mahābhāṣya* are the only worthwhile grammars. This is a conviction which Dayanand obviously came to share.

In *Satyārth Prakāś* Swami Dayanand discusses *Kośas* or dictionaries in the context of *Nirukta* or etymology. Here he specifically condemns *Amarakośa*. Dayanand is not explicit about the faults of *Amarakośa*, but he does give some idea as to why the work is rejected. Dayanand writes, "Several years should not be wasted in the study of other works such as the *Amarakośa* written by *nāstikas*."[44] One of the problems with *Amarakośa* and other dictionaries is that they take several years to master. On the other hand the *Nirukta* of Yāska can be covered in only eight months. Another defect of *Amarakośa* is that it was written by a *nāstika*. *Nāstika* means a skeptic. It is sometimes used to refer to atheists, but it is more often attached to those who do not accept the authority of the Vedas, especially those who from the standpoint of traditional Hinduism are regarded as heterodox. There is some internal evidence that the author of the *Amarakośa* was a Buddhist.[45] This would constitute another reason to reject the text for Dayanand.

In *Satyārth Prakāś* one text on *Chandas* or meter is specifically condemned, *Vṛttaratnākara*. No explanation is given of the deficiencies of this work, other than that it is a book composed by a person with little knowledge. This is a work concerned with classical Sanskrit meters rather than the Vedic meters. Presumably it has been rejected for this reason.

In *Jyotis* two works are specifically mentioned in *Satyārth Prakāś* and one in *Ṛgvedādibhāṣyabhūmikā* that should not be studied. *Ṛgvedādibhāṣyabhūmikā* describes the condemned *Muhūrttacintāmaṇi* as giving "instruction in the effects of auspicious moments and horoscopes."[46] The belief was prevalent in India in Swami Dayanand's time, as it is now, that the movement of heavenly bodies affects human destiny. Thus people wait for the auspicious moment (*muhūrta*) to perform marriages and other ceremonies. Others have horoscopes (*janmapatra*) made so that they will have an idea what the future holds. Swami Dayanand did not believe in *phalajyotis*, or the science of the effect of the movements of heavenly bodies on human life. Dayanand does recommend the study of astronomy in *Jyotis*, along with algebra, arithmetic, geography, geology, and geometry. *Jyotis* in Dayanand's system is a very broadly defined discipline, but it does not contain the one thing that is most central to *Jyotis* as practiced in the modern period—astrology. It is astrological works which Dayanand condemns here.

The list of works censured in connection with Kavya or poetical literature is very heterogeneous indeed. *Nāyikābheda* (literally, "types of female characters") is not the title of an individual work, but refers to a class of literature. There is a rich tradition of erotic poetry in Sanskrit. Works on *Nāyikābheda* are secondary writings in this tradition, concerned with the characteristics of female figures in literature. Presumably Dayanand did not approve of this literature because he regarded it as prurient.

Kuvalayānanda, Raghuvaṃśa, and *Kirātārjunīya* are the titles of individual works. Perhaps the first book is rejected by Dayanand because of its erotic content. *Raghuvaṃśa* and *Kirātārjunīya* are not known for their erotic passages, but may be singled out here on theological grounds. *Raghuvaṃśa* is about Rama and his royal line, the descendants of Raghu. Perhaps there is some reference in this work to the common traditional belief that Rama was an incarnation (or avatar) of the god Vishnu. Swami Dayanand did not believe that God takes on human form, and did not regard Rama as a divine incarnation. It is likely that it is because of this difference in theology that *Raghuvaṃśa* is rejected. *Kirātārjunīya* is a work devoted to describing the encounter of Arjuna (one of the heroes of the *Mahābhārata*) with the god Shiva, who had taken on human form as a member of the Kirāta tribe. This work, too, may be condemned because it contains *avatāravāda*, the theory that God from time to time takes on human form.

Māgha is the name of an author. His best known work is *Śiśupālavadha*, also known as *Māghakāvya*. This book describes the confrontation between Krishna and King Śiśupāla, which results in the former striking off the latter's head. There is not much eroticism here, but perhaps there is a mention of the belief that Krishna was also an avatar of Vishnu. It is possibly on this ground that the works of Māgha are condemned.

The list of Kavya works singled out as unauthoritative by Swami Dayanand contains the titles of three books, the name of one author, and the designation of a class of works. The heterogeneousness of this list indicates something about Dayanand's method in condemning unreliable texts. Apparently Dayanand did not prepare carefully drawn up comprehensive lists of works that are not authoritative. Rather he was content to make a few notes in this area. Much is left to the reader.

For the *Upāṅgas*, the six *darśanas* or philosophical systems, Swami Dayanand names at least one work to be rejected for each system. The lists of these rejected texts are quite similar in *Satyārth Prakāś* and *Ṛgvedādibhāṣyabhūmikā*. In *Satyārth Prakāś* Dayanand does not comment on the defects of these books. In *Ṛgvedādibhāṣyabhūmikā* the explanation is limited to saying that each of these works is opposed to the basic sutra text in its discipline. We are forced to speculate on why Swami Dayanand has rejected these books.

Some works are perhaps rejected because they are not consistent with Dayanand's teachings. In Mimamsa, for example, *Vratārka* is concerned with *vratas*, fasting and other observances to be performed on particular days. Dayanand was not a great believer in these kinds of ritual acts. Hence he rejects this text. *Haṭhapradīpikā* also is condemned because it is inconsistent with Swami Dayanand's beliefs about yoga, as noted at the beginning of this chapter.

Some of the books which Dayanand condemns in connection with the *Upāṅgas* are currently popular texts. *Sāṅkhyatattvakaumudī* and *Vedāntasāra*, for example, are thought of as good introductions to Sankhya and Vedanta. Both works are based only on a part of the original sutra texts of their disciplines. Presumably Swami Dayanand objects to these books on the same basis that he condemned the *Siddhānta Kaumudī* in grammar. Dayanand would not brook any attempt to abridge or rearrange the original sutras, which he regarded as adequate statements in themselves of what must be learned in a given area.

Among the *Upavedas* only one text is identified as unworthy of study, *Śārṅgadhara* in Ayur Veda. Dayanand offers no explanation as to why this work has been censured.

In *Smṛti* (which here refers to law codes) all works are condemned but *Manu* in *Satyārth Prakāś* and *Ṛgvedādibhāṣyabhūmikā*. In both books Dayanand also mentions that there are interpolated (*prakṣipta*) passages in *Manu* which should not be accepted.[47] Unfortunately Dayanand does not spell out which are the interpolated passages, or how they have been determined to be interpolations.

In *Satyārth Prakāś* Swami Dayanand says that all works on tantra are not to be read. In *Ṛgvedādibhāṣyabhūmikā* Dayanand specifically mentions *Rudrayāmala*, and so forth, but all works are intended. In Dayanand's discussion of unauthoritative works there is only a bare condemnation of the tantras, but in another context there is more discussion of this topic.

In the eleventh chapter of *Satyārth Prakāś* Swami Dayanand criticizes various Hindu sects. Here he discusses the tantrics, especially *vāmamārgīs*, at some length. The practices of the tantrics are presented as centering on "the five Ms:" *madya* or liquor, *māṃsa* or meat, *mīna* or fish, *mudrā* or parched or fried grain, and *maithuna* or sexual intercourse. Dayanand paints a lurid picture of a tantric ritual beginning with the consumption of grain, alcohol, meat, and fish and culminating in group sex.[48] If there is an esoteric meaning to this ritual Swami Dayanand does not explore it. In fact, the philosophy of the tantrics is hardly discussed. Their behavior is regarded as sufficient to warrant the condemnation of the sect. Presumably it is on the basis of this censure of the ritual activity of the tantrics that the tantra literature is rejected here.[49]

Another genre that is condemned wholesale here is the Puranas. Again *Satyārth Prakāś* states flatly that all the Puranas and *Upapurāṇas* (minor Puranas) are not to be studied. *Ṛgvedādibhāṣyabhūmikā* mentions the *Brahmavaivarta Purāṇa*, and so forth, but surely all the texts in this category are intended. In the eleventh chapter of *Satyārth Prakāś* there is extensive criticism of the Puranas.[50] They are characterized as sectarian works which contain many falsehoods.

In *Ṛgvedādibhāṣyabhūmikā* Swami Dayanand also rejects all *māhātmya* works. Books which expand upon the greatness of holy places and the benefits to be derived from pilgrimage to them are called *māhātmyas*. Dayanand characterizes these as works which claim that sins can be removed and liberation attained "merely by fasting in month of Mārgaśīrṣa, or on the eleventh of each month, by traveling to Kāśī [Benares], or to other water courses, by remembering the names of the gods, or worshipping lifeless idols."[51] Because the swami did not believe that these acts could wash away sins or secure liberation he condemns the works that enjoin them.

Swami Dayanand also rejected in *Ṛgvedādibhāṣyabhūmikā* texts written by the adherents of heretical sects ("pāṣaṇḍisampradāyanirmittāni sarvāṇi pustakāṇi").[52] As pointed out in the Hindi rendering of this sentence, Dayanand is referring to Shaivas, Vaishnavas, and members of other sectarian groups prevalent in modern Hinduism. Dayanand separately criticizes the Puranas as books by the adherents of these sects. Presumably this further injunction is meant to include all other sectarian writings, condemned for the same reasons that the Puranas have been rejected.

In *Ṛgvedādibhāṣyabhūmikā* Swami Dayanand condemns works propagating *nāstikatva*, which probably means disbelief in the Vedas. The twelfth chapter of *Satyārth Prakāś* is dedicated to the criticism of the great *nāstika* traditions of South Asian history, the Cārvākas (a materialist sect not surviving in the modern period), the Buddhists, and the Jains.[53] It is probably the writings of these groups that are being referred to here.

There is one more large group of works which Swami Dayanand

rejects in *Satyārth Prakāś*, that is, all works in Hindi. We must look to another context to understand this blanket condemnation.

When Swami Dayanand discusses the authority of the Vedas, he argues that those texts were originally communicated by God in Sanskrit for a reason. Dayanand believed that Sanskrit was the mother of all languages, spoken by the united human community in the time before the divisions engendered by the *Mahābhārata* war. Sanskrit is not the exclusive preserve of one nation, but is the legacy of all. Hence Dayanand argues in *Satyārth Prakāś* that the imparting of the Vedas in Sanskrit is a sign of God's impartiality. If God had communicated the Vedas in the language of any one country, then they would have been easy to understand for the native speakers of that language and difficult for others. Instead God communicated the Vedas in Sanskrit which is not the exclusive language of any country, or so the argument goes. Hence, "because comparable effort is required of the people of all nations in studying and teaching [Sanskrit], God is not partial."[54]

Presumably the same argument could be extended to apply to all the works that Dayanand recommends. They are in Sanskrit, and so they are not the exclusive property of any nation. If Hindi books were included in Dayanand's list of authoritative texts that would make it less universal. Hence all Hindi works are excluded.

Swami Dayanand in *Sayārth Prakāś* singles out two Hindi books for special censure, *Rāmcaritmānas* and *Rukmiṇīmaṅgal*.[55] The latter work is on the marriage of Rukmiṇī and Krishna, and it is probably condemned because of its erotic contents. The *Rāmcaritmānas* of Tulsīdās presents the life story of Rama. Presumably Dayanand rejects it because it depicts Rama as an incarnation of Vishnu. The *Rāmcaritmānas* is one of the most popular devotional works in Hindi-speaking north India, and its condemnation by Swami Dayanand is noteworthy.

These are the texts which Swami Dayanand identified as unauthoritative in his major writings. Having reviewed in detail Dayanand's lists of those works which are to be studied and those which are not, next we will present a few general observations suggested by those lists.

GENERAL DISCUSSION OF AUTHORITATIVE AND UNAUTHORITATIVE WORKS

It could be said that Swami Dayanand's body of authoritative texts is not as original as that of unauthoritative ones. Most Hindus in the modern period, even those with a very different viewpoint from Dayanand, would probably be willing to accept the works which the swami designated worthy of study. Dayanand sought to propagate a universal form of Hinduism free of sectarianism. Hence his list of authoritative texts generally includes only works of widely acknowledged repute.

For the reader familiar with Western histories of Indian religion it is striking that Dayanand's lists of authoritative works seem to represent a return to classical Brahmanism. The texts which Dayanand recommends are presumably those that dominated South Asian Hinduism centuries ago, before the development of tantrism and bhakti (devotionalism). The golden age before the *Mahābhārata* war was the Brahmanical period, at least with respect to the literature produced in it.

There is one aspect of Swami Dayanand's curricula that differs strikingly from the usual understanding of Brahmanical teaching, that is, the inclusion of science. In *Jyotis* mathematics and other sciences are to be studied along with astronomy; dissection of cadavers is to be used to facilitate the study of medicine in Ayur Veda; advanced technology, such as the telegraph (which was advanced in Dayanand's day), is a part of *Artha Veda*. At first glance it might seem that the inclusion of science in Dayanand's curricula is a modern innovation. Yet Dayanand would probably argue that he was just restoring the ancient system. For Dayanand believed that science was advanced during the *ārṣa* period.

It is interesting that there is nothing distinctive about Swami Dayanand's curricula with regard to the Vedas. The Samhitas, though theoretically different from the rest of Vedic literature for Dayanand, are to be studied along with the other texts. Dayanand spells out some of the Vedic literature that should be taken up with the Samhitas, but his lists are incomplete. In *Saṃskār Vidhi* there is a relatively extensive enumeration of the works that should be studied along with the Ṛg Veda, but the books which go with the other Vedas are not specified. *Ṛgvedādibhāṣyabhūmikā* is even more vague, only suggesting that the Vedas should be studied along with the *Śākhās*. Dayanand never details what works related to the Vedas are to be studied in what order and for how long.

Part of the reason for Dayanand's vagueness in this area may be that most Indian Vedic scholars in his time were Brahmans who were born into a Vedic school. For students coming from this traditional system there was a ready-made curriculum for studying the Vedas passed down from father to son. Nowadays, thanks in part to the work of the Arya Samaj in making the Vedas more widely available, there are many Vedic scholars who were not trained in the traditional way. For them a syllabus is more necessary.

In spite of the breadth of Dayanand's curricula, the lists of authoritative works are limited in some ways. There is a general emphasis on religion and philosophy. Dayanand does mention other areas of knowledge, but those curricula are vague. The group of disciplines that is the farthest from religion and philosophy, the *Upavedas*, is also the group with the most indefinite syllabi. The topics that Dayanand suggests for the *Upavedas* are only very meagerly covered by the texts that he mentions.

There is not much provision in Swami Dayanand's curricula for pure literature. In Kavya or poetic literature Dayanand recommends *Manu*, the *Rāmāyaṇa*, and the *Mahābhārata*. *Manu* is a law code, not a kavya. The *Rāmāyaṇa* and the *Mahābhārata* are sometimes considered kavyas, but they are certainly not the most developed books in this genre. It is only in Dayanand's lists of unauthoritative works that fully developed kavyas like Kālidāsa's *Raghuvaṃśa* appear. Of course there is a heavy element of eroticism in the Kavya tradition, which could not have been accepted by Dayanand. There are also Kavyas in which eroticism does not play a major role, but they are still not recommended by Dayanand. The idea of reading literature for enjoyment or edification is not present here.

As for the fine arts, there is provision for studying music and even dance in *Gāndharva Veda*, but it is specifically stated that they should be pursued in relation to the Sāma Veda and not just for enjoyment. It is significant that no mention of sculpture or painting is made in connection with *Śilpaśāstra*. One gets the impression that there is little room in Swami Dayanand's program for the arts.[56]

That there are limits to Swami Dayanand's lists of authoritative works is obvious at a glance. This is not accidental. Dayanand did not make a distinction between texts to be studied by the student and books that are more basically authoritative. In a curriculum the virtue of brevity is obvious, since a young person can only spend a limited amount of time in school. This economy has been carried over into the general list of authoritative works. Like the sutra texts for which he had such high regard, Dayanand's goal here is to present a list of reliable texts which is comprehensive yet brief. The comprehensiveness of the lists will be called into question to a certain extent by the material in the following section.

SOURCES QUOTED BY DAYANAND

In this section we will discuss the sources quoted in two of Swami Dayanand Sarasvati's major works, *Satyārth Prakāś* and *Ṛgvedādibhāṣyabhūmikā*. *Saṃskār Vidhi* will not be included here. Since *Saṃskār Vidhi* is concerned with the life-cycle rites, quotations from ritual guides predominate in it. *Satyārth Prakāś* and *Ṛgvedādibhāṣyabhūmikā* are more general works, and hence give a more balanced idea of the texts Dayanand cites. The object of this section is to see how the swami's practice in quoting sources corresponds to his theories as adumbrated in the first two sections of this chapter.

It is important to realize that the quotes in these books are not just embellishments. Both *Satyārth Prakāś* and *Ṛgvedādibhāṣyabhūmikā* are like commentaries. Dayanand usually proceeds by quoting a verse and then commenting on it. Unlike traditional commentaries, the author has drawn his authorities from many sources and arranged them so that he can best elucidate the topic at hand. And Dayanand often breaks out of the general scholiastic structure to make some independent point. Still, the quotations are generally integral to the swami's argument.

This section will be divided into two subsections. The first subsection will be on the sources that Dayanand quotes in general as that information is set forth in Table 3. The second subsection will be on specific contexts where Dayanand has quoted heavily from one source. These two subsections together give an idea of what sources are important in *Satyārth Prakāś* and *Ṛgvedādibhāṣyabhūmikā*.

THE SOURCES THAT DAYANAND QUOTES IN GENERAL

In Table 3 all the works from which Dayanand quoted approvingly in *Satyārth Prakāś* and *Ṛgvedādibhāṣyabhūmikā* are noted.[57] Quotations have only been counted for this table which Dayanand used to support his position. Verses identified as espousing errant views have not been

TABLE 3

SOURCES QUOTED IN DAYANAND'S MAJOR WRITINGS

Group	Discipline	Work	No. of Verses Cited	
			Satyārth Prakāś	*Ṛgvedādibhāṣyabhūmikā*
Vedangas	Kalpa	Āśvalāyana Gṛhya Sūtras	1	0
	Vyākaraṇa	Aṣṭādhyāyī	6	81
		Dhātupāṭha	74	19
		Mahābhāṣya	4	25
	Nirukta	Nighaṇṭu	0	17
		Nirukta	5	54
	Chandas	Piṅgala's Chandaḥ-sūtras	0	2
Total			90	198
Kavya	—	Manu	408	32
		Mahābhārata	22	0
Total			430	32
Upāṅgas	Mimamsa	Sutras	1	4
	Vaisheshika	Sutras	50	3
	Nyaya	Sutras	12	20
		Vātsyāyana's commentary	3	8

Table 3—*Continued*

Group	Discipline	Work	No. of Verses Cited	
			Satyārth Prakāś	*Ṛgvedādibhāṣyabhūmikā*
	Yoga	Sutras	13	66
		Vyāsa's commentary	0	21
	Sankhya	Sutras	10	1
	Vedanta	Sutras	7	6
Total			96	129
Upanishads	—	Kena	0	1
		Kaṭha	6	12
		Praśna	0	1
		Mūṇḍaka	10	7
		Māṇḍūkya	3	2
		Taittirīya	14	6
		Chāndogya	19	15
		Bṛhadāraṇyaka	4	2
Total			56	46
Vedas	—	Ṛg	31	90
		Yajur	47	160
		Sāma	1	3
		Atharva	14	62
Total			93	315

Table 3—*Continued*

Group	Discipline	Work	No. of Verses Cited	
			Satyārth Prakāś	*Ṛgvedādibhāṣyabhūmikā*
Brahmanas	—	Aitareya Śatapatha	2 13	13 118
Total			15	131
Upavedas	Ayur Veda	Suśruta	4	0
Total for authoritative works			784	851
Vedangas	Kalpa	Pāraskara Gṛhya Sūtra	0	3
	Vyākaraṇa	Vārttika	0	8
		Uṇādi Sūtras	0	1
		Paribhāṣāvṛtti Sīradeva	0	1
Upāṅgas	Vedanta	Śaṅkara's commentary on the Sutras	0	1

Table 3—*Continued*

Group	Discipline	Work	No. of Verses Cited	
			Satyārth Prakāś	*Ṛgvedādibhāṣyabhūmikā*
Upanishads	—	Jābāla	2	0
		Kaivalaya	1	0
		Maitrāyāṇi	1	0
		Mūṇḍakya Upaniṣad Gauṛapādīyā Kārikā	2	0
		Śāṭyāyana	0	1
		Śvetāśvatara	5	2
Vedas	—	Ṛg Veda Khila	0	2
		Taittirīya Saṃhitā	1	3
		Pratijñā Pariśiṣṭa	1	0
Brahmanas	—	Taittirīya	1	1
		Sadviṃśa	1	0
		Chāndogya Mantra	1	0
Upavedas	Ayur Veda	Śārṅgadhara	1	0
Other	Aranyakas	Taittirīya	5	11
		Aitareya	0	3

Table 3—*Continued*

Group	Discipline	Work	No. of Verses Cited	
			Satyārth Prakāś	*Ṛgvedādibhāṣyabhūmikā*
	Dharma Sutras	Āpastamba	2	2
	—	Cāṇakyanīti	2	0
	—	Bhartṛhari's Nītiśataka	1	0
	—	Pañcatantra	1	0
Total for unauthoritative works			28	39
Total for all works			812	890

Sources: Dayanand, *Satyārth Prakāś*; idem, *Ṛgvedādibhāṣyabhūmikā*, in *Ṛgveda-Bhāṣyam*, vol. 1, 1-430.

included. The point here is to look at the sources that Dayanand used as authorities in his arguments. Passages quoted to other ends are not relevant. Consistent with this method the last four chapters of *Satyārth Prakāś* have not been counted in this survey. At the end of *Satyārth Prakāś* Dayanand criticizes Hindu sects, anti-Vedic sects of Indian origin, Christianity, and Islam in separate chapters.[58] Most of the quotes in those chapters are from the scriptures of the sects under scrutiny. Those texts are quoted only to be refuted. Hence those quotations have no place in Table 3. The section by Swami Dayanand on his own beliefs which is appended to chapter fourteen of *Satyārth Prakāś* (headed "Svamantavyāmantavyaprakāśaḥ") is included in Table 3.[59]

Here we will make only a few general points on the information contained in Table 3, rather than reviewing every text in the table. We are especially interested to note how Swami Dayanand's own quotation of authorities in Table 3 compares with his theory of authoritative works, which has already been discussed.

On first reading it may appear that Swami Dayanand's practice in quoting authorities is not very consistent with his principles as to which works are worthy of study. Thirty-two of the texts that Dayanand quotes are in his lists of books to be studied, while a full twenty-four works that he quotes are not in the lists. It might seem that Dayanand quotes a great deal in his own writings from texts that are not included in his discussion of authoritative books. There are several points worthy of mention here in mitigation of this impression.

It is important to realize that Swami Dayanand quotes much more frequently from books that are included in his lists of authoritative works than he quotes from books not in the lists. Out of a total of fifty-six works quoted in *Satyārth Prakāś* and *Ṛgvedādibhāṣyabhūmikā*, twenty-four are not mentioned in the lists of texts to be studied or almost 43 per cent. In both Dayanand's books taken together there are a total of 1,702 verses quoted. Of this total only sixty-seven verses are taken from writings not explicitly mentioned in the lists of works to be studied, or less than 4 per cent. While almost half of the books quoted by Swami Dayanand are not included in his enumeration of authoritative works, only 4 per cent of the total verses cited are from those books. Thus 96 per cent of the verses cited are from texts included in the lists of authoritative works.

Also it should be noted that Swami Dayanand does not cite the source of every verse that he quotes in his works.[60] Dayanand made an effort to identify the sources of his quotations, including chapter and verse numbers. Still, many quotes are not accompanied by a reference.

It is very probable that Dayanand himself did not know the source of some of these quotes. Some he must have written out from memory without being able to recall the source, or perhaps without having ever known what the source was, having only heard the passage out of context. The point here is that Dayanand might have made some quotes without knowing for certain whether they were from books in the lists of works to be studied or not.

Of the sources quoted in *Satyārth Prakāś* and *Ṛgvedādibhāṣya-bhūmikā* which do not belong to the lists of books to be read, the following are referred to with a specific citation by Swami Dayanand: *Pāraskara Gṛhya Sutras*,[61] *Vārttika*,[62] *Uṇādi Sūtras*,[63] *Paribhāṣāvṛtti Sīradeva*,[64] *Vedanta Sutras Śaṅkara Bhāṣya*,[65] *Kaivalaya Upanishad*,[66] *Māṇḍūkya Upanishad Gauṛapādīyā Kārikā*,[67] *Śvetāśvatara Upanishad*,[68] *Ṛg Veda Khila*,[69] *Pratijñā Pariśiṣṭa*,[70] *Taittirīya Āraṇyaka*,[71] *Aitareya Āraṇyaka*,[72] *Āpastamba Dharma Sūtras*,[73] *Cāṇakyanīti*,[74] and Bhartṛhari's *Nītiśataka*.[75] Thus only fifteen texts which are not specifically mentioned in the lists of works to be studied are quoted by Dayanand with at least one definite reference. This is a modest number of texts compared with the total number cited.

It could be argued that some of the works quoted by Swami Dayanand which are not explicitly included in the lists of works to be studied are implicitly included. For example, in *Saṃskār Vidhi* Dayanand is not very specific about what books should be studied with the Vedas. No mention is made of the Aranyakas anywhere in Dayanand's lists, but perhaps he intended that they should be studied as a part of Vedic literature in his curriculum in *Saṃskār Vidhi*. Other texts might in this way be subsumed into Dayanand's lists.

Swami Dayanand only quotes one verse approvingly that is drawn from a work in the lists of books that are ~~not~~ to be read, that is, *Śārṅgadhara*.[76] It is significant that the swami does not identify the source of this quote. It is a testimony to the consistency of Dayanand's practice with his theory that this is the only verse that he quotes approvingly from a work that is also condemned in the lists of works that are unauthoritative. One out of 1,702.

It is interesting to consider the proportion of verses quoted from different groups of disciplines from the lists of authoritative works. These proportions are presented in Table 4.

TABLE 4

VERSES QUOTED BY DAYANAND FROM GROUPS AS A PROPORTION OF ALL VERSES QUOTED FROM AUTHORITATIVE WORKS

Group	*Satyārth Prakāś*	*Ṛgvedādibhāṣyabhūmikā*
Vedangas	11%	23%
Kavya	55	4
Upāṅgas	12	15
Upanishads	7	5
Vedas	12	37
Brahmanas	2	15
Upavedas	1	0[a]

[a] The total here is not 100 per cent because of rounding.

A significant proportion of quotes are from the Vedas in both *Satyārth Prakāś* and *Ṛgvedādibhāṣyabhūmikā*. In *Ṛgvedādibhāṣyabhūmikā* the Vedas are quoted more than any other group of texts. This is to be expected since *Ṛgvedādibhāṣyabhūmikā* is an introduction to Dayanand's Vedic commentaries, and explains his philosophy specifically with respect to the Vedas. In *Satyārth Prakāś* where Dayanand's exposition is not tied to any book or group of books the Vedas are not quoted so heavily. In *Satyārth Prakāś* there is not the very strong emphasis on the Vedas that one might expect to find given Dayanand's theory of their unique inerrancy.

Among the Vedas the most frequently quoted in both *Satyārth Prakāś* and *Ṛgvedādibhāṣyabhūmikā* is the Yajur Veda. The texts of the Ṛg Veda and the Atharva Veda are much longer than the Yajur Veda. The Ṛg Veda contains over ten thousand mantras and the Atharva Veda is composed of over five thousand mantras, while the Yajur Veda has around two thousand mantras. Still, about half of the Vedic mantras quoted in *Satyārth Prakāś* and *Ṛgvedādibhāṣyabhūmikā* are from the Yajur Veda. Swami Dayanand was trained in the Yajur Veda as a boy by his father.[77] He planned to write commentaries on all four of the Vedas, but was only able to complete the Yajur Vedic commentary before his death.[78] Dayanand was in the process of commenting on the Ṛg Veda when he died, and his commentary is available through Ṛg Veda 7.60. Despite the formidable amount of work on the Ṛg Veda that Dayanand did complete during his lifetime, the Yajur Veda is still preferred in his quotations.[79]

In *Satyārth Prakāś* the predominant group in terms of total number of verses quoted is Kavya. Of the Kavya texts the work that is important is *Manu*. Only twenty-two verses are quoted from the *Mahābhārata*, and none from the *Rāmāyaṇa*, while a staggering 408 verses are quoted from *Manu*. Over half of the verses quoted from authoritative works in *Satyārth Prakāś* are from *Manu*. Although *Saṃskār Vidhi* will not be analyzed here, it is worth noting that in the general passages in that work *Manu* is relied upon heavily. Particularly in the chapter on the duties of the householder *Manu* is important.[80] One gets the impression from *Satyārth Prakāś* and *Saṃskār Vidhi* that *Manu* is a major source for Dayanand. It is interesting that *Manu* does not play such a significant role in *Ṛgvedādibhāṣyabhūmikā*.

Having said something about the groups most heavily cited, a word should be added about the least quoted group, the *Upaveda*s. It was noted in the previous section that though the curricula for the *Upaveda*s are very broadly defined, they are also very vague. To this assertion may now be added the observation that Swami Dayanand in his major works hardly quotes from the *Upaveda*s at all. In both Dayanand's lists of authoritative works and among the books that he quotes the *Upaveda*s are a kind of empty set.

These are some of the salient points that emerge from consideration of Table 3. Now we will go on to discuss works heavily quoted in specific contexts in *Satyārth Prakāś* and *Ṛgvedādibhāṣyabhūmikā*.

SOURCES QUOTED HEAVILY BY DAYANAND IN SPECIFIC CONTEXTS

In both *Satyārth Prakāś* and *Ṛgvedādibhāṣyabhūmikā* there are passages in which Swami Dayanand offers a long series of quotations from a single work. It is interesting to look at these passages. They shed some light on what texts are important for Dayanand, and how he uses the authorities that he quotes.

In the first chapter of *Satyārth Prakāś* Swami Dayanand explains the many names that are used to refer to God. In general he explains each divine name with reference to the verb root from which it is derived. The verb roots are cited here as found in the *Dhātupāṭha*, though there is no explicit mention of that text. In all seventy-four roots are cited in just twenty-six pages.[81] This chapter is a fine example of the way the Dayanand reinterprets the Hindu tradition. The list of divine names includes many that are generally regarded as referring to different divinities—Agni, Vāyu, and so forth. Yet Dayanand takes all these names as referring to the one God of his monotheistic theology. He interprets the different names as stressing the various aspects of this one God. In this process the use of the *Dhātupāṭha* is very important. By interpreting the names etymologically Dayanand considers only the connotation of the words, and not the traditional understanding of the words as names denoting individual divine beings. There are no further references to the *Dhātupāṭha* in *Satyārth Prakāś*, but there are several quotes from that text in *Ṛgvedādibhāṣyabhūmikā*. The *Dhātupāṭha* is a limited but very powerful tool in Dayanand's reinterpretation of the Hindu tradition.

The *Vaisheshika Sutras* are heavily quoted in the third chapter of *Satyārth Prakāś*. This chapter is a broad one, concerned with what is to be studied and taught. In the context in question Swami Dayanand is explaining certain basic aspects of philosophy. The *Vaisheshika Sutras* are quoted in a discussion of substances and qualities (*dravya* and guna). Here Dayanand quotes forty-seven sutras practically in a string.[82] Clearly in this technical area Dayanand is dependent on this one text. The *Vaisheshika Sutras* are quoted only a few times in *Satyārth Prakāś* other than in the immediate context, and there only a handful of references to these sutras in *Ṛgvedādibhāṣyabhūmikā*. The use of the *Vaisheshika Sutras* is less interesting than that of the *Dhātupāṭha*. The sutras are used to explain a traditional topic in the traditional way.

Swami Dayanand set forth his philosophy of statecraft in the sixth chapter of *Satyārth Prakāś*. Here the law code of *Manu* has pride of place, with 189 verses quoted in just fifty pages.[83] In this chapter other sources are quoted, but none to any considerable extent. *Manu* is quoted many times in *Satyārth Prakāś* outside this chapter, and is quoted a significant number of times in *Ṛgvedādibhāṣyabhūmikā* as well.

It is interesting to note that *Manu* does not occupy such an important place in *Ṛgvedādibhāṣyabhūmikā* as it does in *Satyārth Prakāś*. *Manu* is not quoted even once in the brief chapter in *Ṛgvedādibhāṣyabhūmikā* on statecraft.[84] The difference is partly one of focus. *Ṛgvedādibhāṣyabhūmikā* is a work specifically on the Vedas. In the chapter on statecraft in *Ṛgvedādibhāṣyabhūmikā* Swami Dayanand is not so concerned with providing a complete plan for the state as he is in explaining what the Vedas have to say on this topic. In *Satyārth Prakāś*, where the discussion is not bound to any text, *Manu* comes into its own as a natural guide in matters of state. It is a testimony to Swami Dayanand's originality that the sources that he quotes heavily are quite different in *Satyārth Prakāś* and *Ṛgvedādibhāṣyabhūmikā*.

In *Ṛgvedādibhāṣyabhūmikā* there are two places where the Yajur Veda is quoted in an especially regular fashion. The chapter on the creation of the world consists largely of a commentary on the "Puruṣa Sūkta."[85] And in the chapter on the five great sacrifices (*pañcamahāyajña*) Dayanand quotes heavily from the Yajur Veda.[86]

The "Puruṣa Sūkta" is found in Ṛg Veda 10.90 and Yajur Veda 31 with textual variations. It is the version of the Yajur Veda that Dayanand follows here. In the "Puruṣa Sūkta" the creation of the world is described as the sacrifice of a primeval person, the purusha. Philosophical commentators have offered various explanations of this primeval person, some opining that he is a sort of demiurge. Dayanand's own interpretation is that this is none other than the supreme being. Consistent with this view Dayanand reinterprets Yajur Veda 31.14. In this mantra the body of the primeval person is transformed through the sacrifice into the parts of the cosmos. In Dayanand's theology there is no room for any sacrifice of God, and he interprets the passage to mean that sacrifices are performed with materials given by God. The swami also reads this mantra as referring to the past, the present, and the future. For Dayanand it is not that one sacrifice occurred in the past, but that sacrifices have occurred in the past, do occur in the present, and should continue to occur in the future. By this interpretation Swami Dayanand rather undoes the image of the cosmogonic self-sacrifice of the primeval person which is central to this hymn. Still, his interpretation does serve to make the hymn consistent with his philosophy as a whole.

In the short section on the *pitṛyajña* in the chapter on the five great sacrifices in *Ṛgvedādibhāṣyabhūmikā* Dayanand relies heavily on Yajur Veda 19, quoting eighteen verses in sixteen pages. It should be noted that according to Dayanand not all of the five great sacrifices are sacrifices in the narrow sense of the term. Specifically the *pitṛyajña* and the *atithiyajña* involve service to others and are devoid of ritual. Traditionally the *pitṛ*s ("fathers"), who are the objects of the *pitṛyajña*, are regarded as the manes of the sponsor of the sacrifice. Dayanand argued that the *pitṛyajña* should only be performed for the living, for one's elders and those who are learned or virtuous. In support of this notion Dayanand goes through some of the mantras of the nineteenth chapter of the Yajur Veda which contains an invocation of the *pitṛs*. Dayanand reinterprets these mantras consistent with his own belief as to what the meaning of *pitṛ* is.

These two passages from the Yajur Veda are quoted at length by Dayanand to demonstrate his reinterpretation of them. As will be noted later, Dayanand's procedure here is unique. In the case of the other sources that he quotes extensively in specific contexts there is no example of a text being quoted to be reinterpreted.

The *Yoga Sutras* enjoy great importance in Swami Dayanand's discussion of *upāsanā*, or worship, in *Ṛgvedādibhāṣyabhūmikā*. Here Dayanand quotes fifty-one sutras, often following the order of the original text.[87] In this context Dayanand frequently reproduces Vyāsa's commentary on individual sutras. Throughout *Ṛgvedādibhāṣyabhūmikā* Dayanand quotes an original text and then comments on that text in Sanskrit, which is followed by a Hindi translation of his commentary. In this chapter the system breaks down. For several sutras Dayanand quotes Vyāsa's commentary, but does not offer any comment.[88] It is noteworthy that Swami Dayanand regarded Vyāsa's commentary as so clear and consistent with his own approach that it could be quoted without comment. Nevertheless Vyāsa is not quoted outside this chapter in *Ṛgvedādibhāṣyabhūmikā*, and he is not quoted at all in *Satyārth Prakāś*. There are only a few other references to the *Yoga Sutras* in *Ṛgvedādibhāṣyabhūmikā*. There are several citations to the *Yoga Sutras* scattered throughout *Satyārth Prakāś*. Dayanand's interpretation of the *Yoga Sutras* is not very different from the traditional understanding.[89]

Finally in the chapter on grammar in *Ṛgvedādibhāṣyabhūmikā* the crucial work is Pāṇini's *Aṣṭādhyāyī*. Here fifty-seven sutras are quoted from that grammar in the explanation of Vedic usage.[90] To explicate Pāṇini's text Dayanand frequently quotes the *Mahābhāṣya*, Patañjali's commentary on the *Aṣṭādhyāyī*. There are also a few references to the *Vārttikas*, another layer of commentary on Pāṇini's sutras. There are several other references to the *Aṣṭādhyāyī* to be found in other contexts in *Ṛgvedādibhāṣyabhūmikā*. Only a few quotes from this great grammatical work are to be found in *Satyārth Prakāś*. It is understandable that in a book that is more technical such as *Ṛgvedādibhāṣyabhūmikā* there would be more references to the *Aṣṭādhyāyī*. This is especially true since the central texts of *Ṛgvedādibhāṣyabhūmikā* are the Vedas, which are difficult books with many grammatical anomalies. Dayanand wrote a partial commentary on the *Aṣṭādhyāyī*, which is a further indication of his interest in that work.[91] Still, his understanding of that text was not revolutionary.

In most of these passages Dayanand quotes a traditionally respected work with an interpretation which is not inconsistent with the way that work is traditionally understood. This is basically true of the passages discussed on the *Vaisheshika Sutras*, *Manu*, the *Yoga Sutras*, and the *Aṣṭādhyāyī*. Dayanand's use of the *Dhātupāṭha* as a lexical aid is not unusual, but the conclusions that he reaches with the help of the *Dhātupāṭha* are very original indeed. The *Dhātupāṭha* is not Dayanand's subject in the context referred to here, rather it is a tool used to analyze his subject. In the passages described on the Yajur Veda Dayanand's interpretation of that text differs quite radically from the traditional understanding. Dayanand goes through the text verse by verse to argue for the plausibility of his interpretation. These few passages give some idea of the variety of ways that the traditional authorities are used by Swami Dayanand.

In conclusion of this section only three points must be made. The analysis of the sources which Dayanand quotes reveals that his quotations are generally consistent with his lists of authoritative and unauthoritative works described in the preceding section of this chapter. Several works are quoted which are not in Dayanand's lists, but the number of verses quoted from these works is very small. Various arguments might be advanced to account for several of even these few quotes. Swami Dayanand generally quotes from books in his lists of authoritative works.

The second point is that Dayanand's usage is less consistent with the theory regarding the unique authority of the Vedas described in the first section of this chapter. The Vedas are quoted by Dayanand, but not to the degree that one might expect given their special status. Based on Dayanand's practice in quoting it seems clear that the foundation for this philosophy is the *ārṣa* literature and the Vedas taken as a whole. The Vedas do not have any outstanding prominence, but are quoted along with the *ārṣa* texts. In other words, the difference between the *anārṣa* and *ārṣa* literature is very marked when one considers the authorities that Dayanand quotes. The difference between the Vedas and the *ārṣa* literature is not marked.

Finally among the contexts in which one source is heavily quoted there are two passages where Dayanand quotes extensively from the Yajur Veda. In both cases Dayanand offers an interpretation of the passage which differs strikingly from the traditional understanding. These are the only occasions among those discussed in this section where Dayanand felt it was necessary to reinterpret the source. In terms of the overall pattern of quotations the Vedas do not stand out against the *ārṣa* literature. Yet on the basis of the passages where one source is extensively quoted, the Vedas are different. The traditional understanding of the *ārṣa* texts is accepted by Dayanand, but the Vedas must be reinterpreted.

FUNDAMENTALIST SCRIPTURALISM AND THE ARYA SAMAJ

In this chapter we have seen further evidence of the similarity in the area of scripture between the Arya Samaj and the Christian and Islamic fundamentalist movements described earlier. All three groups base themselves on an inerrant religious text. The infallible authority according to Bob Jones University is the Bible. In the Jama'at-i Islami it is the Qur'an. For Arya Samajists it is the Vedas. Despite this common element, it should be noted that in the theory of Maulana Maududi and Swami Dayanand there are religious texts of a secondary character which are admitted to be reliable to a limited extent. Christian fundamentalists in their eagerness to demonstrate the centrality of the Bible to their faith have been much less willing to confess the authority of any other book.

This is not to say that all of the beliefs of North American Protestant fundamentalism are explicitly articulated in the Bible. James Barr has argued that support for the doctrine of the trinity, for example, is not very great even in the New Testament. This idea was only fully developed in the patristic period and later. But most Christian fundamentalists do not quote the church fathers, so their debt to the tradition on this point is not noted.[92] The desire of North American Protestant fundamentalists to demonstrate that their theology is based on the one unimpeachable book precludes an admission of the significance of other sources.

According to the data presented in this chapter a similar strategy is manifest in the writings of Swami Dayanand. Theoretically the Vedas are the only texts which are inerrant. The Vedas are the source of all truth, such that anything good which is found in the *ārṣa* literature is only a reflection of the Vedas. Yet the great distinctiveness of the Vedas in principle is not so obvious in practice. In Dayanand's curricula there does not seem to be a singular focus on the Vedas. The swami's major works contain more quotes from *ārṣa* books than the infallible Vedas. As in the case of North American Protestant fundamentalism, the Arya Samaj maintains that its teachings are derived from the one perfect authority, while the importance of other works goes unacknowledged.

NOTES

1. Swami Dayanand Sarasvati, "The Autobiography of Dayanand Saraswati, Swami" *Theosophist*, November 1880, 25. I have retained the italics and spelling of the original. Dayanand's autobiographical fragments appeared in the *Theosophist* in three installments (in October 1879, December 1879, and November 1880). A small book was recently published including a facsimile of handwritten manuscripts of the first two installments of the autobiography in Hindi dating back to Dayanand's time (either written entirely in his hand or with corrections by him). Swami Ḍayanand Sarasvati, *Ātma-Kathā,* Maharṣi Dayānand-Nirvāṇ-Śatābdī Saṃskaraṇ (Ajmer: Vaidik Pustakālay, 1983). Because Dayanand did not know English, someone else must have translated his Hindi original for the *Theosophist.* So these manuscripts are an important guide to what Dayanand actually wrote. Unfortunately the editors were not able to locate a manuscript for the third installment, which contains the story in our text. Since the Hindi original is not available, perhaps the English translation of the *Theosophist* is the closest that we can come to Dayanand's version of this event.
2. This explanation accounts for the "Narichakars" in the *Theosophist:* Narichakar = *nāḍī* + *cakra*. I am less sure what is meant by "Narichakant." Judging by the titles of the works which are mentioned, the translator's method of transliterating Devanagari is difficult. I might add that *kamal*, which usually means lotus, in the context of hatha-yoga refers to the centers of energy (which are sometimes depicted as shaped like a lotus). Without seeing Dayanand's original Hindi it is hard to come to any certain conclusion, but it seems that "heart" is a very misleading translation for *kamal*.
3. Jordens in several places discusses the development of Dayanand's views with regard to Hindu scripture (e.g., Jordens, *Dayānanda Sarasvatī*, 54-59). We will concern ourselves here only with the swami's mature thought, which is the basis of the teachings of the Arya Samaj.
4. The translation is my own. The original reads: "Ved satyavidyāoṃ kā pustak hai. Ved kā paṛhnā paṛhānā aur sunnā sunānā sab āryyoṃ kā param dharm hai." Lekh Rām, *Jīvancaritra: Maharṣi Swāmī Dayānand Sarasvatī*, ed. Bhavānīlāl Bhārtīy, trans. Raghunandansiṃh, 2d printing (Delhi: Ārṣ Sāhitya Pracār Trust, Vikram Saṃvat 2041), 329. See the note on this *niyam* in the previous chapter for an interpolation that has crept into it over time. Observe that the Vedas are the only works mentioned in the ten *niyams*, the *ārṣa* literature is nowhere to be found in them.

5. For more detail on Dayanand's theory of history see the subsection "Fundamentalism as Antievolutionary" in Chapter 2.
6. Dayanand, *Satyārth Prakāś*, 313-314.
7. Idem, *Ṛgvedādibhāṣyabhūmikā*, in *Ṛgveda-Bhāṣyam*, vol. 1, 19.
8. Idem, *Satyārth Prakāś*, 315-316.
9. Ibid., 315.
10. Dayanand makes the crucial distinction between works that are *svataḥ pramāṇa* and those that are *parataḥ pramāṇa* in *Ṛgvedādibhāṣyabhūmikā* (p. 316) and in *Satyārth Prakāś* (p. 120).
11. The term *ārṣa* is used by Dayanand in *Ṛgvedādibhāṣyabhūmikā* on p. 321.
12. Dayanand, *Satyārth Prakāś*, 119.
13. In *Satyārth Prakāś* Dayanand writes that in the case of one *ārṣa* text, *The Laws of Manu*, only the interpolated *ślokas* are not worthy of study. Dayanand, *Satyārth Prakāś*, 120-121. It seems clear that at least in the case of *Manu* Dayanand believed that the text was originally totally perfect, and it is only later interpolators who have introduced errors into the text. Perhaps Dayanand believed that all the *ārṣa* literature was once perfectly free of error. Compare the following passage in *Ṛgvedādibhāṣyabhūmikā*: "In this way the system of rule along with councils continued to operate up to the honorable maharaja Yuddhiṣṭhir, the testimony to which is accurately written in books of the *Mahābhārata* about the dharma of rajas and so forth and in scriptures on dharma [*dharmaśāstra*] such as *Manusmṛti* and so forth. In them some things have been interpolated [*prakṣipt*], leaving aside that everything else is good." Dayanand, *Ṛgvedādibhāṣyabhūmikā*, in *Ṛgveda-Bhāṣyam*, vol. 1, 273. This would seem to indicate that both *Manu* and the *Mahābhārata* were wholly reliable, until material was added later. But note that this text is only present in the Hindi of *Ṛgvedādibhāṣyabhūmikā* (which was written by pandits in Dayanand's employ) and not in the Sanskrit (which was written by the swami himself).
14. Dayanand, *Ṛgvedādibhāṣyabhūmikā*, in *Ṛgvedā-Bhāṣyam* vol. 1, 316.
15. Idem, *Satyārth Prakāś*, 119.
16. Ibid., 122.
17. The word *apramāṇa* is used in *Ṛgvedādibhāṣyabhūmikā* by Dayanand on p. 322.
18. Jones has written, "*Ārsha* texts included the Vedas and all others written while Vedic scholarship still persisted." Jones, *Arya Dharm*, 31. Here I have argued that the Vedas fall into a separate category from the *ārṣa* literature. The key passage on this question runs as follows: "Eta īśvaroktā Vedās tadvyākhyānamayā

Brāhmaṇādayo granthā ārṣā Vedānukūlāḥ satyadharmavidyāyuktā yuktipramāṇasiddhā eva mānanīyāḥ santi." Dayanand, *Ṛgvedādibhāṣyabhūmikā*, in *Ṛgvedā-Bhāṣyam*, vol. 1, 321. I would translate this sentence: "The Vedas, which were composed by God, and the works such as the Brahmanas, which are commentaries on the Vedas, which were composed by the rishis [that is, which are *ārṣa*], which are consistent with the Vedas, which are bound to the knowledge of true religion, and which are proven by arguments and authorities, they [the Vedas and the *ārṣa* works] are to be accepted." According to this reading, *ārṣa* in this sentence is only one of a long string of qualifications of the works which should be regarded as authoritative *other than the Vedas*. Note that the second of the rules adopted at the founding of the Bombay Arya Samaj in 1875 makes a distinction between the Vedas and *ārṣa* literature. Lekh Rām, *Jīvancaritra: Maharṣi Swāmī Dayānand Sarasvatī*, ed. Bhavānīlāl Bhārtīy, trans. Raghunandansiṃh, 2d printing (Delhi: Ārṣ Sāhitya Pracār Trust, Vikram Saṃvat 2041), 255.

19. Dayanand, *Ṛgvedādibhāṣyabhūmikā*, in *Ṛgvedā-Bhāṣyam*, vol. 1, 94.
20. The most important class of literature that Dayanand regarded as wrongly attributed to a rishi is the Puranas, as we will discuss below.
21. Dayanand, *Satyārth Prakāś*, 49-51.
22. Idem, *Ṛgvedādibhāṣyabhūmikā*, in *Ṛgvedā-Bhāṣyam*, vol. 1, 316. Similar light imagery is used to describe the authority of the Vedas by the Vedic commentator Sāyaṇa and the Vedanta philosopher Śaṅkara. For Sāyaṇa see *Ṛgveda-Saṃhitā*, ed. N. S. Sontakke and T.N. Dharmadhikari, 2d ed. (Pune: Vaidika Saṃśodhana Maṇḍala, 1972), 1: 3-4. For Śaṅkara see his commentary on *Vedanta Sutras* 2.1.1, in J. Muir, *Original Sanskrit Texts on the Origin and History of the People of India, Their Religion and Institutions*, vol. 3, *The Vedas: Opinions of Their Authors and of Later Indian Writers on Their Origin, Inspiration, and Authority*, 2d ed. (London: Truebner, 1873), 187.
23. *Satyārth Prakāś* and *Ṛgvedādibhāṣyabhūmikā* have already been cited. The full reference for the third work is Swami Dayanand Sarasvati, *Saṃskāra-Vidhiḥ* [Rules of rituals], ed. Yudhiṣṭhir Mīmāṃsak, Āryasamāj-Śatābdī-Saṃskaraṇ (Bahalgarh [Sonipat]: Ram Lal Kapoor Trust, 1974). In English there is *The Sanskar Vidhi (The Procedure of the Sacraments) of Swami Dayanand Saraswati*, trans. Vaidyanath Shastri (Delhi: Sārvadeśik Ārya Pratinidhi Sabhā, n.d. [The "Publisher's Note," dated 1985, identifies this as the 2d ed.]).

24. Dayanand, *Satyārth Prakāś*, 110-119; idem, *Ṛgvedādibhāṣya-bhūmikā*, in *Ṛgvedā-Bhāṣyam*, vol. 1, 316-319; idem, *Saṃskār Vidhi*, 129-132.
25. "Atha Granthaprāmāṇyāprāmānyaviṣayaḥ," is how the chapter is headed. Dayanand, *Ṛgvedādibhāṣyabhūmikā*, in *Ṛgvedā-Bhāṣyam*, vol. 1, 316.
26. See Jordens, *Dayānanda Sarasvatī*, 32-39 on Dayanand's guru Virjānand.
27. The reference to the *Avyayārtha* of Āptamuni may not be to a specific work. *Avyayārtha* may only refer to the topic; and *āptamuni* may not be the name of an individual, but may refer to a class of people, "accomplished ascetics" (which is what *āptamuni* literally means).
28. In *Satyārth Prakāś* Dayanand presents evidence of interpolations in the *Mahābhārata*. Dayanand, *Satyārth Prakāś*, 468.
29. Dayanand, *Satyārth Prakāś*, 115.
30. Idem, *Ṛgvedādibhāṣyabhūmikā*, in *Ṛgvedā-Bhāṣyam*, vol. 1, 321.
31. Idem, *Satyārth Prakāś*, 118.
32. Idem, *Ṛgvedādibhāṣyabhūmikā*, in *Ṛgvedā-Bhāṣyam*, vol. 1, 319.
33. Idem, *Saṃskār Vidhi*, 131.
34. Arya Samajists criticize both Śaṅkara and Rammohun Roy for stopping short at the Upanishads and not penetrating to the Vedic Samhitas in their studies.
35. Dayanand's curricula in *Satyārth Prakāś* and *Saṃskār Vidhi* include some notes on the length of time that should be devoted to each discipline. In *Satyārth Prakāś* he allots four years each to the study of Ayur Veda and *Dhanur Veda*. No time limits are mentioned for the other two *Upavedas*. Dayanand, *Satyārth Prakāś*, 117-118. In *Saṃskār Vidhi* Dayanand recommends three years each for the study of Ayur Veda, *Dhanur Veda*, and *Gāndharva Veda*, and six years for the study of *Artha Veda*, for a hefty total of fifteen years to be spent on the *Upavedas*. Dayanand, *Saṃskār Vidhi*, 132.
36. "Jaise *Suśrut* meṃ śastra likhe haiṃ, banākar śarīr ke sab avayavoṃ ko cīr ke dekheṃ, tathā jo us meṃ śārīrakādi vidyā likhī haiṃ, sakṣāt kareṃ." Dayanand, *Saṃskār Vidhi*, 132. Yudhiṣṭhir Mīmāṃsak, an important scholar on Dayanand and the editor of this edition of *Saṃskār Vidhi*, adds a curious footnote. He points out that some later editions have *śārīrika* in place of *śārīraka*. Mīmāṃsak rejects this reading, because "Another name for the *Vedanta Sutras* is the *Śārīraka Sutras*, not the *Śārīrika Sutras*." (*Saṃskār Vidhi*, 132, n. 2). But surely it is a question here not of an alias for the *Vedanta Sutras*, but of texts having to do with the body. On this point either *śārīraka* or *śārīrika* is possible, as both are adjectives meaning "bodily" from the noun *śarīra*

"body." Sir Monier Monier-Williams, *A Sanskrit-English Dictionary*, rev. ed. (Oxford: Clarendon Press, 1979), 1066.

37. The masculine and feminine pronouns are used advisedly here. In opposition to traditional Hindus, Dayanand affirmed that girls as well as boys should be allowed to study the Vedas. (See, for example, Dayanand, *Satyārth Prakāś*, 124-128.) As Kenneth Jones notes the Arya Samaj was a leader in women's education in Punjab, but there was an emotionally charged debate in the Samaj over whether primary education for girls was sufficient or more should be offered. (Jones, *Arya Dharm*, 103-108.) The time when women might enter the medical profession in India was, of course, still distant in Dayanand's day.
38. Dayanand, *Satyārth Prakāś*, 117-118.
39. "Parantu bhaḍuve veśyā aur viṣayāsaktikārak vairāgiyoṃ ke gardabhaśabdavat vyarth ālāp kabhī na kareṃ." Dayanand, *Satyārth Prakāś*, 118.
40. That is, "vimān, tār, bhūgarbhādi vidyāoṃ." Dayanand, *Saṃkār Vidhi*, 132.
41. Dayanand, *Satyārth Prakāś*, 110-121; idem, *Ṛgvedādibhāṣyabhūmikā*, in *Ṛgvedā-Bhāṣyam*, vol. 1, 321-322.
42. Idem, *Ṛgvedādibhāṣyabhūmikā*, in *Ṛgvedā-Bhāṣyam*, vol. 1, 321.
43. Idem, *Satyārth Prakāś*, 114.
44. Ibid., 115.
45. Claus Vogel, *Indian Lexicography*, A History of Indian Literature, ed. Jan Gonda, vol. 5, fascicle 4 (Wiesbaden: Otto Harrassowitz, 1979), 310.
46. The text reads "muhūrttajanmapatraphalādeśavidhāyakāḥ." Mīmāṃsak's edition has *mūhūrtta-* (Dayanand, *Ṛgvedādibhāṣyabhūmikā*, in *Ṛgvedā-Bhāṣyam*, vol. 1, 321) while another generally reliable edition reads *muhūrtta-* (Swami Dayanand Sarasvati, *Dayānand-Granthmālā*, Nirvāṇ-Śatābdī-Saṃskaraṇ, 2d reprint [Ajmer: Paropkāriṇī Sabhā, 1983], vol. 2, 543). The latter reading is, of course, the likely one.
47. Dayanand, *Satyārth Prakāś*, 120-121; idem, *Ṛgvedādibhāṣyabhūmikā*, in *Ṛgvedā-Bhāṣyam*, vol. 1, 321.
48. Idem, *Satyārth Prakāś*, 441-444.
49. Similarly Maulana Maududi regarded the *vāmamārga* as the source of sexually licentious practices in Hinduism. "These are indeed the impious remnants of the movement started by Bam-marg, which spread like plague in India at the zenith of her civilization." Maulana S. Abu'l-A'la Maududi, *Purdah and the Status of Woman in Islam*, trans. and ed. al-Ash'ari, 2d ed. (Lahore: Islamic Publications, 1975), 16.
50. Dayanand, *Satyārth Prakāś*, 514-530.

51. Idem, *Ṛgvedādibhāṣyabhūmikā*, in *Ṛgvedā-Bhāṣyam*, vol. 1, 321.
52. Ibid.
53. Idem, *Satyārth Prakāś*, 627-740.
54. Ibid., 315.
55. Ibid., 121.
56. By the same token, among the signs of increasing degeneracy in Islamic kingdoms after the rightly guided caliphs Maulana Maududi noted that "fine arts like dancing, music, and painting which are strictly un-Islamic found patronage from those who had been forbidden to practise these 'ugly' arts." Maulana S. Abu'l-A'la Maududi, *A Short History of the Revivalist Movement in Islam*, trans. al-Ash'ari, 2d rev. ed. (Lahore: Islamic Publications, 1972), 29.
57. All the numbers in this section are based on my own reckoning.
58. Dayanand, *Satyārth Prakāś*, 425-950.
59. Ibid., 951-961.
60. I am indebted to Dayanand's editors, especially Yudhiṣṭhir Mīmāṃsak, for the work that they have done in tracking down Dayanand's quotes.
61. Dayanand, *Ṛgvedādibhāṣyabhūmikā*, in *Ṛgvedā-Bhāṣyam*, vol. 1, 340.
62. Ibid., 237, 407, 416.
63. Ibid., 230.
64. Ibid., 411.
65. Ibid., 41
66. Idem, *Satyārth Prakāś*, 17.
67. Ibid., 330.
68. Ibid., p. 293; idem, *Ṛgvedādibhāṣyabhūmikā*, in *Ṛgvedā-Bhāṣyam*, vol. 1, 22-23.
69. Idem, *Ṛgvedādibhāṣyabhūmikā*, in *Ṛgvedā-Bhāṣyam*, vol. 1, 344.
70. Idem, *Satyārth Prakāś*, 318.
71. Ibid., 68; idem, *Ṛgvedādibhāṣyabhūmikā*, in *Ṛgvedā-Bhāṣyam*, vol. 1, 1, 49, 123-124, 127, and 128-129.
72. Idem, *Ṛgvedādibhāṣyabhūmikā*, in *Ṛgvedā-Bhāṣyam*, vol. 1, 98.
73. Idem, *Satyārth Prakāś*, 146, 412; idem, *Ṛgvedādibhāṣyabhūmikā*, in *Ṛgvedā-Bhāṣyam*, vol. 1, 360.
74. Idem, *Satyārth Prakāś*, 218.
75. Ibid., 952.
76. Ibid., 415.
77. Jordens, *Dayānanda Sarasvatī*, 4.
78. Some of the text was only published posthumously.
79. This evidence contradicts Arvind Sharma's contention that Dayanand came to "focus on the Saṃhitā and especially on the *Ṛgveda-saṃhitā* alone." Arvind Sharma, "Svami Dayananda

Sarasvati and Vedic Authority," in *Religion in Modern India*, ed. Robert E. Baird (Delhi: Manohar, 1981), 182. Dayanand did emphasize the Vedas in his later works, but there is no distinction made between the four Samhitas on a theoretical level, and it is actually the Yajur Veda which is more prominent in Dayanand's quotes. Sharma's source here is R. C. Majumdar, general ed., *British Paramountcy and Indian Renaissance*, part 2, History and Culture of the Indian People, vol. 10 (Bombay: Bharatiya Vidya Bhavan, 1965), 112. Majumdar in turn cites Bipin Chandra Pal, *Memories of My Life and Times* (Calcutta: Yugayatri Prakashak, 1951), vol. 2, 77-78. Pal in his description of Dayanand's writings admits that he is relying upon his memory (on p. 78). Pal wrote his memoirs near the end of his life (he died in 1932), and his account of the Arya Samaj is based on experiences in Punjab that he had several decades earlier (while residing in Lahore from 1889 to 1890). When he lists Dayanand's writings Pal mentions the swami's commentary on the Ṛg Veda but not the commentary on the Yajur Veda. Apparently Pal's memory did not serve him well on this detail, and his assertion that Dayanand's teaching was based on "particularly the Rigveda-Samhita" (on pp. 77-78) is simply an historical error.

80. This chapter is headed, "Atha Gṛhāśramasaṃskāravidhiṃ Vakṣyāmaḥ." Dayanand, *Saṃskār Vidhi*, 211-221.
81. Dayanand, *Satyārth Prakāś*, 99-108.
82. Ibid., 22-47.
83. Ibid., 220-269.
84. Idem, *Ṛgvedādibhāṣyabhūmikā*, in *Ṛgvedā-Bhāṣyam*, vol. 1, 255-273.
85. Ibid., 137-152.
86. Ibid., 294-310.
87. Ibid., 191-207.
88. See Dayanand's discussion of *Yoga Sutras* 1.25, 1.26, 1.27, and 1.28, for example. Dayanand, *Ṛgvedādibhāṣyabhūmikā*, in *Ṛgvedā-Bhāṣyam*, vol. 1, 196.
89. Dayanand's yoga is original in that it is based solely on the *Yoga Sutras* and Vyāsa's commentary. Dayanand had no use for hatha-yoga, for example, as has been noted.
90. Dayanand, *Ṛgvedādibhāṣyabhūmikā*, in *Ṛgvedā-Bhāṣyam*, vol. 1, 406-420.
91. Idem, *Aṣṭādhyāyī-Bhāṣyam*, 2 vols., 2d ed. (Ajmer: Paropkāriṇī Sabhā, Vikram Saṃvat 2018 and 2034).
92. James Barr, *Fundamentalism* (Philadelphia: Westminster Press, 1978), 176-177.

4

THE CONTEXT OF THE ARYA THEORY ABOUT THE VEDAS

In the first chapter of this book we analyzed a Christian and an Islamic fundamentalist movement in light of the definition of fundamentalism spelled out in the introduction. The second chapter was a study of a Hindu fundamentalist movement, the Arya Samaj, in terms of the same definition. The third chapter was focused on Swami Dayanand Sarasvati, the founder of the Arya Samaj. Specifically in that chapter we surveyed the texts that Swami Dayanand identified as authoritative in his major works, and those which he labeled unauthoritative. The books from which Dayanand actually quoted were compared with his theory of authoritative and unauthoritative works. In this chapter we concentrate on the swami's theories about the Vedas.

We have had more than one occasion in this study to restate Swami Dayanand's claim that the Vedas are the only texts which are totally free of error. In chapter two we pointed out the similarity between North American Protestant fundamentalism and the Arya Samaj in their belief in scriptural inerrancy. It was also suggested that a more basic and interesting similarity between the scripturalism of the two movements lies in their attempts to stretch the authority of their sacred texts into new areas. The first section of this chapter will be dedicated to filling out these arguments. We will look again at the Vedas not only from the perspective of the Arya Samaj, but also from the viewpoints of Western scholars and traditional Hindus.

Having articulated the ways that Swami Dayanand's understanding of the Vedas is traditional and the ways that it is novel in the first section of this chapter, we will go on to examine in more depth in the second section how Dayanand substantiated his interpretation of the

Vedas in the introduction to his commentaries on those texts, the work entitled *Ṛgvedādibhāṣyabhūmikā*. The swami maintained that his reading of the Vedas is supported by the most ancient and authoritative secondary sources. This was not just a proposition that Dayanand defended on the theoretical level, rather he also tried to demonstrate it through quotation of those works in commenting on Vedic mantras. What books did Dayanand rely on to support his reading of Vedic mantras in *Ṛgvedādibhāṣyabhūmikā*, and how did he use those texts? These are the questions that we hope to answer in the second section below.

The two sections in this chapter are different approaches to the issue of the role of the Vedas in the writings of Swami Dayanand and in the life of the Arya Samaj. The first section gives a sense of perspective about the context in which Swami Dayanand claimed that the Vedas are inerrant. The second section introduces the reader to the problem that those claims present to the person who tries to defend them. The chapter encourages the reader to think seriously about the substance of the Arya Samaj's position and the evidence which has been marshaled to support it.

THE VEDAS IN PERSPECTIVE

To gain some perspective on Swami Dayanand's theories about the Vedas first we will discuss the conclusions that Western scholars have reached about those texts, and contrast them with the position of the founder of the Arya Samaj. The theories of the academic community in the West were just beginning to crystalize around the time that Dayanand wrote his major works. That the swami took these theories seriously is indicated by the many disagreements with Western scholars that he voiced in his books, a few of which will be noted below. Yet the purpose of this section is not to describe the debates that Dayanand had with Western academics on specific points, rather it is simply to outline the fundamentally different conclusions about the Vedas that have been reached in the Western academic world and in the Arya Samaj.

After discussing the perspective of Western scholars we will turn to traditional Hindu ideas about the Vedas as expressed in philosophical works and in religious texts. There are many similarities between Dayanand's theories about the Vedas and those of the adherents of the orthodox Hindu philosophical schools. We will indicate some of them in this section. Then we will go on to point out the very different perspective on the Vedas that can be found in many Hindu religious works.

THE WESTERN SCHOLARLY PERSPECTIVE

According to Western scholars the term Veda actually encompasses a large body of diverse religious literature. The Vedas are often divided into four strata: the Samhitas, the Brahmanas, the Aranyakas, and the Upanishads. The Samhitas are further broken down into the four groups: Ṛg, Yajur, Sāma, and Atharva. These groups can be analyzed yet again as there are different recensions of the Vedic Samhitas which have been preserved by different schools. The Samhitas are made up largely of hymns to the Vedic gods. The Brahmanas are commentaries on the Samhitas which focus especially on ritual questions. The Aranyakas continue the philosophical reflections on the meaning of the sacrifice which are found in the Brahmanas. The Upanishads carry this abstraction even further, often supporting a monistic metaphysics.

For scholars the Samhitas, Brahmanas, Aranyakas, and Upanishads represent four layers of Vedic literature, each later than the one preceding it and each with its own characteristic concerns. Yet it is also true that these groups of texts cannot be perfectly divided. For example, the Samhita of the Black Yajur Veda includes commentary on its own verses, which might seem more appropriate in a Brahmana than in a Samhita. These strata are confused in other ways. To take a couple of other instances, the *Śatapatha Brāhmaṇa* actually includes the *Bṛhadāraṇyaka Upaniṣad*, and the *Īśa Upaniṣad* is also a hymn in the Yajur Veda Samhita.

Although certain dates in the Vedic period are hard to come by, one scholar has concluded that the oldest parts of the Ṛg Veda Samhita may have been composed as early as the thirteenth century B.C.E. It is impossible to identify an end to the era in which this literature was written—texts have been composed which call themselves Upanishads up until recent centuries. Nonetheless the main body of the Samhitas, Brahmanas, Aranyakas, and the early Upanishads must have been completed before the time of the Buddha, around the second half of the sixth century B.C.E.[1]

It is the Vedic Samhitas which will be the focus of this chapter. The Samhitas were composed by the rishis. Some scholars have understood these sages to be visionary poets who sometimes described their work as the product of a kind of revelation. The authors of many of the mantras are unknown, and the traditional lists of the rishis of the hymns of the Vedas are in part fanciful. Still, in some of the mantras the name of the author is recorded.[2]

Though the Vedic Samhitas contain no historical narratives as such, scholars have attempted to extract some references to history from them. Most important is the general acknowledgement that some of the hymns of the Ṛg Veda contain accounts of the battles of the Indo-Europeans as they migrated to the east and south across the South Asian subcontinent. In these hymns the poets sometimes refer to the Indo-Europeans as *āryans* and to their opponents, the indigenous peoples of the subcontinent, as *dāsas*. The references to this migration in the Ṛg Veda are mixed with mythological material. In some contexts it is difficult to determine if the enemies of the *āryans* are humans or demons. Occasionally one comes across what appears to be the name of a historical king or warrior in the Samhitas, but again it is not easy to separate history and legend.[3]

The Samhitas are made up largely of hymns to the Vedic deities, who are closely related to nature and who are worshipped in sacrifice. Indra, the most celebrated divinity in the Ṛg Veda, is the god of thunder and the preeminent warrior. Agni, the god of fire, is another important Vedic deity. Not just the earthly fire, Agni is also the sun in the celestial realm and lightning in the atmosphere. Because Agni is also the sacrificial fire, he is known as a priest and a messenger bringing the offerings to the gods.[4] Many of the mantras of the Ṛg Veda Samhita are found again in the Yajur and Sāma Vedas, where they have been rearranged for ritual purposes. Although it contains a limited amount of the same material, the Atharva Veda Samhita is of a somewhat different character, including a number of charms and spells.

Though active debate continues on many of the issues presented above, this account will suffice as a general statement of the conclusions of Western scholars on the nature of Vedic literature. It will be seen that the position of the Arya Samaj on the Vedas as reflected in the writings of Swami Dayanand differs in many ways.

Swami Dayanand argued that the use of the term Veda should be restricted to the Samhitas. The rest of the literature that is usually considered Vedic, the Brahmanas, the Aranyakas, and the Upanishads, are only commentaries on the Samhitas and so their authority is not equal to that of the Samhitas. The Brahmanas and other works are only authoritative to the extent that they are consistent with the Samhitas.[5]

According to Swami Dayanand the Vedas were promulgated at the time of the creation of the world almost two billion years ago.[6] This date is determined by adding up the length of the epochs of world history that have passed up to the present according to the Hindu tradition. Dayanand specifically rejects the conclusions of Western scholars in this area. "By explaining this much it should be known that when it is said by European professors like Wilson and Max Mueller that the Vedas were composed by humans, and that there is no sruti, and that 2,400, or 2,900, or 3,000, or 3,100 years have passed since the creation of the Vedas, this is all basically wrong."[7]

As this quote implies, it was not men who were the authors of the Vedas in Dayanand's theory but God (*īśvara*). He communicated the Vedas to the sages Agni, Vāyu, Āditya, and Aṅgiras after creating the world.[8] The rishis whose names are associated with individual mantras in the tradition should not be understood as the authors of those mantras. They are merely the ones by whom "the real meaning of the mantra became known."[9]

This is not the first time that God has communicated the Vedas to the human community according to Dayanand. "The words and letters, the meaning, and the connection between the words and meaning which exist in this kalpa in the Vedas were just so formerly and they will be so in future."[10] According to a Hindu theory of history the universe goes through a never-ending cycle of creation, dissolution, and re-creation. The period between a creation and dissolution is known as a kalpa. Dayanand argued that not only were the Vedas manifested at the beginning of the present kalpa, but that they have been made manifest in every kalpa endlessly in the past and they will be made manifest in every kalpa in the future. It is for this reason that the Vedas are permanent (*nitya*) according to Swami Dayanand.[11]

We can better grasp what Dayanand intended here by looking at his argument in a different context. Dayanand claimed that there are three eternally existing (*anādi*) entities: God, souls (*jīvas*), and the material universe (*jagat*). Dayanand admitted that after the dissolution or pralaya at the end of a kalpa the universe and souls cease to exist in the form that we now know them, but at the beginning of the next kalpa they come into existence again. They are eternal "by means of a continual succession" ("pravāheṇa").[12] *Pravāha* literally means "current," like the current of a river. We think of a river as continuing to exist even though it may run dry in the hot season. In the same way souls and the universe come into existence again and again with each re-creation of the world. The Vedas, too, are not manifest in the period after a pralaya, but they are communicated to people each time the world is re-created.

In considering Dayanand's ideas about the continual manifestation of the Vedas it would probably be wrong to place a great deal of emphasis on God's will in this process. Swami Dayanand wrote that the Vedas issue forth from God "like breath naturally" ("niśvāsavat sahajatayā").[13] The manifestation of the Vedas upon the creation of the world is something that God does repeatedly, always in the same way. In this context it might even be appropriate to translate "sahajatayā" not as "naturally" but as "automatically." Dayanand affirmed repeatedly in the introduction to his commentaries on the Vedas that the Samhitas contain all knowledge.[14] The Vedas are the knowledge of God which is vouchsafed to humans at the beginning of each kalpa.

The Vedas are always the same in every new creation because they are God's knowledge. God is outside time and does not undergo change (he is *nirvikār* according to the principles of the Arya Samaj), and so his knowledge is changeless.[15] In *Satyārth Prakāś* Dayanand considered whether it is appropriate to call God "trikāldarśī" (one who sees the three times, that is, past, present, future). Dayanand concluded that because God's knowledge is changeless it is not appropriate to speak of the past and future in relation to him. Humans know things as having existed in the past and then slipping out of existence. They also encounter things that do not exist in the present but which come to exist in the future. But God's understanding is different. "The knowledge of the highest lord remains present always, unitary and undivided."[16]

It follows from this argument that there cannot be any references to historical individuals or places in the Vedas. Unlike the Brahmanas, Dayanand insisted, in the Vedas there is not "a trace of history."[17] God's knowledge is not of temporal things, but only of ideas which are eternal. Consistent with this principle Dayanand tended to reinterpret allegorically what are usually understood as the names of individuals when they occur in the Vedas. For example, Kaśyapa, mentioned in Ṛg Veda 9.114.2 and many other places in Vedic literature, has been understood as a rishi among other things. But Dayanand reads the term as referring to God. To support this interpretation Dayanand offers an etymological explanation of the word Kaśyapa. Kaśyapa is derived from *paśyaka* ("seer") according to Dayanand (with metathesis of the initial and final consonants), which refers to God, who sees all.[18] This identification of Kaśyapa with God is supported by a reference to the *Śatapatha Brāhmaṇa*.[19]

In commenting on the Vedas Swami Dayanand reinterpreted not

only the names of men, but the names of the gods as well. Because Dayanand believed that there is only one God, omniscient and omnipotent, he did not agree that many deities are praised in the Vedas. In general Dayanand interpreted what have sometimes been understood as divine names on two levels: the *vyāvahārika* (related to the practical world) and the *pāramārthika* (related to the highest end of human existence, that is, God).[20] Agni, for example, is understood not only as the earthly fire but also as God, the one who enlightens everything.[21] Indra is not an anthropomorphic god-king in Dayanand's theory, but still suggests sovereignty. In one context the founder of the Arya Samaj took Indra as referring to that which gives power in the world, the sun, and that which is the source of all power, God.[22] The notion that the Vedas are marked by a primitive nature mysticism, that the ancient Aryans worshipped the sun, wind, rains, and so forth was rejected by Dayanand in no uncertain terms. "Nowadays when some modern Indians or Europeans have said or do say that in the Vedas there is worship of material gods ["bhautikadevatā"], this is quite false."[23]

Dayanand's theory of the timelessness of the Vedas bears a complex relationship to his notions about modern scientific knowledge and technology in those texts. In *Ṛgvedādibhāṣyabhūmikā* Dayanand maintained that there are mantras which deal with the gravitational attraction of celestial bodies.[24] In that same work he also cited a Vedic mantra in discussing telegraphy.[25] As has been shown elsewhere in this book, Swami Dayanand held that the ancient Aryans were a technologically advanced people. The great Indian epics give evidence of this, or so Dayanand believed. But it would not be appropriate to speak of the Vedas as a manifestation of any level of technology, primitive or advanced, since they are timeless. It is necessary to make a distinction here between the ideas of modern science and the technology of modern science. To the extent that gravitation is understood as a natural law, as a principle which theoretically describes the way matter must always operate, its presence in the Vedas is consistent with their timelessness. On the other hand, it is hard to see how there could be any place for the telegraph as a machine in the Vedas. Yet what Dayanand is dealing with here is not really telegraph machines, but with the knowledge that it takes to make telegraph machines. The heading of the chapter at issue is "Atha Tāravidyāmūlaṃ Saṃkṣepataḥ." ("Now Briefly the Basis of the Knowledge of the Telegraph."). Modern technology as such does not have a role in the Vedas, but the knowledge upon which that technology is based, and all knowledge, has its roots in the Vedas.[26]

It is striking that Swami Dayanand's ideas disagree with those of modern Western scholars on so many points. While the Vedas include the Brahmanas, Aranyakas, and Upanishads in addition to the Samhitas for most scholars, Dayanand limited the term to just the Samhitas. Western academics have dated the composition of the Vedas to the second or first millennium B.C.E., an estimate that is off by nearly two billions years by Dayanand's reckoning. And for Dayanand this most recent revelation of the Vedas was just one in a series of manifestations of texts which have existed eternally. Dayanand maintained that the author of the Vedas was God himself. The rishis who are identified as the authors by scholars were merely the individuals who grasped the meaning of God's words. The attempts by historians to develop some ideas about ancient India from the Vedas are bound to fail in Dayanand's system, because the Vedas are timeless. Finally while Western scholars have identified a number of gods in the Vedas, Dayanand maintained that there is only one.

Given these differences it is small wonder that Louis Renou, the great French Vedic scholar, characterized the Arya Samaj's reading of the Vedas as "a vigorous (and from our point of view, extremely aberrant) interpretation."[27] Jan Gonda is hardly kinder when he writes of Dayanand's "socio-politic, by no means scientific, interpretation."[28] Though the Arya Samaj's interpretation of the Vedas is unacceptable to Western scholars, some aspects of it do have some precedent in traditional Hindu thought. It is to the traditional Hindu understanding of the Vedas that we now turn.

THE HINDU PHILOSOPHICAL PERSPECTIVE

Here we will briefly compare Swami Dayanand's position on the Vedas with that of the orthodox Hindu philosophical schools. In the process it will be necessary to attend to some of the differences between those schools. For despite general agreement on the authority of the Vedas, philosophers have disagreed about their character. "All schools of Hindu Philosophy are unanimous in accepting the Veda as the supreme scripture which informs us about things which cannot be known otherwise (*ajnāta jnāpanam*); but as to the nature of the Vedic revelation, there is no unanimity."[29] We will begin with the school that concerns itself most directly with the exegesis of the Vedas, Mimamsa.

Mimamsa is the philosophical school which expounds the dharma of ritual. This dharma is unchanging, and so must be the Vedas which are the guide to it. The Vedas have existed for all eternity (they are *nitya*), and they have no author. The rishis were merely transmitters of the Vedas, not their makers. Hence the Vedas are *apauruṣeya* (from *a* [not] + *pauruṣeya* [related to a person, or *puruṣa*]), they do not depend upon the authority of any person. Rather the Vedas enjoy independent authority (*svatantraprāmāṇya*).[30]

As the Vedas are timeless, they do not contain the names of historical people or places. Mimamsa tends to reinterpret not only the names of people in the Vedas, but also those of the gods. We can take as an example the explanation of the great Mimamsa commentator Śabara of a passage from the Taittirīya Samhita (one of the schools of the Black Yajur Veda). The Prajāpati mentioned there, Śabara argues, cannot be the creator-god, but must be some "eternal object: wind, sky, or sun."[31] Since Mimamsa is primarily concerned with the Vedas as they relate to ritual, it focuses mostly on the Brahmanas rather than the Samhitas, Aranyakas, or Upanishads. According to Mimamsa the most important statements in the Veda are the *vidhis*, specific ritual injunctions. For some adherents of Mimamsa the Vedic Samhitas are only *arthavāda*, explanations of the occasion for *vidhis* which are not as significant as the rules themselves.[32]

Nyaya, the philosophical school concerned with logic and dialectics, takes issue with some of the Mimamsa theory with regard to the Vedas. Along with Mimamsa Nyaya accepts the authority (*prāmāṇya*) of the Vedas. Nyaya goes to some lengths to prove that the Vedas are free of error, especially the faults of falsehood, internal contradiction, and redundancy.[33] Still, Nyaya cannot accept that the Vedas have existed through all eternity (so for Nyaya the Vedas are *anitya*), and it criticizes the absurdity of the notion of a book without an author (so the Vedas are *pauruṣeya*). The authority of the Vedas depends not upon their timelessness but upon the reliability of their author (or authors). In Vaisheshika, Nyaya's companion philosophical school, this author is identified as God.[34]

Vedanta, known for its monistic metaphysics, is closely linked to Mimamsa as its companion philosophical school. Nevertheless the position of Vedanta with regard to the Vedas to a degree reconciles the conflicting theories of Mimamsa and Nyaya. Like Mimamsa Vedanta asserts that the Vedas are eternal (*nitya*). The great Vedanta philosopher Śaṅkara wrote that just as the sun illumines objects but requires no other light to shine itself, so the authority of the Vedas does not depend on any other work (the Vedas possess *nirapekṣaprāmāṇya*).[35] In another passage in the same work Śaṅkara seemed to imply that the Vedas are manifest in the same form at the beginning of each kalpa.[36] Vedanta also maintains that there are no references to historical individuals in the Vedas.

Following Nyaya's speculation about the author of the Vedas to a certain extent, Vedanta allows that the Vedas come from *brahman*, the immaterial essence which is the substratum of the universe. Several different theories have been advanced by adherents of Vedanta to explain how the Vedas, which have no origin, might still have an originator, but these subtleties need not detain us. Vedanta largely ignores the Samhitas, Brahmanas, and Aranyakas in favor of the Upanishads, which contain passages that are especially consonant with, and important to, Vedanta's philosophy. In its emphasis upon these Upanishadic texts Vedanta overturns Mimamsa's evaluation of *vidhi* and *arthavāda*: for Vedanta the ritual injunctions of the *vidhi* are much less important than the speculative passages contained in the *arthavāda*.

As should be clear from even this brief summary, though all of the orthodox Hindu philosophical schools accept the authority of the Vedas, there has been substantial disagreement about how that authority might best be established. Among the many theories that have been advanced to demonstrate the normative force of the Vedas the two most important have been Mimamsa's (and Vedanta's) argument that the Vedas are authoritative because they are eternal, and Nyaya's argument that the Vedas are authoritative because of the reliability of their author (or authors). Swami Dayanand embraced both of these arguments in his *Ṛgvedādibhāṣyabhūmikā*. With Mimamsa and Vedanta Dayanand accepted that the Vedas are *nitya*. Like Nyaya Dayanand insisted that we can trust the Vedas because their author was reliable. Dayanand did not shrink from eclecticism in his attempt to prove that the Vedas are authoritative.[37]

Aside from the important issue of proving the Vedas' authority, some of Swami Dayanand's theories about those texts are consistent with the position of Vedanta, which is not surprising given that Vedanta has been the dominant philosophical school in India for several centuries.[38] Like Mimamsa and Vedanta Dayanand argued that there are no references to temporal things in the Vedas, and that the rishis did not write them. With regard to Dayanand's belief in the re-creation of the Vedas in each kalpa, there does seem to be some evidence that Śaṅkara also accepted this idea.[39] On these points Swami Dayanand's views on the Vedas were more or less consistent with those of the Vedanta philosophers.

There is one key element of Dayanand's interpretation of the

Vedas that has no parallel in any of the orthodox philosophical schools, that is, the idea that the term Veda should be restricted to the Samhitas. Because Mimamsa is concerned primarily with ritual, its focus is on the Brahmanas, which describe Vedic ceremonies at some length. The Samhitas receive consideration only because portions of them are recited in rituals. Vedanta relies upon Vedic literature for support for its monistic metaphysics, and so it concentrates mostly on the Upanishadic passages where that support can be found. Discussions of the Samhitas are rare in Vedanta in comparison with analysis of the Upanishads. The other philosophical schools are not as concerned with Vedic literature in general as Mimamsa and Vedanta, hence even less attention is devoted to the Samhitas in Sankhya, Yoga, Nyaya, and Vaisheshika. Swami Dayanand's retrieval of the Vedic Samhitas has no precedent in the philosophical schools. It is also remarkably inconsistent with the tendency of most Hindu religious literature, which will be demonstrated in the next section.

THE PERSPECTIVE OF HINDU RELIGIOUS LITERATURE

Scholars have often noted that the litmus test of orthodoxy in the Hindu tradition is acceptance of the Vedas. As Renou writes, "the Veda is precisely the sign, perhaps the only one, of Indian orthodoxy."[40] One of the most important general terms for a heretic in Sanskrit literature is *nāstika*. This word (which literally reflects the denial of the skeptic--*na asti* means "it is not") may originally have referred to those who deny the existence of another world, but it came to be used most characteristically for those who deny the existence or the authority of the Vedas.[41] Only those groups which acknowledge Hinduism's most ancient scriptures are admitted to be orthodox.

Despite the general admission of the authority of the Vedas, throughout the history of Hinduism works have claimed equality with, or even priority to, those ancient texts. As early as the *Chāndogya Upaniṣad* there is an admission of a fifth Veda in addition to the Ṛg, Yajur, Sāma, and Atharva, called the Itihāsa-Purāṇa, the legends and ancient lore.[42] The *Muṇḍaka Upaniṣad* goes even further when it divides knowledge (*vidyā*) into two classes. The higher knowledge, the *parā vidyā*, is that by which the imperishable is known. The lower knowledge, the *aparā vidyā*, includes the four Vedic Samhitas along with other classes of literature.[43] Clearly for this Upanishad knowing the Samhitas is only a propaedeutic to the study of a more exalted truth.

Both of the great Sanskrit epics, the *Rāmāyaṇa* and the *Mahābhārata*, claim equality with the Vedas.[44] The *Bhagavad Gītā* (which is a part of the *Mahābhārata*) occasionally speaks of the Vedas in positive terms, but only when they are understood to reveal Krishna. Krishna himself says, "I make my dwelling in the hearts of all: from Me stem memory, wisdom, the dispelling [of doubt]. Through all the Vedas it is I who should be known, for the maker of the Vedas' end am I, and I the Vedas know."[45] The *Gītā* disparages the ritualism that is characteristic of Vedic religion. "As much use as there is in a water-tank flooded with water on every side, so much is there in all the Vedas for the Brāhman who discerns."[46] What is required to attain God, says Krishna to Arjuna, is not knowledge of the Vedas but devotion, bhakti. "Not by the Vedas or grim-ascetic-practice, not by the giving of alms or sacrifice can I be seen in such a form as you did see Me; But by worship-of-love addressed to [Me,] none other, Arjuna, can I be known and seen in such a form and as I really am: [so can my lovers] enter into Me."[47] The *Bhagavad Gītā* is the first major work of Hindu devotionalism. In it we see that the Vedas, and the rites with which they are associated, have been displaced by a new religiosity.

The authority of the Vedas is undermined in the Puranas as well. Repositories of Hindu mythology, the Puranas were important in the rise of devotionalism. The *Bhāgavata Purāṇa* repeats the claim that *itihāsa* and *purāṇa* are the fifth Veda.[48] In another passage in the *Bhāgavata* the devotee must go beyond the the Veda as well as the world. "When the Divine Being regards any man with favour, that man, sunk in the contemplation of the soul, abandons all thoughts which are set upon the world and the Veda."[49] As in the *Bhagavad Gītā*, the religion of the Vedas is regarded as inferior to that of the *Bhāgavata Purāṇa* by the author of that text.

Kabīr, the iconoclastic devotional poet who probably lived in the fifteenth century C.E., continued this tradition of criticizing the Vedas. Like others Kabīr understood the Vedas to be tied to worldliness:

> I was just tagging along
> in the wake of the world and the Veda.

Then the Satguru met me on the path
and He put a Lamp in my hand.[50]

To the extent that empty scripturalism can be an obstacle to the struggle for spiritual realization. the Vedas are condemned by Kabīr.

Hey swan, clear your mind
in the morning. They've set
so many snares, knit the net
of three qualities
and trapped the world.
If the landlord is a butcher,
why think about the tenants?
Those who have no devotion
are called devotees;
they fling away nectar
and swallow poison.
The brightest ones have sunk,
not listening to what I said.
What I said was, tie your bundle tight,
stay alert day and night.
Kaliyug's crafty gurus entice the world
to destroy it.
Veda and Koran are traps laid
for poor souls to tumble in.
Kabir says, if you meet the one
who can extricate you,
you won't forget it.[51]

For Kabīr, as for other Hindu authors from the Upanishads onward, the Vedas advocate religious practices which have been surpassed. These thinkers do not assert that the Vedas are not authoritative—that is a philosophical question which is more or less beside the point. It would be more accurate to say that the Vedas are outmoded. The Hindu tradition has been marked by a number of historic shifts despite the philosophers' continuing insistence upon Vedic authority. Even during the Vedic period itself in the Upanishads we see a new religious sensibility based on renunciation of the world. The Upanishadic sages identified the sacrificial system of the Samhitas and Brahmanas with the world which they had renounced. In the *Bhagavad Gītā* another new religious value comes to the fore, devotionalism.

Though the *Gītā* does not accept the renunciation of the Upanishads, it agrees with the Upanishads in their condemnation of the Vedas. For the *Gītā* the Vedas are a scripture that is closely tied to sacrifices undertaken for selfish motives. In later devotional literature, like the Puranas and Kabīr's writings, the Vedas continue to be a symbol of empty ritualism and scripturalism.

What these authors have attacked is not the Samhitas, or even Vedic literature as a whole, but a certain type of religion which they identify as Vedic and its Brahman proponents. Although these later texts may caricature the nature of Vedic religion for polemic purposes, they do give an indication of the fate of the Samhitas in Hinduism. There have been several noteworthy attempts to understand the Vedic Samhitas, especially around the time of Sāyaṇa in the fourteenth century C.E.[52] But the vast majority of effort has been expended on questions of ritual and the recitation required in ritual. The Upanishads rather than the Samhitas have been the subject of most debates beyond narrow technical questions. So for later Hinduism the Vedic Samhitas are texts which are to be used in ritual, generally in small fragments.

We can now summarize the traditional view of the Samhitas. In Hinduism the Samhitas are a part of the Vedas. For orthodox Hindu philosophers the Samhitas share in the authority that is admitted to the Vedas as a whole. Yet the Samhitas themselves have been the subject of relatively little philosophical inquiry. In Hindu religious literature the Samhitas have suffered an even worse fate. Rarely the subject of any close reading, the Samhitas have been disparaged along with the rest of the Vedas as texts which are a part of an outmoded ritualistic religion. Against this background the radical nature of Dayanand's assertion of the authority of the Vedic Samhitas becomes glaringly obvious.

Swami Dayanand did not accept that the Vedic Samhitas were only useful in a narrow ritual context. On the contrary, the swami claimed that the Vedas contain all knowledge and hence that they are relevant to all areas of life. Whether Dayanand was discussing religion, or caste, or even steam engines he did not hesitate to quote the Vedas. Though his position appears to be a strikingly radical departure from traditional Hinduism, the swami maintained that it was consistent with the most ancient and authoritative works about the Vedas. This claim will be the subject of the next section.

THE SUPPORT FOR DAYANAND'S THEORIES ABOUT THE VEDAS

In the last section of this chapter we brought out the ways that Swami Dayanand's theories about the Vedas are consistent with the Hindu tradition and the ways that they are a departure from it. In this section we will look in more detail at how Dayanand attempts to substantiate his reading of the Vedas with the help of the tradition. It is important to realize that Dayanand claimed that his interpretation of the Vedas is a continuation of the earlier understandings of those texts. When questioned by his hypothetical interlocutor in *Ṛgvedādibhāṣyabhūmikā* about whether he is writing a new commentary or promulgating those of the former teachers (*pūrvācārya*), Dayanand maintained that he only reproduced the interpretation of the ancient sages. He even went so far as to say that his commentary is "merely a collection" of the views of older works. Dayanand assured his reader that "no unauthoritative, new, arbitrary [commentary] is being composed."[53]

If Swami Dayanand's commentary on the Vedas just repeats the interpretation of the ancients, then what was the point of even writing it? To this Dayanand responded that in addition to the writings of the authoritative teachers of old there are other works on the Vedas which are now available. Dayanand specifically mentioned the great medieval commentators on the Vedas (Rāvaṇa, Uvaṭa, Sāyaṇa, Mahīdhara, and others), the European scholars who have followed them, and the modern Indian students of the Vedas who have adopted the perspective of the Europeans. Swami Dayanand set his own interpretation of the Vedas over against all these works. In contrast to the ancient texts these more recent books contain novelties in Vedic interpretation which have no authority. Dayanand presented his own interpretation of the Vedas as wholly grounded in the ancient authoritative works on the Vedas, hence his interpretation of Vedas is fully reliable.

In this section we will test Dayanand's claim that his interpretation of the Vedas is based on the ancient *ārṣa* literature. Specifically we will analyze the secondary sources that Dayanand cited to support his interpretation of individual Vedic mantras *Ṛgvedādibhāṣyabhūmikā*. The texts which the swami used were such that they allowed him a certain latitude in his commentary. Still, we will note a few examples where Dayanand seems clearly to have rejected the reading of the work cited, despite its authority. In the conclusion we will be discussing the significance of these apparent contradictions.

DAYANAND'S USE OF SECONDARY SOURCES

When one analyzes Swami Dayanand's use of secondary sources in the interpretation of Vedic mantras in *Ṛgvedādibhāṣyabhūmikā*, it is necessary to acknowledge first that many mantras are cited without a direct commentary in that work, and many more are commented upon without the support of any citation. Of the 342 Vedic mantras quoted or referred to in *Ṛgvedādibhāṣyabhūmikā* ninety-one are not commented upon. Many of the Vedic verses without any commentary are cited in the chapter on grammar, where brief fragments of mantras are given as examples of Vedic usage.[54] Another context where several Vedic mantras are referred to without comment is in the chapter on the contents of the Vedas (headed, "Atha Vedaviṣayavicāraḥ"). Here Dayanand cited thirty-four mantras in succession as proof texts for his contention that in the Vedas only worship of God is enjoined, and not worship of material divinities like the sun and moon.[55]

In these passages and others almost 27 per cent of the Vedic mantras referred to in *Ṛgvedādibhāṣyabhūmikā* are cited without any commentary. We cannot analyze these citations to come to an appreciation of Dayanand's interpretation of Vedic mantras because these mantras really are not interpreted, rather they are cited without explanation as examples of Vedic usage or as evidence in some argument in which they play only an incidental role.

Having eliminated the mantras without commentary from consideration, we are left with 251 Vedic verses cited with some explication in *Ṛgvedādibhāṣyabhūmikā* out of the total of 342 verses. Of these, 179 mantras are commented upon without the citation of any secondary source. There are only seventy-two Vedic verses explicated with the help of some other authority. Thus it would seem that though Dayanand argued that his Vedic interpretation is consistent with the teachings of the ancient commentators, in *Ṛgvedādibhāṣyabhūmikā* very often he did not go to the trouble of demonstrating that consistency.

The judgment that Swami Dayanand was frequently willing to advance his own interpretation of the Vedas without demonstrating its basis in authoritative works is mitigated to an extent by attention to context. For example, Dayanand occasionally quoted a string of verses from the same Vedic hymn in *Ṛgvedādibhāṣyabhūmikā*, only some of which are commented on with the support of other texts. In this situation one might argue that Dayanand's interpretation of an individual mantra is dependent upon the authorities that he quotes in the immediate context, even though those authorities are not cited for the specific verse in question. But even if we eliminate every Vedic hymn which contains any mantra which is commented upon by Dayanand with a reference to a secondary source, we are still left with many verses interpreted without any support. In *Ṛgvedādibhāṣyabhūmikā* there are eighty-five mantras which Dayanand explained without relying on any secondary text excluding those which are contained in hymns in connection with which a secondary source is cited in the interpretation of another mantra. The conclusion stands that very often in *Ṛgvedādibhāṣyabhūmikā* Swami Dayanand was content to set forth his own explication of Vedic mantras with no citation of secondary sources.

There are still seventy-two Vedic verses in *Ṛgvedādibhāṣya-bhūmikā* which Swami Dayanand explained with the help of some secondary source. It is interesting to look in detail at the works which Dayanand cites in explaining Vedic mantras. In Table 5 all of the secondary sources which Swami Dayanand referred to in support of his interpretation of Vedic verses are listed.[56] The number of mantras in connection with which they are cited has also been noted.[57] This table might be compared with the pattern of Dayanand's quotes in Table 3 of chapter three. As in Table 3, here too there are references to works which Dayanand did not explicitly designate as authoritative, though they make up a relatively small proportion of the total secondary sources cited. Generally Swami Dayanand relied upon works included in his lists of authoritative books in explaining Vedic mantras.

Among the unauthoritative works which Dayanand quoted in interpreting Vedic mantras in *Ṛgvedādibhāṣyabhūmikā* those from the Vedic group are worthy of comment. These citations especially suggest questions of the limits of the Vedic canon in the swami's thought. In the table we have noted one reference to a Ṛg Veda Khila. In his discussion of Ṛg Veda 10.75.5 Dayanand cited a mantra that runs:

> Sitāsite sarite yatra saṃgathe tatrāplutāso divam utpatanti
> Ye vai tanvaṃ vi sṛjanti dhīrās te janāso amṛtatvaṃ bhajante.[58]

The Ṛg Vedic Khilas are mantras which are not a part of the Śākalya recension of the Ṛg Veda Samhita, which is the only version of the text that survives to the present.[59] Though not accepted within the Samhita itself, these mantras were still preserved.[60] They were collected into a sort of an appendix, which is often published at the end of the Samhita text in printed editions. The mantra quoted here is

TABLE 5
SECONDARY SOURCES CITED IN COMMENTING ON VEDIC MANTRAS IN *ṚGVEDĀDIBHĀṢYABHŪMIKĀ*

Group	Discipline	Work	Number of Mantras Commented Upon
Vedangas	Nirukta	Nighaṇṭu	10
		Nirukta	34
	Vyākaraṇa	Aṣṭādhyāyī	8
		Dhātupāṭha	5
		Mahābhāṣya	1
Upanishads	—	Kena	1
		Taittirīya	1
		Chāndogya	4
		Bṛhadāraṇyaka	2
Brahmanas	—	Aitareya	4
		Śatapatha	37
Total for authoritative works			107
Vedangas	Vyākaraṇa	Vārttika	1
		Uṇādi Sutras	1
Vedas	—	Ṛg Veda Khila	1
		Taittirīya Saṃhita	3
Other	Aranyakas	Aitareya	3
Total for unauthoritative works			9

Source: Dayanand, *Ṛgvedādibhāṣyabhūmikā*, in *Ṛgveda-Bhāṣyam*, vol. 1, 1-430.

included in the Vaidika Saṃśodhana Maṇḍal edition of the Ṛg Veda Samhita after Khila 3.14.1.[61] The editors note that this mantra is interpolated following Ṛg Veda 10.75.5, the text upon which Dayanand is commenting.

When Swami Dayanand quoted this mantra he noted that it is from a "supplementary part of the text" ("pariśiṣṭa"), but he did not comment further on the status of the Ṛg Veda Khilas. Did Dayanand regard the Khilas as a part of the Ṛg Veda, or should they be understood to be on a par with the *ārṣa* literature? Dayanand does not answer this question here (or anywhere in his writings to my knowledge), but his quotation of a Khila text implies that he did allow them some authority.

Even more puzzling is Swami Dayanand's quotation of a mantra from the Taittirīya Samhita in explaining a Vedic verse in *Ṛgvedādibhāṣyabhūmikā*.[62] There are two main recensions of the Yajur Veda, the Black and the White. The Samhita texts of the Black Yajur Veda are more expansive than those of the White Yajur Veda, with occasional glosses of obscure terms. Hence adherents of the White Yajur Veda school have claimed that they have preserved the Samhita with greater purity—that the Samhita of the Black Yajur Veda contains commentatorial interpolations.[63]

Dayanand generally quoted the Mādhyandina Samhita of the White Yajur Veda in his works. In at least one place in his writings it seems that he accepted the idea that the Black Yajur Veda Samhita has not been purely preserved, since he argued that it contains non-Vedic commentatorial material.[64] If the Black Yajur Veda Samhita was not acknowledged to be a reliable part of the Vedas by Dayanand, was it at least granted some authority as a kind of Vedic commentary? The swami is silent on this point. Reliance upon the Taittirīya Samhita (which is a Black Yajur Veda text) as a secondary source might serve as evidence for the conclusion that Dayanand did admit some authority for the Black Yajur Veda. But it is significant that in this context Dayanand quoted a single line from the Taittirīya Samhita, without indicating the provenance of that line. It is only from a footnote by a later editor that the reader learns that this quote is in fact from the Taittirīya Samhita.[65] Such a fragmentary and anonymous reference is not very strong evidence for the authority of the Black Yajur Veda given that Swami Dayanand otherwise generally ignored it.

Having discussed some of the unauthoritative works which Swami Dayanand quoted in explaining Vedic mantras in *Ṛgvedādibhāṣyabhūmikā*, let us turn our attention to authoritative ones.

Even a superficial perusal of Table 5 reveals that two texts are quite important in Dayanand's commentary on Vedic verses, the *Śatapatha Brāhmaṇa* and the *Nirukta*. Two other works are relatively less important, but still quoted several times, the *Nighaṇṭu* and the *Aṣṭādhyāyī*. In considering Dayanand's use of these four texts, the analyst is struck by the flexibility which they allow the interpreter of the Vedas. These works gave Swami Dayanand the latitude that he needed to support his original understanding of the Vedas.

The *Śatapatha Brāhmaṇa* is the work which Dayanand quoted most often to support his interpretation of Vedic mantras in *Ṛgvedādibhāṣyabhūmikā*. The *Śatapatha* is the Brahmana connected with the White Yajur Veda. Like other Brahmanas it contains not only rules for Vedic rituals, but also some speculation on the meaning of the mantras used in those rituals. This speculation is often expressed in equations between more or less homologous entities.[66] For example, much of the third *brāhmaṇa* of the fourth *adhyāya* of the fourteenth *kāṇḍa* of the *Śatapatha Brāhmaṇa* is devoted to a series of triads which spring from the mention of three kinds of food in the first verse. The three kinds of food are identified with mind, speech, and breath. Mind, speech, and breath are, in turn, equated with the three worlds (terrestrial, atmospheric, and celestial); the three Vedas (Ṛg, Yajur, and Sāma); gods, manes, and men; father, mother, and offspring; and what is known, what is to be known, and what is unknown.[67]

In *Ṛgvedādibhāṣyabhūmikā* Swami Dayanand generally quoted only isolated verses or fragments of verses from the *Śatapatha Brāhmaṇa* without explaining their context. When Dayanand quoted *Śatapatha Brāhmaṇa* 14.4.3.11 to show that the three worlds are mind, speech, and breath, he did not bother to explain all the other triads in that *brāhmaṇa*.[68] Because Dayanand might use any part of any of the equations of the *Śatapatha Brāhmaṇa* in the interpretation of a given Vedic mantra, that text afforded him a range of options from which to choose ideas supportive of his reading.

In its prevalence as a secondary source in interpreting Vedic verses in *Ṛgvedādibhāṣyabhūmikā*, the *Nirukta* is a close second to the *Śatapatha Brāhmaṇa*. Since the *Nirukta* is a commentary on the *Nighaṇṭu*, let us discuss the latter book first. The *Nighaṇṭu* is a work on Vedic vocabulary which is made up of a series of lists of words. Most of these lists are composed of synonymous terms, but some are organized on other principles (lists of words with multiple meanings, for example, or of deities of the same realm). Actually even in the lists of words which express one meaning, many of the terms included are not quite synonymous. The *Nighaṇṭu* seems to include words which are equated only in metaphorical usage. For instance, in *Nighaṇṭu* 1.1 the list of words synonymous with *pṛthivī*, which usually means "earth," includes not only well known synonyms such as *mahī* and *bhūmi*, but less closely related terms like *go*.[69] The word *go* usually means "cow," but in several texts including the *Nighaṇṭu* it is used for "earth" because the earth is "the milk-cow of kings."[70]

Swami Dayanand picked up on the equation *go* = *pṛthivī* in his commentary on Yajur Veda 3.6 in the chapter on planetary motion in *Ṛgvedādibhāṣyabhūmikā*. This mantra is not about a calf grazing near its mother in Dayanand's reading, rather it is about the movement of celestial bodies through space.[71] This is just one sample of the creative interpretations that the heterogeneous word lists of the *Nighaṇṭu* might be used to support.

Now we can return to the *Nirukta*, which explains the *Nighaṇṭu* in the context of Vedic usage. Most of the *Nirukta* is made up of commentaries on Vedic mantras illustrating the meanings of the words to be found in the *Nighaṇṭu*. Often these terms are explained etymologically—the very term *nirukta* means "the etymological interpretation of a word" in Sanskrit. Frequently the *Nirukta* offers several different definitions of the word in question.

For instance, beginning its commentary on the list of celestial deities in *Nighaṇṭu* 5.6, the *Nirukta* takes up the Aśvins in the first five sections of the twelfth chapter. First the *Nirukta* offers two different explanations of the derivation of the term Aśvin. The Aśvins are so called because they pervade everything (from the verb root *as*), or because they have horses (from the noun *aśva*). The author of the *Nirukta* still is not satisfied, and goes on to ask, "Who then are the Aśvins?" In answer to this question he cites several theories. Some say that the Aśvins are heaven and earth, others maintain that they are day and night, while still others claim that they are the sun and moon. According to the historians (the *aitihāsikas*) they were two meritorious kings.[72] The *Nirukta* continues describing the nature of the Aśvins for several more sections, but this much will probably suffice to give an idea of the variety of explanations for a given term that one might find in that text.

For an example of how Swami Dayanand made use of this material, one can turn to his commentary on Ṛg Veda 1.116.3-4 in *Ṛgvedādibhāṣyabhūmikā*.[73] These mantras make reference to the mythical story of the rescue of Bhujyu, the son of Tugra, by the Aśvins in a ship traveling through water and air.[74] Dayanand quoted the mantra to establish that there is some reference to steam-powered land, water, and airborne craft in the Vedas.[75] In Dayanand's interpretation the Aśvins are not the gods of the popular understanding of the myth, rather they are the forces involved in the production and operation of these crafts. To support this reading the swami quoted *Nirukta* 12.1. Particularly important to Dayanand's argument is the *Nirukta*'s idea that the Aśvins are the heaven and earth ("dyāvāpṛthivyau"). Relying upon the association of the celestial realm with brightness in Hindu cosmology, Dayanand understood *div* to be the fire by which his craft is propelled. Dayanand read *pṛthivī* as the element earth, from which come the wood, iron, and other materials with which the craft is made. The *Nirukta*'s other definitions of Aśvin are not so important to Dayanand's interpretation of Ṛg Veda 1.116.3-4, and he does not discuss them.[76] This is just one indication of the way that Swami Dayanand took advantage of one of the interpretative alternatives presented by the *Nirukta*.

To the discussion of Swami Dayanand's use of the *Nirukta* in the preceding paragraph one interesting point might be added. Even proper names are not exempt from etymological analysis in the *Nirukta*. In *Nirukta* 12.1 we have a couple of different explanations of the word Aśvin. Elsewhere in *Ṛgvedādibhāṣyabhūmikā* Dayanand quoted the *Nirukta*'s derivations for Aṅgiras,[77] Vṛtra,[78] and Viṣṇu.[79] We noted in the previous section that Dayanand did not accept that one can find the names of historical persons or places in the Vedas, nor did the swami believe in the mythological figures usually discerned in those texts. Relying upon the *Nirukta*'s etymological explanation of proper names, Swami Dayanand focused on the connotation of the elements of those names, ignoring their common significance.

To this point we have briefly surveyed three works which are important in Swami Dayanand's interpretation of Vedic mantras in *Ṛgvedādibhāṣyabhūmikā*: the *Śatapatha Brāhmaṇa*, the *Nighaṇṭu*, and the *Nirukta*. Only one text remains which was used by Dayanand in the interpretation of a significant number of Vedic verses: the *Aṣṭādhyāyī*. The *Aṣṭādhyāyī* is the compendious work on Sanskrit grammar by Pāṇini. Although not a commentary on the Vedas, like the *Śatapatha Brāhmaṇa* and the *Nirukta*, the *Aṣṭādhyāyī* does contain many rules on Vedic usage. Swami Dayanand exploited the flexibility of these rules in his interpretation of Vedic verses in *Ṛgvedādibhāṣyabhūmikā*. The most interesting example of this is what Dayanand did with Vedic verbs. There are a few different rules in the *Aṣṭādhyāyī* which allow great latitude in reading verbs in the Vedas. Swami Dayanand relied upon these rules to advance his theory of the timelessness of the Vedas.

Because the God who wrote the Vedas is beyond time, there are no historical narratives in those texts in Dayanand's theory. But what of the passages where the Vedas seem to describe a past event? Are they temporal? For the swami the answer to this question is an emphatic no. Let us take one complicated but noteworthy example. The thirty-second hymn of the first book of the Ṛg Veda deals with Indra and Vṛtra. According to the usual interpretation Indra is a warrior-god, while Vṛtra is a serpent-demon. This hymn describes the heroic battle of long ago in which Indra succeeded in destroying his rival. Dayanand had no use for warrior-gods or serpent-demons, and he offered a very different explanation of Ṛg Veda 1.32. According to Swami Dayanand this hymn describes in metaphorical language ("alaṃkāra") the releasing of the waters by the clouds (which are Vṛtra) after they have been smitten by the sun (which is Indra). This hymn does not describe an event that took place in the distant past, Dayanand argued, but one which goes on continually in the present. One of several secondary sources which the swami cited to support this interpretation of Ṛg Veda 1.32 is *Aṣṭādhyāyī* 3.4.6.[80] This rule allows that a past tense verb might be used in place of the present in the Vedas.[81]

There are also a few other contexts in the *Ṛgvedādibhāṣya-bhūmikā* where Dayanand quoted the *Aṣṭādhyāyī* to justify changing the tense[82] or person of a verb[83] in line with a universal interpretation of the application of a Vedic mantra. With the support of the *Aṣṭādhyāyī* Dayanand was able to read mantras which seem to refer to the distant past as if they are actually speaking of the present. He also took verses which are apparently directed at specific individuals and glossed them so that they address a more general audience. These reinterpretations are a very good example of the way that Swami Dayanand used his secondary sources to draw a meaning out of the Vedas which is consistent with his own theories.

We have seen that many Vedic mantras were cited by Swami Dayanand in *Ṛgvedādibhāṣyabhūmikā* without a direct commentary. Of the verses which are interpreted, more often than not Dayanand did not quote any authority to support his reading. When the swami quoted some secondary source it was liable to be one that allowed him a certain flexibility in demonstrating consistency with his interpretation of the Vedas. This is true for all four of the texts which Dayanand quoted most heavily in glossing Vedic mantras in *Ṛgvedādibhāṣyabhūmikā*. The *Śatapatha Brāhmaṇa*, the *Nighaṇṭu*, and the *Nirukta* on occasion offer a series of parallel explanations of a word or a Vedic verse. From these

Dayanand chose the option most consistent with the conclusion that he himself had reached. The *Aṣṭādhyāyī* also permits some latitude in reading the Vedas, which Swami Dayanand fully exploited. With these elastic authorities the founder of the Arya Samaj attempted to demonstrate that his reading of Vedic mantras is consistent with the ancient *ārṣa* literature.

DAYANAND'S MISUSE OF SECONDARY SOURCES

When Swami Dayanand quoted some secondary source in commenting on a Vedic mantra in *Ṛgvedādibhāṣyabhūmikā* it was generally one that allowed him a measure of flexibility. This is not to say that these works might properly be used to support an infinite number of different interpretations. On the contrary, there are instances where Dayanand's authorities clearly adopt one reading. Among these examples there are a limited number of cases where Dayanand did not follow the interpretation of the text which he cited. These divergences might well be said to weaken Swami Dayanand's claim that his interpretation of the Vedas is based upon *ārṣa* works.

At the outset it is difficult to judge in many cases whether the interpretation of a Vedic mantra which Swami Dayanand advanced is consistent with the secondary source cited in *Ṛgvedādibhāṣyabhūmikā* without going to that source. The swami's quotations of his authorities are often limited to single verses or even fragments of verses. Frequently it is hard to make out what the original is driving at from such a brief quote.

Even when the scholar considers the context of the material that the swami quoted, it can be difficult to judge if his use of that material is really appropriate. To take one example: Yajur Veda 31.7 says that the Vedas were produced from the sacrifice, the *yajña*. Dayanand identified the sacrifice with Vishnu, and then argued that Vishnu is God. So the swami said that the mantra means that the Vedas were produced by God. To support the equation of *yajña* with Vishnu Dayanand quoted *Śatapatha Brāhmaṇa* 1.1.2.13: "Yajño vai viṣṇuḥ." "Vishnu is the sacrifice."[84] Here the *Śatapatha Brāhmaṇa* is explaining why the sacrificer intones a part of Yajur Veda 1.9 ("Viṣṇus tvā kramatām") as he mounts the cart which contains the offerings for the new and full-moon sacrifices.[85]

The context of Dayanand's equation of *yajña* and Vishnu is quite different from that of the passage from the *Śatapatha Brāhmaṇa* which he quoted. In *Ṛgvedādibhāṣyabhūmikā* Swami Dayanand reproduced the same phrase on two other occasions, each time arguing that the *yajña* is God.[86] In these cases also Dayanand quoted the phrase without reference to its context in the *Śatapatha Brāhmaṇa*. Using the *Śatapatha Brāhmaṇa* in this way would only be legitimate if "Yajño vai viṣṇuḥ" was intended as a general proposition. Otherwise it would not be appropriate to gloss the word *yajña* as Vishnu wherever one finds it.

The difficulty in judging the appropriateness of Swami Dayanand's use of his sources in interpreting the Vedas is mitigated to a certain extent in those places where Dayanand and the authorities that he quoted are both commenting on the same mantra. In such cases the problems related to context are not so great. Table 6 includes all of the occasions in *Ṛgvedādibhāṣyabhūmikā* where Dayanand in commenting on a Vedic mantra refers to a secondary source which also cites the same mantra.

The first observation that must be made on the basis of the data in this table is that when Dayanand cited secondary sources in the interpretation of Vedic verses in *Ṛgvedādibhāṣyabhūmikā*, very often his source was not commenting on the same verse. Of the 107 mantras commented upon with reference to authoritative secondary sources in Table 5 only thirteen have made it into Table 6. This reinforces the reader's general impression that Dayanand did not attend too closely to context when he looked in other books for support for his Vedic interpretation.

Swami Dayanand's commentaries on the Vedic mantras included in Table 6 are generally more or less consistent with the secondary sources that he cited. But there are a few occasions where it is clear that Dayanand did not follow the authority which he quoted. The most striking example of this is in the swami's discussion of Yajur Veda 23.[87] It was noted in chapter two that Swami Dayanand took strong exception to the medieval commentator Mahīdhara's sexual reading of this hymn. This is a subject that merits further scrutiny. It is appropriate to begin with the interpretation of the *Śatapatha Brāhmaṇa* since Dayanand regarded that text as authoritative and he quoted it in this context.

Parts of Yajur Veda 23 are recited during the great royal horse sacrifice known as the *aśvamedha*. The verses related to this ceremony are explained in the second *adhyāya* of the thirteenth *kāṇḍa* of the *Śatapatha Brāhmaṇa*. In *Śatapatha Brāhmaṇa* 13.2.8.1-2 the ritual

TABLE 6
OCCASIONS WHERE DAYANAND AND HIS SECONDARY SOURCES ARE COMMENTING ON THE SAME VEDIC MANTRA IN *ṚGVEDĀDIBHĀṢYABHŪMIKĀ*

Mantra	Pages in *Ṛgvedādibhāṣyabhūmikā*	Reference to Secondary Source
Ṛg Veda 1.6.1 (=Yajur Veda 23.5)	189-190	Śatapatha Brāhmaṇa 13.2.6.1
Ṛg Veda 1.164.33	324-325	Nirukta 4.21
Ṛg Veda 1.164.46	83 and 371	Nirukta 7.18
Ṛg Veda 10.75.5	343-344	Nirukta 9.26
Yajur Veda 1.5	116	Śatapatha Brāhmaṇa 1.1.1.4, 5
Yajur Veda 5.15 (see Ṛg Veda 1.22.17)	341	Nirukta 12.19
Yajur Veda 23.19	374-375	Śatapatha Brāhmaṇa 13.2.8.4-5
Yajur Veda 23.20	378	Śatapatha Brāhmaṇa 13.2.8.5
Yajur Veda 23.22	379	Śatapatha Brāhmaṇa 13.2.9.6
Yajur Veda 23.24	380	Śatapatha Brāhmaṇa 13.2.9.7
Yajur Veda 23.26	381-382	Śatapatha Brāhmaṇa 13.2.9.2-5
Yajur Veda 23.30	384	Śatapatha Brāhmaṇa 13.2.9.8
Yajur Veda 31.16	148	Nirukta 12.41

Sources: Dayanand, *Ṛgvedādibhāṣyabhūmikā*, in *Ṛgveda-Bhāṣyam*, vol. 1, 1-430; *Śatapatha-Brāhmaṇam*, ed. Ganga Prasad Upadhyaya, 3 vols. (Delhi: Research Institute of Ancient Scientific Studies, 1967-1970); and Lakshman Sarup, ed., *The Nighaṇṭu and the Nirukta: The Oldest Indian Treatise on Etymology, Philology and Semantics* (Delhi: Motilal Banarsidass, 1984), Part 3.

slaughter of the horse is described. Prior to this, mantras from Yajur Veda 23 are explained that are intoned as the horse is prepared for its execution. But it is the mantras that can be found after 13.2.8.1-2 which most concerned Swami Dayanand. Here the *Śatapatha Brāhmaṇa* relates an unusual ritual in which the wives of the king who is the sponsor of the sacrifice first circumambulate the equine victim. Then the king's favorite wife lies down beside the dead horse and commands it to impregnate her. This is followed by a colloquy between the king's wives and the ritual officiants which is of a sexually explicit nature.

The *Śatapatha Brāhmaṇa* not only describes these ceremonies, but also offers an interpretation of them which relates to the royal context. We might quote as an example Julius Eggeling's translation of *Śatapatha Brāhmaṇa* 13.2.9.6:

> [The Adhvaryu addresses one of the attendant maids, Vâg. S. XXIII, 22,] 'That little bird,'--the little bird, doubtless, is the people (or clan),—'which bustles with (the sound) "ahalak,"'—for the people, indeed, bustle for (the behoof of) royal power,—"thrusts the "pasas" into the cleft, and the "dhâraka" devours it,'—the cleft, doubtless, is the people, and the 'pasas' is royal power; and royal power, indeed, presses hard on the people; whence the wielder of royal power is apt to strike down people.[88]

It seems that we are dealing here with a fertility ritual, which was becoming subject to reinterpretation even as early as the *Śatapatha Brāhmaṇa*.[89]

In his commentary on the Yajur Veda Mahīdhara devoted some attention to the twenty-third *adhyāya*. In explaining Yajur Veda 23.5-32 (which includes the mantras cited in the second *adhyāya* of the thirteenth *kāṇḍa* of the *Śatapatha Brāhmaṇa* in connection with the *aśvamedha*) Mahīdhara frequently quoted the *Śatapatha Brāhmaṇa*.[90] In Table 7 we have noted all of the secondary sources cited by Mahīdhara in his commentary on Yajur Veda 23.5-32. It should be pointed out that while Mahīdhara discussed in detail the fertility ritual described above, he paid no attention to the *Śatapatha Brāhmaṇa*'s royal reinterpretation. We might refer again to Yajur Veda 23.22, on which the commentary from the *Śatapatha Brāhmaṇa* was just quoted. Mahīdhara just glosses *gabha* as *yoni*, which is another word for vulva, and *pasas* as *liṅga*, or "penis." There is no sign in Mahīdhara's commentary of the *viś* (the people) or *rāṣṭra* (royal power) that one finds in the *Śatapatha Brāhmaṇa*.[91]

TABLE 7
SECONDARY SOURCES CITED BY MAHĪDHARA IN COMMENTING ON YAJUR VEDA 23.5-32

Mantra in the Yajur Veda	Sources Cited by Mahīdhara	
	Śatapatha Brāhmaṇa	Other Works
23.5	13.2.6.1	Aṣṭādhyāyī 3.1.135
23.6	—	Nirukta 2.6
23.7	—	Aṣṭādhyāyī 7.4.65
23.8	—	—
23.9	—	—
23.10	13.2.6.10-13	—
23.11	—	—
23.12	13.2.6.14, 16	—
23.13	13.2.7.2, 4, 6-7[a]	Yajur Veda 6.9, 24.1
23.14	13.2.7.8, 10	—
23.15	13.2.7.11	—
23.16	13.2.7.12	Vārttika 3 on Aṣṭādhyāyī 3.1.48
23.17	13.2.7.13	Yajur Veda 6.10
23.18	13.2.8.2	Yajur Veda 6.11, 12, Aṣṭādhyāyī 6.1.118

[a] Weber has *Śatapatha Brāhmaṇa* 13.2.7.5 rather than 13.2.7.6, but it seems that this is an error. Compare *Śatapatha-Brāhmaṇam*, ed. Ganga Prasad Upadhyaya, 3: 1709.

Table 7—*Continued*

Mantra in the Yajur Veda	Sources Cited by Mahīdhara	
	Śatapatha Brāhmaṇa	Other Works
23.19	—	—
23.20	13.2.8.5	—
23.21	—	—
23.22	—	Aṣṭdhyāyī 5.3.71, 85, Nirukta 5.16
23.23	—	—
23.24	—	—
23.25	—	—
23.26	—	—
23.27	—	—
23.28	—	Nighaṇṭu 3.2
23.29	—	Aṣṭādhyāyī 1.4.82, 3.4.6, 5.2.115
23.30	—	Aṣṭādhyāyī 3.1.103, 7.4.34, and Vārttika 1.2 on Aṣṭādhyāyī 4.1.4
23.31	—	—
23.32	13.2.9.9	Aṣṭādhyāyī 3.2.75, 171, and 6.4.41

Source: Albrecht Weber, ed. *The Vajasaneyi-Saṃhitā in the Mādhyandina and the Kānva-Śākhā with the Commentary of Mahidhara*, 2d ed., Chowkhamba Sanskrit Series, no. 103 (Benares: Chowkhamba Sanskrit Series Office, 1972), 709-722.

While Mahīdhara ignored one side of the *Śatapatha Brāhmaṇa*'s interpretation of Yajur Veda 23, Swami Dayanand in *Ṛgvedādibhāṣyabhūmikā* ignored the other. From Table 8 it is clear that the *Śatapatha Brāhmaṇa* was an important source for Dayanand's understanding of the twenty-third *adhyāya* of the Yajur Veda in the present context.[92] Here the swami, who castigated Mahīdhara for his obscene commentary, presented the *Śatapatha Brāhmaṇa*'s reinterpretation of the fertility ritual connected with Yajur Veda 23, but he overlooked the ritual itself. To take the same instance yet a third time, in the swami's explanation of Yajur Veda 23.22 *pasas* is only *rāṣṭra*, or "royal power," and not "penis," and *gabha* is only *viś*, or "the people," not "vulva."[93]

Swami Dayanand maintained this univocal reading in spite of the rather obvious contrary interpretation of the *Śatapatha Brāhmaṇa*, even in passages that he quoted. For example, in the part of *Śatapatha Brāhmaṇa* 13.2.8.5 that Dayanand reproduced in commenting on Yajur Veda 23.20 the former text twice has the phrase "mithunasyāvarudhyai." The queen addresses the slain horse "in order to attain copulation," the *Śatapatha Brāhmaṇa* explains. Yet even here the swami's interpretation only concerns proper governance, and not sexual intercourse.[94] Swami Dayanand maintained his own interpretation despite the contrary evidence in a secondary source which he actually quoted.

The impression that Swami Dayanand has not given an adequate account of the *Śatapatha Brāhmaṇa*'s interpretation of this passage from Yajur Veda 23 is reaffirmed when we turn our attention to the second *brāhmaṇa* of the fifth *adhyāya* of the thirteenth *kāṇḍa* of the *Śatapatha Brāhmaṇa*. Here the fertility ritual that we have described is recounted in even greater detail. For example, the speakers in the obscene colloquy are identified. With Yajur Veda 23.22 the priest known as the *adhvaryu* addresses a maiden *(kumārī)*, who replies to him with 23.23. Then the *brahman* priest directs Yajur Veda 23.24 at the *mahiṣī*, the first wife of the king, whose attendants respond with 23.25. This is followed by Yajur Veda 23.26, which the *udgātṛ* priest speaks to the *vāvātā* (the king's favorite wife, inferior only to the *mahiṣī*), whose attendants utter 23.27 in response. After this the *hotṛ* priest turns to the *parivṛktā* (which means "the despised woman," she is a queen who is less favored by the king than the *mahiṣī* or *vāvātā*) with Yajur Veda 23.28, to which those accompanying her answer 23.29. Finally the *kṣattṛ*, who is a servant of the crown, addresses the king's fourth wife (the *pālāgalī*) with Yajur Veda 23.30, and her companions respond with 23.31.[95]

TABLE 8

SECONDARY SOURCES CITED BY DAYANAND IN COMMENTING ON YAJUR VEDA 23.19-31

Mantra in the Yajur Veda	Sources Cited by Dayanand	
	Śatapatha Brāhmaṇa	Other Works
23.19	13.2.2.14-17, 19, 13.2.3.1 13.2.8.4-5, 13.3.3.5	Aitareya Brāhmaṇa 1.21,[a] Nirukta 7.24
23.20	13.2.8.5	--
23.21	--	--
23.22	13.2.9.6	--
23.23	--[b]	--
23.24	13.2.9.7	--
23.26[c]	13.2.9.2-5	--
23.28	--[c]	--
23.29	--	--
23.30	13.2.9.8	--
23.31	--[b]	--

Source: Dayanand, *Ṛgvedādibhāṣyabhūmikā*, in *Ṛgveda-Bhāṣyam*, vol. 1, 374-385.

---

a Dayanand quoted from the twenty-first verse of the first *pañcikā*, which might also be numbered the fourth verse of the fourth *adhyāya* of the first *pañcikā*. Arthur Berriedale Keith, *Rigveda Brahmanas: The Aitareya and Kauṣītaki Brāhmaṇas of the Rigveda*, Harvard Oriental Series, ed. Charles Rockwell Lanman, vol. 25 (Cambridge, Mass.: Harvard University Press, 1920), 122.

b This mantra is cited with the previous one by Dayanand. The secondary sources noted for the latter might be said to apply to both.

c Yajur Veda 23.28 is cited with 23.26. The secondary sources noted for the latter might be said to apply to both.

In *Śatapatha Brāhmaṇa* 13.2 only a few of these mantras are commented upon, and the emphasis is on the sense of the verses themselves and their royal reinterpretation--the parties to the colloquy are never named.[96] So *Śatapatha Brāhmaṇa* 13.5.2 adds an important element to our understanding of the rituals in which the twenty-third *adhyāya* of the Yajur Veda is used. Unfortunately Swami Dayanand did not quote these later verses.

Anticipating this objection, the editor of *Ṛgvedādibhāṣya-bhūmikā* Yudhiṣṭhir Mīmāṃsak maintains that *Śatapatha Brāhmaṇa* 13.5.2 is an interpolation and not a reliable reflection of the opinion of the author of that work. Specifically Mīmāṃsak suggests that the use of the word *pariśiṣṭa* in 13.5.2.1 definitely marks what follows as a later addition to the *Śatapatha Brāhmaṇa*.[97] This evidence is far from probative, for *pariśiṣṭa* can mean many different things.[98] Most importantly, one must be clear that this argument is not made by Dayanand himself. It seems that the swami was content to quote the passages from the *Śatapatha Brāhmaṇa* which were easier to reconcile with his own interpretation, while remaining silent on those that were less consistent.

There is one more interesting issue suggested by *Śatapatha Brāhmaṇa* 13.2 which Swami Dayanand did not confront directly, but which is worthy of consideration nonetheless. One of the great causes of the Arya Samaj has been vegetarianism. Arya Samajists have been especially aggressive in their attacks on animal sacrifice in religious ceremonies. Western scholars believe that the slaughter and oblation of animals was at the heart of Vedic religion, but Arya Samajists reject this notion. In *Satyārth Prakāś* Dayanand argued that animal sacrifice was introduced into Hinduism by tantrics. Vedic mantras which have been related to the killing of animals are simply misunderstood. Any passages in the authoritative *ārṣa* literature which enjoin the killing of animals were interpolated by tantrics.[99]

Although he did not express his views on this issue at such great length in *Ṛgvedādibhāṣyabhūmikā*, it is clear that here, too, Dayanand did not accept animal sacrifice as a part of Vedic religion. At one point in glossing a passage from the *Śatapatha Brāhmaṇa* on the *aśvamedha* or horse sacrifice, the swami wrote: "Protection of the state is the sacrifice of Kshatriyas known as the *aśvamedha*, and not killing a horse and oblating its limbs."[100] But *Śatapatha Brāhmaṇa* 13.2.8.1-2 clearly describes the slaughter of the horse in the *aśvamedha*, using the verb root *han*, "to strike, to kill." Although Dayanand quoted *Śatapatha Brāhmaṇa* 13.2.8.4-5 in his analysis of Yajur Veda 23, he never said anything about 13.2.8.1-2. From the beginning of his discussion, the swami reinterprets *aśva* (horse) as a symbol of royal power. He gives no indication that there is any ceremony involving an actual horse being described in the *Śatapatha Brāhmaṇa*. Thus Dayanand avoided discussing the issue of the killing of an animal in Vedic ceremonial, though it is clear that this is what the *Śatapatha Brāhmaṇa* demands.

It is difficult to avoid the general conclusion that Swami Dayanand was not completely faithful to the *Śatapatha Brāhmaṇa* in his interpretation of the twenty-third *adhyāya* of the Yajur Veda. At the same time it seems obvious that Dayanand was not completely fair to Mahīdhara in his criticism of the medieval commentator. The swami only cites passages from Mahīdhara that are obscene, leaving out other material. For example, Mahīdhara opens his commentary on Yajur Veda 23.19 with a discussion of the circumambulation of the sacrificial victim by the kings' wives, before going on to describe the queen's sexual address to the dead horse.[101] When Dayanand quoted Mahīdhara on this verse he only reproduced the sexual injunction and not the circumambulation.

It is also significant that in his quotes of Mahīdhara the swami did not include a single one of the medieval commentator's citations of secondary works. In comparing Table 7 and Table 5 it is striking that the texts which Mahīdhara referred to in connection with Yajur Veda 23.5-32 are some of the same ones that are important in Dayanand's commentaries on Vedic mantras in *Ṛgvedādibhāṣyabhūmikā*. On the basis of the passages that the swami quoted the reader might get the impression that Mahīdhara's commentary is without support from secondary sources. When the reader investigates Mahīdhara's original, he or she finds that his interpretation is shored up by just those texts which Dayanand identified as authoritative. By his selective quotation the swami has created a false impression about Mahīdhara's work.

Our discussion of Swami Dayanand's interpretation of Yajur Veda 23, the *Śatapatha Brāhmaṇa*, and Mahīdhara's commentary has been so lengthy that it might be helpful to repeat the main conclusions that have arisen from it once again by way of summary. In discussing the ritual application of Yajur Veda 23.18-32 the *Śatapatha Brāhmaṇa* presents a fertility ceremony and offers a royal reinterpretation of that ceremony. In his commentary on the Yajur Veda Mahīdhara describes the same fertility rite, but he does not concern himself with the royal significance of it. Dayanand, on the other hand, did not admit that any obscene ritual is involved here, and he limited his attention to the reinterpretation of the *Śatapatha Brāhmaṇa*. Because Mahīdhara's viewpoint included what Dayanand wished to exclude and excluded what the swami sought to emphasize, it is totally rejected.

The swami's method with regard to the *Śatapatha Brāhmaṇa* is consistent with what we find in other contexts in *Ṛgvedādibhāṣyabhūmikā*. Dayanand often chose to focus on the allegorical significance of a myth or rite while denying any reality to that myth or rite in itself. For example, we have already noted that Dayanand regarded the story of Indra and Vṛtra in Ṛg Veda 1.32 as an allegory for the release of the rains under the heat of the sun. For the swami there was no Indra who was a warrior-god or Vṛtra who was a serpent-demon. In a similar manner, the swami maintained that in Yajur Veda 23 there are no horses or priests or queens but only allegorical figures related to proper governance. Because Dayanand's conclusions here pick up on just one aspect of the interpretation of Yajur Veda 23 in the *Śatapatha Brāhmaṇa*, he is forced to ignore the other aspects of that interpretation. Though the *Śatapatha Brāhmaṇa* was included among the lists of authoritative works, and though it is the text most heavily quoted in the interpretation of Vedic mantras in *Ṛgvedādibhāṣyabhūmikā*, Swami Dayanand was still capable of misreading that work in order to justify his own conclusions.

To demonstrate that this deliberate misreading of the *Śatapatha Brāhmaṇa* is not an isolated case, a few other examples of Swami Dayanand's creative use of secondary sources might be in order. One of the more blatant instances again concerns the *Śatapatha Brāhmaṇa*. At the end of a long commentary on Ṛg Veda 8.28.1, Yajur Veda 14.31, and Atharva Veda 10.7.23 and 27 Dayanand quoted *Śatapatha Brāhmaṇa* 14.4.2.22 to show that only one God is to be worshipped according to authoritative literature.[102] In the *Śatapatha Brāhmaṇa* it is clear in this context that the thing which is to be worshipped is the self (the Atman), which is not different from the whole world. We have already noted in this chapter that Dayanand believed that there are three eternally existing (*anādi*) entities, God (*īśvara*), souls (*jīvas*), and the material world (*jagat*). The idea of an Atman which is not different from all of these three entities was not consistent with Dayanand's philosophy. So the swami was at some pains to choose a passage from the *Śatapatha Brāhmaṇa* which does not obviously contradict his teachings.

In order to arrive at such a quote it was actually necessary for Dayanand to do a little editing. Not only did he fail to reproduce the context of the sentence quoted, but he omitted a phrase from the middle of that sentence. Here is translation of the sentence which Dayanand quoted, with the material that he left out of his quote in italics. "So whoever worships another divinity [than his Self], *thinking 'He is one and I another,'* he knows not. He is like a sacrificial animal for the gods."[103] In this case Dayanand was forced to chop up the passage in the *Śatapatha Brāhmaṇa* so that it would contain nothing contrary to his philosophy.

Let us review just one more example of a quote taken out of context from the *Śatapatha Brāhmaṇa* in *Ṛgvedādibhāṣyabhūmikā*. In his public debates Swami Dayanand repeatedly tried to prove that there is no image worship in the Vedas. Against this contention traditional Hindu pandits pointed to the occurrences of the word *pratimā* in the Vedas, a word which came to mean "idol" among other things in classical Sanskrit. Dayanand set down his response to this argument in *Ṛgvedādibhāṣyabhūmikā*, where he claimed that in the Vedas and *ārṣa* literature *pratimā* means the same thing as *pratimāṇa*, or "measure."

To substantiate this claim the swami quoted *Śatapatha Brāhmaṇa* 10.4.3.20 in commenting on Atharva Veda 3.10.3.[104] The passage from the former work which Dayanand quoted reads: ". . . they are the counterpart [the original is *pratimā*] of the muhūrtas: there are ten thousand and eight hundred of them, for so many muhūrtas there are in a year."[105] It may seem plausible to the reader from just this quote that the *Śatapatha Brāhmaṇa* is speaking here of some unit of measure of time, but that is not in fact the case.

This text is drawn from a long passage which consists of a series of speculations on the meaning of the fire altar. In the verse in question the *lokampṛṇā*, a kind of brick used in building the altar, is being discussed. We have already mentioned the homologies that are characteristic of the *Śatapatha Brāhmaṇa*. Here we have an equation of the altar and the year. One of the elements of this formula is the *lokampṛṇā* brick, which is the counterpart (the *pratimā*) in the altar to the *muhūrta* in the year. If Dayanand quoted the entirety of *Śatapatha Brāhmaṇa* 10.4.3.20 then it would be clear that his interpretation of the verse is strained, since it would make no logical sense for a brick to be a unit of measure (a *pratimāṇa* which is how Dayanand takes *pratimā*) for a period of time. But Swami Dayanand did not quote all of the verse, so his argument appears plausible.

Rather than leave the impression that Swami Dayanand practiced this kind of creative quotation only with respect to the *Śatapatha Brāhmaṇa*, let us take one example from the *Nirukta* on the by now familiar story of Indra and Vṛtra. In commenting on Ṛg Veda 1.32.5 Swami Dayanand quoted *Nirukta* 2.16 and 17 to support his contention that this hymn is about meteorological phenomena and not about warrior-gods and serpent-demons.[106] Both of these sections in the *Nirukta* are focused on mantras from Ṛg Veda 1.32, mantras which continue the tale of Indra and Vṛtra, so it is quite appropriate to quote them in connection with 1.32.5.[107] In 2.16 the author of the *Nirukta* has lent some support to Dayanand's climatic interpretation of the story of Indra and Vṛtra. He allows that Vṛtra is a cloud which gives up its rain. But after advancing this explanation, the *Nirukta* admits that another is possible.

> Indeed, the descriptions of Vedic stanzas and the narratives of the Brāhmaṇas (depict him), no doubt, as a serpent. By expanding his body, he blocked the channels (of the rivers). When he was killed, waters flowed forth.[108]

Here the *Nirukta* acknowledges the mythological understanding of the battle of Indra and Vṛtra as one alternative for interpreting Ṛg Veda 1.32. Dayanand did not quote this part of *Nirukta* 2.16, rather he only reproduced some of the earlier material on the meteorological reading of the verse. Hence Dayanand's quotation of the *Nirukta* makes it seem as if that text is more consistent with the swami's view than it actually is.

Throughout this section the focus has been on the secondary sources which Swami Dayanand used to back up his interpretation of Vedic mantras in *Ṛgvedādibhāṣyabhūmikā*. In the course of our explication we have dealt with one work which the swami quoted in order to demonstrate its inaccuracy, Mahīdhara's commentary on the Yajur Veda. Before concluding the section we might consider a second example of Swami Dayanand's one-sided interpretation of a work which he regarded as unreliable, a work by the German-born English Vedic scholar Max Mueller.

In *Ṛgvedādibhāṣyabhūmikā* Dayanand offers three alternative readings for Ṛg Veda 1.6.1. According to the first and third options this mantra concerns the yogi's contemplation (*upāsanā*) of God. By the second interpretation the mantra is about the sun which attracts and illumines the planets. The key to Dayanand's understanding of Ṛg Veda 1.6.1 is the words *bradhna* and *aruṣa*. In his first reading of the mantra *bradhna* is glossed *sarvānandavardhaka*, "who causes all bliss to increase" or God, and *aruṣa*, which is understood as an adjective modifying *bradhna*, is explained with *ahiṃsaka*, "who does no violence." In the second reading *bradhna* is Āditya, the sun, and *aruṣa* (again modifying *bradhna*) is *agnimaya*, "composed of fire." Finally in the third gloss *bradhna* is *sarvāvayavavṛddhikara prāṇa*, "the vital breath which leads to the increase of all the limbs," and *aruṣa* (modifying *bradhna*) is *sarvamarmastha*, "which is situated in all vulnerable spots."[109]

To these various readi. gs Swami Dayanand contrasted Max Mueller's idea that *bradhna aruṣa* in Ṛg Veda 1.6.1 refers to a horse. The swami did admit that the *Nighaṇṭu* gives *bradhna* and *aruṣa* as synonyms of *aśva* ("horse"), but he was not convinced by this evidence. In fact, Dayanand did not even go to the trouble of finding the specific reference, merely saying, "Someplace in the *Nighaṇṭu bradhna* and *aruṣa* are mentioned as synonyms of *aśva*."[110] Dayanand argued that such a reading is not possible here, because it would not make any sense in this context. The swami added disparagingly, "I don't know if this meaning was grabbed by Mr. Max Mueller from the heavens or from hell."[111]

Review of Max Mueller's original interpretation undermines Dayanand's strong condemnation. It is true that Mueller translated *bradhna aruṣa* as "the bright red steed."[112] But in his extensive notes on this phrase Mueller added "Arusha, meaning originally red, is used as a proper name of the horse or of the rising sun." The European scholar interpreted the verse as a "description of sunrise" in which "Indra is taken as the god of the bright day, whose steed is the sun."[113] Thus it seems obvious that Max Mueller's reading of Ṛg Veda 1.6.1 might easily be reconciled with Dayanand's second interpretation of the same mantra.

Why is it that Dayanand so strongly attacked Mueller's comments even though they might well have been brought into accord with his own? It seems that Dayanand judged Mueller on the basis of his translation, without regard for his notes. To the extent that this translation is based on the primary and not the allegorical sense of the mantra, to the extent that in this translation horses are still horses and not yet the sun, Mueller's work was unacceptable to Swami Dayanand. Regardless of the reason for Dayanand's criticism of Mueller, it is clear that the swami misrepresented the European scholar's interpretation of Ṛg Veda 1.6.1 by delineating only one aspect of that interpretation.

After demonstrating in the previous subsection that his secondary sources allowed some flexibility in the interpretation of Vedic mantras, here we have added evidence that Swami Dayanand still found it necessary to misuse those sources on occasion. Most often Dayanand ignored the context of a passage quoted when that context was inconsistent with the point that he was trying to make or with his teaching on some other issue. We have even presented a couple of examples from *Ṛgvedādibhāṣyabhūmikā* where the swami offered such a selective reading of a work which he did not regard as authoritative, which served to make that work more vulnerable to attack. Swami Dayanand's interested reading of his sources undermines his claim that his interpretation of the Vedas is consistent with the ancient and largely authoritative *ārṣa* literature.

CONCLUSION

In this chapter we have examined not only Swami Dayanand's theories about the Vedas, but also his attempts to support those theories through the citation of secondary sources. In the first section we noted that it is not so much Dayanand's claim of inerrancy which distinguishes his position on the Vedas from the traditional understanding—the Vedas have long been held to be free of error—rather it is his attempt to use that literature as an authority in all areas of life. According to Swami Dayanand this position is not new, but marks a return to the situation that pertained in the ancient period. Dayanand believed that access to the proper understanding of the Vedas is to be had through the old works which were written in that period, the *ārṣa* literature. It is these *ārṣa* texts that Dayanand quoted in his commentaries on Vedic mantras, to show that his interpretation was not arbitrary but a reiteration of the antique view. It could be argued that Swami Dayanand's interpretation of the Vedas stands or falls on its consistency with the works that he identifies as authoritative.

In the second section of this chapter we analyzed the secondary sources that Dayanand actually quoted in commenting on Vedic verses in *Ṛgvedādibhāṣyabhūmikā*. Many mantras in that book are glossed without the aid of any secondary work. Yet in those cases where some supporting text is cited, it is generally one that Dayanand dubbed authoritative. Still, there is substantial evidence in this chapter that Swami Dayanand was not above wrenching a quote out of its context in order to bend to it to his interpretation of the Vedas, regardless of the acknowledged reliability of the book from which it was drawn. It would be wrong to leave the reader with the impression that this was his constant practice. In most of the cases where Dayanand has quoted some text to corroborate his reading of a Vedic mantra in *Ṛgvedādibhāṣya-bhūmikā* that reading seems to be more or less consistent with the work cited. Even so, it cannot be denied that there are also many passages where it seems as if the swami was determined to proceed with his own interpretation of a Vedic verse, despite what other works might say.

While it is easy to point to examples where Swami Dayanand misused his sources, proving that his reading of the Vedas is wrong is a different matter. Dayanand was a master of reinterpretation. If one had the opportunity to confront him with some passage in an authoritative work which is in conflict with his commentary on a Vedic mantra, he might well reinterpret that passage so that the difficulty is removed. Even if such an attempt was unavailing, the swami would have a powerful weapon in reserve. According to the founder of the Arya Samaj the *ārṣa* literature is largely authoritative, but not perfectly so. Presented with an irreconcilable conflict, Dayanand could claim that the secondary work is just plain wrong and discard it.

The only conclusion that an academic can establish is that Swami Dayanand was sometimes less than scrupulous in his use of secondary sources. The scholar can follow along behind the swami, looking at the context of the passages that he quoted, and make some judgement about the relative adequacy of his rendering of the sense of those passages. Unlike the fundamentalist, the academic does not have access to an absolutely certain truth. So he or she must be content with modest conclusions.

NOTES

1. Jan Gonda, *Vedic Literature (Saṃhitās and Brāhmaṇas)*, A History of Indian Literature, ed. Jan Gonda, vol. 1, fascicle 1 (Wiesbaden: Otto Harrassowitz, 1975), 20, 22.
2. Ibid., 65-78.
3. Ibid., 128-131.
4. A.A. Macdonell, *Vedic Mythology*, Grundriss der Indo-Arischen Philologie und Altertumskunde, ed. G. Buehler, vol. 3, part 1A (Strassburg: Karl J. Truebner, 1897), for Indra, 55-66, for Agni, 88-101.
5. Dayanand, *Ṛgvedādibhāṣyabhūmikā*, in *Ṛgveda-Bhāṣyam*, vol. 1, 94-105.
6. To be exact Dayanand said that at the time of writing the *Ṛgvedādibhāṣyabhūmikā* (Vikram Saṃvat 1933 or around C.E. 1876) 1,960,852,976 years had passed since the creation of the world. Dayanand, *Ṛgvedādibhāṣyabhūmikā*, in *Ṛgveda-Bhāṣyam*, vol. 1, 24-25.
7. Dayanand, *Ṛgvedādibhāṣyabhūmikā*, in *Ṛgveda-Bhāṣyam*, vol. 1, 31.
8. Ibid., 19.
9. Ibid., 395.

10. Ibid., 34.
11. Ibid., 33-48.
12. Ibid., 21.
13. Ibid., 12. Dayanand is commenting on *Śatapatha Brāhmaṇa* 14.5.4.10 here.
14. To quote one of many examples, "sarvavidyāmayīṃ vedavidyām." Dayanand, *Ṛgvedādibhāṣyabhūmikā*, in *Ṛgveda-Bhāṣyam*, vol. 1, 18.
15. *Nirvikār* is one of the qualities of God according to the second *niyam* of the Arya Samaj. Lekh Rām, *Jīvancaritra: Maharṣi Swāmī Dayānand Sarasvatī*, ed. Bhavānīlāl Bhārtīy, trans. Raghunandansiṃh, 2d printing (Delhi: Ārṣ Sāhitya Pracār Trust, Vikram Saṃvat 2041), 329.
16. Dayanand, *Satyārth Prakāś*, 299. For another discussion of God's knowledge of the three times with a seemingly different conclusion, see Dayanand, *Ṛgvedādibhāṣyabhūmikā*, in *Ṛgveda-Bhāṣyam*, vol. 1, 88.
17. Dayanand, *Ṛgvedādibhāṣyabhūmikā*, in *Ṛgveda-Bhāṣyam*, vol. 1, 96.
18. The *Taittirīya Āraṇyaka* makes a similar argument, though Dayanand did not note this. *Taittirīya Āraṇyaka* 1.8, cited by the editor of *Ṛgvedādibhāṣyabhūmikā*, in *Ṛgveda-Bhāṣyam*, vol. 1, 338, n. 1.
19. *Śatapatha Brāhmaṇa* 7.5.1.5, quoted by Dayanand, *Ṛgvedādibhāṣyabhūmikā*, in *Ṛgveda-Bhāṣyam*, vol. 1, 338. In this passage the *Śatapatha Brāhmaṇa* establishes the equation Kaśyapa = Prajāpati by quite a different set of arguments, which I will not reproduce here.
20. Dayanand, *Ṛgvedādibhāṣyabhūmikā*, in *Ṛgveda-Bhāṣyam*, vol. 1, 398-401. The edition used here reads "vyāvāhārika" (on p. 400), but the *Granthmālā* has "vyāvahārika," which is correct. Swami Dayanand Sarasvati, *Dayānand-Granthmālā*, Nirvāṇ-Śatābdī-Saṃskaraṇ, 2d reprint (Ajmer: Paropkāriṇī Sabhā, 1983), vol. 2: 621.
21. For example, Dayanand, *Ṛgvedādibhāṣyabhūmikā*, in *Ṛgveda-Bhāṣyam*, vol. 1, 287-293.
22. Dayanand, *Ṛgvedādibhāṣyabhūmikā*, in *Ṛgveda-Bhāṣyam*, vol. 1, 329-333.
23. Ibid., 82.
24. Ibid., 160-164.
25. Ibid., 234-236.
26. Here I agree with Dayanand's editor that in the chapter on telegraphy in *Ṛgvedādibhāṣyabhūmikā* one must attend to Dayanand's use of the terms "tāraviḍyāmūla" and "tāravidyābīja." Dayanand, *Ṛgvedādibhāṣyabhūmikā*, in *Ṛgveda-Bhāṣyam*, vol. 1,

234, n. 1 and 235, n. 1. I am less impressed with the editor's arguments in this context about the technological advancement of the ancient Aryans (pp. 234, n. 3 and 235, n. 2). As I have argued above, I think any discussion of technology per se is out of place here.

27. Louis Renou, *The Destiny of the Veda in India*, ed. Dev Raj Chanana (Delhi: Motilal Banarsidass, 1965), 4.
28. Gonda, 54.
29. K. Satchidananda Murty, *Revelation and Reason in Advaita Vedānta* (Waltair: Andhra University, 1959; New York: Columbia University Press, 1959), 212.
30. Sheldon Pollock, "The 'Revelation' of 'Tradition': *Śruti, Smṛti*, and the Sanskrit Discourse of Power," forthcoming in *Lex et Litterae: Festschrift Botto*. I am grateful to Professor Pollock for allowing me to see the manuscript of this article.
31. Śabara's commentary on *Mimamsa Sutras* 1.2.20, paraphrased by Satchidananda Murty, 217.
32. Renou, 42-43.
33. *Nyaya Sutras* 2.1.57 and following, discussed in Renou, 32.
34. J. Muir, *Original Sanskrit Texts on the Origin and History of the People of India, Their Religion and Institutions*, vol. 3, *The Vedas: Opinions of Their Authors and of Later Indian Writers on Their Origin, Inspiration, and Authority*, 2d ed. (London: Truebner, 1873), 127.
35. Śaṅkara in his commentary on *Vedanta Sutras* 2.1.1, quoted by Muir, 187. Muir actually has "prāmaṇyaṃ" here, but this is apparently an error. For the correct reading "prāmāṇyaṃ" see J.L. Shastri, ed., *Brahmasūtra-Śāṃkarabhāṣyam* (Delhi: Motilal Banarsidass, 1980), 351.
36. Śaṅkara in his commentary on *Vedanta Sutras* 1.3.30, discussed by Satchidananda Murty, 50.
37. I disagree here with Arvind Sharma, who has argued that Dayanand's proof of Vedic authority follows Nyaya rather than Mimamsa and Vedanta because it is based not on the eternity of the Vedas but on the reliability of their author. Arvind Sharma, "Svami Dayananda Sarasvati and Vedic Authority," in *Religion in Modern India*, ed. Robert D. Baird (Delhi: Manohar, 1981), 185. As indicated in the text, in Dayanand's work it is not a question of either Mimamsa-Vedanta or Nyaya, but rather of both Mimamsa-Vedanta and Nyaya.
38. It should be added, though, that Dayanand had no use for Vedanta's monism. Dayanand believed that there are three eternally existent entities, which is a Nyaya doctrine. On Nyaya, see Satchidananda Murty, 199. Dayanand criticized the Vedanta's theory that

ultimately all is *brahman*. Dayanand, *Satyārth Prakāś*, 300-310.

39. I understand that Mimamsa denied the perpetual dissolution and re-creation of the world, so the Arya Samaj and Mimamsa differ on this issue. Satchidananda Murty, 213.

40. Renou, 2.

41. Renou notes that *nāstika* has also been used for atheists. Renou, 60, n. 11 (Note that the numbering of the endnotes does not correspond at this point to the numbering of the text.). This seems to be how Dayanand uses the term in the *Ṛgvedādibhāṣyabhūmikā* (on p. 256). In *Satyārth Prakāś* the more usual sense of *nāstika* is more prominent. Twice Dayanand quotes *The Laws of Manu* 2.21:

> That twice-born person who despises these two sources [sruti and smriti] relying upon dialectics
> Should be outcasted by good people, a *nāstika* and reviler of the Vedas.

Dayanand, *Satyārth Prakāś*, 90 and 401.

42. *Chāndogya Upaniṣad* 7.1.2, quoted by Muir, 32-33.

43. *Muṇḍaka Upaniṣad* 1.1.4-5, quoted by Muir, 30-31.

44. Muir, 29-30.

45. R.C. Zaehner, *The Bhagavad-Gītā* (London: Oxford University Press, 1976), 366 (*Gītā* 15.15). The phrase in brackets was inserted by Zaehner.

46. Zaehner, 51 (*Gītā* 2.46).

47. Ibid., 319-320 (*Gītā* 11.53-54). Again the brackets are Zaehner's.

48. *Bhāgavata Purāṇa* 1.4.20, quoted in Muir, 41-42. *Itihāsa* is the genre which includes the epic *Mahābhārata* and *Rāmāyaṇa*. *Purāṇa* is the genre of mythological literature currently under discussion. It is likely that the *Bhāgavata Purāṇa* is referring here to these two well known bodies of literature. The passage cited above from the *Chāndogya Upaniṣad* may not make reference to these genres, since they probably did not exist in the form that we now know them at such an early date. For speculation on the sense of *itihāsa* and *purāṇa* in the Vedic period see Gonda, 407-409.

49. *Bhāgavata Purāṇa* 4.29.42 and following, quoted in Muir, 34-35.

50. Ch. Vaudeville, *Kabīr* (Oxford: Oxford University Press, 1974), vol. 1: 155.

51. Linda Hess and Shukdev Singh, trans. *The Bījak of Kabir* (San Francisco: North Point Press, 1983), 51-52.

52. The date is from Renou, 22.

53. Dayanand, *Ṛgvedādibhāṣyabhūmikā*, in *Ṛgveda-Bhāṣyam*, vol. 1, 370.

54. Thirty-six Vedic mantras without commentary are cited in fourteen pages. Dayanand, *Ṛgvedādibhāṣyabhūmikā*, in *Ṛgveda-Bhāṣyam*, vol. 1, 407-420.

55. Dayanand, *Ṛgvedādibhāṣyabhūmikā*, in *Ṛgveda-Bhāṣyam*, vol. 1, 83-85.
56. Only citations in support of Dayanand's reading have been counted in this survey. Works whose interpretation of the mantras in question Dayanand rejected have not been included in this table.
57. The total number of references in Table 5 is 116. Earlier in this paragraph it was noted that there are only seventy-two mantras commented on in *Ṛgvedādibhāṣyabhūmikā* with secondary sources. The apparent discrepancy is due to the fact that Dayanand explained some mantras with the help of more than one authority. If a mantra is explained with quotations from the *Śatapatha Brāhmaṇa* and the *Nirukta*, for example (as is Yajur Veda 31.1 on p. 137), then it has been counted twice: once in connection with the *Śatapatha Brāhmaṇa* and again in connection with the *Nirukta*.
58. Actually Dayanand only quotes part of the mantra: "Sitāsite [. . .] yatra saṃgathe tatrāplutāso divam utpatanti . . . ." Dayanand, *Ṛgvedādibhāṣyabhūmikā*, in *Ṛgveda-Bhāṣyam*, vol. 1, 344.
59. For a brief discussion of the schools of the Ṛg Veda, see Gonda, 15-19.
60. The Vaidika Saṃśodhana Maṇḍal's edition of the Ṛg Veda Samhita includes a general introduction to the Khilas. *Ṛgveda-Saṃhitā*, ed. N.S. Sontakke and C.G. Kashikar, 2d ed. (Pune: Vaidika Saṃśodhana Maṇḍal, 1983), 4: 891-907.
61. *Ṛgveda-Saṃhitā*, ed. N.S. Sontakke and C. G. Kashikar, 2d ed. (Pune: Vaidika Saṃśodhana Maṇḍal, 1983), 4: 949.
62. In commenting on Atharva Veda 15.6.10-12 Dayanand quotes a fragment of Taittirīya Samhita 1.5.1.1. Dayanand, *Ṛgvedādibhāṣyabhūmikā*, in *Ṛgveda-Bhāṣyam*, vol. 1, 98, especially n. 4.
63. Gonda, 327.
64. Swami Dayanand Sarasvati, *Satyārth Prakāś*, 1st ed. (Benares: Star Press, 1875), 332, quoted by the editor Yudhiṣṭhir Mīmāṃsak in Dayanand, *Satyārth Prakāś*, 321, n. 1.
65. The other references to the Taittirīya Samhita in Table 3 of chapter three are also without a citation in Dayanand's text. Dayanand, *Satyārth Prakāś*, 144, especially n. 4, and idem, *Ṛgvedādibhāṣyabhūmikā*, in *Ṛgveda-Bhāṣyam*, vol. 1, 411, especially n. 1.
66. Brian K. Smith has cast some light on the logic behind these homologies in *Reflections on Resemblance, Ritual, and Religion* (New York: Oxford University Press, 1989), especially 69-81.
67. *Śatapatha-Brāhmaṇam*, ed. Ganga Prasad Upadhyaya (Delhi: Research Institute of Ancient Scientific Studies, 1970), 3: 1872-1874 (*Śatapatha Brāhmaṇa* 14.4.3.1, 8-17). This is the same text can be found in *Bṛhadāraṇyaka Upaniṣad* 1.5.1, 3-10, translated in Robert Ernest Hume, *The Thirteen Principal Upanishads*, 2d ed.

(Delhi: Oxford University Press, 1985), 86-88.

68. Dayanand, *Ṛgvedādibhāṣyabhūmikā*, in *Ṛgveda-Bhāṣyam*, vol. 1, 77.

69. Lakshman Sarup, ed., *The Nighaṇṭu and the Nirukta: The Oldest Indian Treatise on Etymology, Philology and Semantics* (Delhi: Motilal Banarsidass, 1984), Part 3, 1. This edition includes all three parts of Sarup's text in one volume.

70. Monier Monier-Williams, *A Sanskrit-English Dictionary* (Oxford: Clarendon Press, 1979), 363. This is a reprint of the revised 1899 edition.

71. Dayanand, *Ṛgvedādibhāṣyabhūmikā*, in *Ṛgveda-Bhāṣyam*, vol. 1, 156-157.

72. Sarup, Part 3, 206 (*Nirukta* 12.1). An English translation of these sections can be found in Part 2, 184.

73. Dayanand, *Ṛgvedādibhāṣyabhūmikā*, in *Ṛgveda-Bhāṣyam*, vol. 1, 223-225.

74. A.A. Macdonell, *Vedic Mythology*, Grundriss der Indo-Arischen Philologie und Altertumskunde, ed. G. Buehler, vol. 3, part 1A (Strassburg: Karl J. Truebner, 1897), 52.

75. The description of the steam locomotion of these vehicles is most clear in the Hindi translation. In connection with the flying craft it reads (Dayanand, *Ṛgvedādibhāṣyabhūmikā*, in *Ṛgveda-Bhāṣyam*, vol. 1, 232-233): "When one must make the vehicle ["vimān"] go up, then one should keep closed the upper mouth of the steam chamber ["bhāphghar"]. And when wants to descend from higher to lower, then one should open the upper mouth carefully ["anumān se" (?)]. In the same manner when one must make it go east, then one should open the western [mouth] after closing the eastern. And if one must make it go west, one should open the eastern [mouth] after closing the western." It should be recalled that Dayanand himself only wrote the Sanskrit text of *Ṛgvedādibhāṣyabhūmikā*—the Hindi translation was written by pandits in his employ. Although the Hindi text is more clear about the functioning of this engine, the Sanskrit implies that it is steam propulsion that is at work here, frequently mentioning that fire and water power the craft.

76. The Hindi translation attempts to relate several of the *Nirukta*'s other definitions of Aśvin to the building and driving of these craft in a more extended discussion of *Nirukta* 12.1 which is not present in Dayanand's Sanskrit text. Dayanand, *Ṛgvedādibhāṣyabhūmikā*, in *Ṛgveda-Bhāṣyam*, vol. 1, 226.

77. Dayanand, *Ṛgvedādibhāṣyabhūmikā*, in *Ṛgveda-Bhāṣyam*, vol. 1, 5, quoting Nirukta 3.17. Dayanand was commenting here on Atharva Veda 10.7.34.

78. Dayanand, *Ṛgvedādibhāṣyabhūmikā*, in *Ṛgveda-Bhāṣyam*, vol. 1, 330-331, quoting *Nirukta* 2.16-17. Dayanand was commenting here on Ṛg Veda 1.32.5 and 7.
79. Dayanand, *Ṛgvedādibhāṣyabhūmikā*, in *Ṛgveda-Bhāṣyam*, vol. 1, 341, quoting *Nirukta* 12.19. Dayanand was commenting here on Yajur Veda 5.15.
80. Dayanand, *Ṛgvedādibhāṣyabhūmikā*, in *Ṛgveda-Bhāṣyam*, vol. 1, 331. Dayanand was commenting here on Ṛg Veda 1.32.5, 7.
81. Śrīśa Chandra Vasu, trans. and ed., *The Siddhānta Kaumudī of Bhaṭṭoji Dīkṣita*, 2d ed. (Delhi: Motilal Banarsidass, 1982), vol. 3: 17-18. This is a reprint of the 2d ed., dated 1962. In this edition the original volumes 2, 3, and 4 are bound together as the second volume.
82. Dayanand quoted *Aṣṭādhyāyī* 3.4.6 again to justify reading a past tense as present in commenting on Yajur Veda 31.11 (Dayanand, *Ṛgvedādibhāṣyabhūmikā*, in *Ṛgveda-Bhāṣyam*, vol. 1, 145).
83. Dayanand quoted *Aṣṭādhyāyī* 3.1.85 to justify reading the verb in the second person as third in commenting on Ṛg Veda 1.116.3-4 (Dayanand, *Ṛgvedādibhāṣyabhūmikā*, in *Ṛgveda-Bhāṣyam*, vol. 1, 223-225). He also changed past tense to present here. Dayanand quoted *Aṣṭādhyāyī* 3.1.85 again in commenting on YV 15.54 to change second person to third (Dayanand, *Ṛgvedādibhāṣya-bhūmikā*, in *Ṛgveda-Bhāṣyam*, vol. 1, 353).
84. Dayanand, *Ṛgvedādibhāṣyabhūmikā*, in *Ṛgveda-Bhāṣyam*, vol. 1, 11.
85. *Śatapatha-Brāhmaṇam*, ed. Ganga Prasad Upadhyaya (Delhi: Research Institute of Ancient Scientific Studies, 1967), 1: 11. For an English translation, see Julius Eggeling, *The Śatapatha-Brāhmaṇa According to the Text of the Mādhyandina School*, part 1, The Sacred Books of the East, ed. F. Max Mueller, vol. 12 (Oxford: Clarendon Press, 1882), 15.
86. Dayanand, *Ṛgvedādibhāṣyabhūmikā*, in *Ṛgveda-Bhāṣyam*, vol. 1, 120 (where the swami is commenting on Atharva Veda 12.5.3) and 178 (where he is commenting on Yajur Veda 18.29). For the first of these quotes (the one on p. 120) Dayanand did not note the source. In note 3 the editor supplies *Śatapatha Brāhmaṇa* 13.1.8.8 and *Kauṣītaki Brāhmaṇa* 4.2. *Yajño vai viṣṇuḥ* can be found in *Śatapatha Brāhmaṇa* 13.1.8.8 (and also 1.1.3.1) and *Kauṣītaki Brāhmaṇa* 4.2 as well as *Śatapatha Brāhmaṇa* 1.1.2.13, but since the latter reference is the one that Dayanand gave for the phrase in the places where he did note its source in *Ṛgvedādibhāṣyabhūmikā* (on pp. 11 and 178 [with an error in the citation by Dayanand emended by the editor]) it would seem to be more appropriate to supply that reference here also.

87. Dayanand, *Ṛgvedādibhāṣyabhūmikā*, in *Ṛgveda-Bhāṣyam*, vol. 1, 374-386. The swami was commenting here on Yajur Veda 23.19-24, 26, and 28-31.
88. Julius Eggeling, *The Śatapatha-Brāhmaṇa According to the Text of the Mādhyandina School*, part 5, The Sacred Books of the East, ed. F. Max Mueller, vol. 44 (Oxford: Clarendon Press, 1900), 325. The brackets are in the original, as is all the other punctuation. The phrase in brackets is not in the Sanskrit of the *Śatapatha Brāhmaṇa*, but was supplied by Eggeling to indicate the speaker of the quoted verse. An *adhvaryu* is a type of priest. "Vāg. S. XXIII, 22" is Yajur Veda 23.22, the mantra from which all the material in single quotation marks is taken. The force of the original verse from the Yajur Veda may not be clear because of Eggeling's discrete translation. *Pasas* is one of the Sanskrit words for penis. In the original, the word which Eggeling renders "cleft" is *gabha*, or vulva. *Dhārakā* also means "vulva."
89. About this ritual Eggeling writes, "This barbarous ceremony was evidently an old indigenous custom too firmly established in popular practice to be easily excluded from the sacrificial ritual. That it had nothing to do with Vedic religion and was distasteful to the author of the *Brāhmana* is evident from the brief way in which he refers to it, and from the far-fetched symbolic explanations attached to the formulas and discourses." Eggeling, *The Satapatha-Brāhmana According to the Text of the Mādhyandina School*, part 5, The Sacred Books of the East, vol. 44, 321-322, note 3. At any rate it seems clear from his delicate translation that the ritual was distasteful to Eggeling himself.
90. Albrecht Weber, ed., *The Vajasaneyi-Saṃhitā in the Mādhyandina and the Kānva-Śākhā with the Commentary of Mahidhara*, 2d ed., Chowkhamba Sanskrit Series, no. 103 (Benares: Chowkhamba Sanskrit Series Office, 1972), 709-722.
91. Ibid., 717-718.
92. I have only included Yajur Veda 23.19-24, 26, and 28-31 in the table because they are the only verses which Dayanand cited in this passage. Elsewhere in *Ṛgvedādibhāṣyabhūmikā* one finds discussion of other mantras from the same hymn. For Yajur Veda 23.9-10, see Dayanand, *Ṛgvedādibhāṣyabhūmikā*, in *Ṛgveda-Bhāṣyam*, vol. 1, 165-166. For Yajur Veda 23.62, see ibid., 170.
93. Dayanand, *Ṛgvedādibhāṣyabhūmikā*, in *Ṛgveda-Bhāṣyam*, vol. 1, 379-380.
94. Ibid., 378.
95. *Śatapatha-Brāhmaṇam*, ed. Ganga Prasad Upadhyaya, 3: 1754-1756 (*Śatapatha Brāhmaṇa* 13.5.2.4-8). Eggeling, *The Satapatha-Brāhmana According to the Text of the Mādhyandina School*, part

5, The Sacred Books of the East, vol. 44: 386-387.

96. On Yajur Veda 23.22, see *Śatapatha Brāhmaṇa* 13.2.9.6; on 23.24, see 13.2.9.7; on 23.26, see 13.2.9.2-5; and on 23.30, see 13.2.9.8.

97. Dayanand, *Ṛgvedādibhāṣyabhūmikā*, in *Ṛgveda-Bhāṣyam*, vol. 1, 386, n. 2 and 387, n. 2.

98. It is significant the editors of our Sanskrit and English editions of the *Śatapatha Brāhmaṇa* do not indicate that they regard this passage as interpolated. *Śatapatha-Brāhmaṇam*, ed. Ganga Prasad Upadhyaya, 3:1754. Eggeling, *The Satapatha-Brāhmana According to the Text of the Mādhyandina School*, part 5, The Sacred Books of the East, vol. 44: 386.

99. Dayanand, *Satyārth Prakāś*, 444-446.

100. Dayanand, *Ṛgvedādibhāṣyabhūmikā*, in *Ṛgveda-Bhāṣyam*, vol. 1, 272. Dayanand is commenting here on *Śatapatha Brāhmaṇa* 13.1.6.3.

101. Albrecht Weber, ed., *The Vajasaneyi-Saṃhitā in the Mādhyandina and the Kānva-Śākhā with the Commentary of Mahidhara*, 2d ed., Chowkhamba Sanskrit Series, no. 103 (Benares: Chowkhamba Sanskrit Series Office, 1972), 716.

102. Dayanand, *Ṛgvedādibhāṣyabhūmikā*, in *Ṛgveda-Bhāṣyam*, vol. 1, 78.

103. This version is from Hume's translation of *Bṛhadāraṇyaka Upaniṣad* 1.4.10, which is that same as *Śatapatha Brāhmaṇa* 14.4.2.22. Robert Ernest Hume, *The Thirteen Principal Upanishads*, 84. The brackets are in Hume's text and indicate material that he has added to clarify the sense. The italics are mine.

104. Dayanand, *Ṛgvedādibhāṣyabhūmikā*, in *Ṛgveda-Bhāṣyam*, vol. 1, 349.

105. Julius Eggeling, *The Satapatha-Brāhmana According to the Text of the Mādhyandina School*, part 4, The Sacred Books of the East, ed. F. Max Mueller, vol. 43 (Oxford: Clarendon Press, 1897), 360. A *muhūrta* is a unit of time of slightly less than fifty minutes duration.

106. Dayanand, *Ṛgvedādibhāṣyabhūmikā*, in *Ṛgveda-Bhāṣyam*, vol. 1, 330-331.

107. *Nirukta* 2.16 comments on Ṛg Veda 1.32.10, and 2.17 comments on Ṛg Veda 1.32.11.

108. Sarup, Part 2, 31. The original Sanskrit can be found in Part 3, 52.

109. Dayanand, *Ṛgvedādibhāṣyabhūmikā*, in *Ṛgveda-Bhāṣyam*, vol. 1, 189-190.

110. Ibid., 190. The reference is to *Nighaṇṭu* 1.14.

111. Dayanand, *Ṛgvedādibhāṣyabhūmikā*, in *Ṛgveda-Bhāṣyam*, vol. 1, 190. The editor of our edition of *Ṛgvedādibhāṣyabhūmikā* has

added a couple of words to this sentence in brackets. I assume that he intends them as clarifications. They do not substantially alter the meaning of the sentence.

112. F. Max Mueller, *Rig-Veda-Sanhita: The Sacred Hymns of the Brahmans*, vol. 1 (London: Truebner, 1869), 3. Although the title page indicates that this is volume 1, no further volumes were published with this title. Rather a second edition of this work was published as F. Max Mueller, *Vedic Hymns*, part 1, The Sacred Books of the East, ed. F. Max Mueller, vol. 32 (Oxford: Clarendon Press, 1891).

113. Mueller, *Rig-Veda-Sanhita*, 6. Mueller discusses his interpretation of *aruṣa* in his first note on Ṛg Veda 1.32.1, which stretches from p. 6 through p. 18.

5

RELIGION, POLITICS, AND THE STUDY OF FUNDAMENTALISM

This book was undertaken with the assumption that one can learn something by studying the Arya Samaj (or any Hindu movement) in comparative perspective. Some scholars might question that assumption, asking, "Why not just study the Arya Samaj in its own terms?" I am not at all sure that such an approach would be even possible. When confronting a movement a historian of religions (like any other historian) must take the welter of discrete bits of information and try to construe them in terms of more general categories. When a Western scholar is working on non-Western materials, she or he is liable to think in terms of categories that are cross cultural. Those general notions may not be self-consciously articulated in a book which aims to describe a movement "in its own terms," but they would still be operative. For the sake of clarity, if nothing else, I believe that it is advisable to be explicit about the categories that inform a study.

If the reader is willing to admit that cross cultural comparison is fruitful in general, that still does not justify this particular cross cultural comparison. There is ample evidence in this book of the value of analyzing the Arya Samaj as a fundamentalist movement. For example, within this context the importance of the Vedas in the program of the Arya Samaj becomes much more obvious than if the Samaj is regarded simply as a social reform organization. This does not mean that this study is comprehensive. My analysis of the Arya Samaj as a fundamentalist movement does not exhaust the possibilities for describing this group. Undoubtedly there will be future works that will approach the Arya Samaj from different angles, which will make a contribution toward our understanding of it. This study adds to that effort because it casts valuable new light on the Arya Samaj, by looking at the Samaj from a different perspective.

Yet it must be admitted that something is to be lost in the choice of any perspective. If this had been a book on the Arya Samaj as a social reform movement then some aspects of that organization's activities would have been more fulsomely analyzed than they are here. And I think that there are special problems with the study of fundamentalism across cultures, which I want to try to articulate in this conclusion.

The use of the word "fundamentalist" to describe groups in non-Western societies became popular in the 1980s. At that time fundamentalists were very active in politics in America, which may have had an impact on how people understood what fundamentalism is all about. Fundamentalists are people who drag their religious agenda into politics, some might argue. Because they understand fundamentalism to be about religion and politics, journalists used the word "fundamentalist" to describe groups in other cultures (especially in the context of Islam) which define their political stance in terms of their religious convictions.

This perceived nexus of religion and politics is something that has proved seductive to the scholars who are studying fundamentalism across cultures. Probably the largest group in the United States dedicated to the study of fundamentalism worldwide is the Fundamentalism Project. In his definition of fundamentalism Martin Marty, the director of the Project, wrote that "fundamentalists are not always activists, militants, belligerents, or terrorists."[1] And yet it was a concern with public policy that led to the development of the Fundamentalism Project. This began when Edward H. Levi became the president of the American Academy of Arts and Sciences, the body that funds the Fundamentalism Project.

> Upon assuming office Levi determined that the Academy's resources would be marshalled most productively in the service of an interdisciplinary program of policy studies with the objective being a holistic presentation of the interrelationships among policy questions and among proposed solutions. The social, political, and religious roots of the conflict in the Middle East seemed a concern of suitable complexity and global significance for such an enterprise. . . . In consultation with the Council of the Academy and other fellows, including Martin E. Marty, Levi refined the study by globalizing and specifying its subject: public

> policy-makers would most benefit from a detailed exposition and analysis of manifest political, economic, and social consequences of the recent worldwide religious resurgence.[2]

Thus the Fundamentalism Project was born, intended from the outset to assist "public policy-makers." Among those associated with the Project there is even the anticipation that this study in and of itself might have a salutary impact upon political conflict. As Associate Project Director R. Scott Appleby has admitted, "Some of our colleagues on the project even hope that it will contribute in some small way to the lessening of tension among peoples and the increase of tolerance."[3] With this statement the Fundamentalism Project is in danger of moving from a study that is about politics to a study that is political. Even if the Project does not make this leap, it is fair to say that as its concerns are oriented towards public policy, so it is likely to describe a fundamentalism that is political in nature.

Bruce Lawrence begins his study of Jewish, Christian, and Islamic fundamentalisms by denying that fundamentalism can be understood purely as a political phenomenon. "Fundamentalism is not a political gambit, to seize public power through appeal to aggrieved parties." But Lawrence goes on to affirm that there is a connection between fundamentalism and politics. "Fundamentalists *do* relate to the public sphere. They *do* care about political power, economic justice, and social status. But they are above all religiously motivated individuals, drawn together into ideologically structured groups, for the purpose of promoting a vision of divine restoration."[4] The word to conjure with here is ideology. As Lawrence argues in his conclusion, "Though it has religious labels, fundamentalism functions as an ideology. Fundamentalist leaders are self-proclaimed churchmen or observant Jews or faithful Muslims, but they are in reality ideologues because they must operate within the modernist hegemony while challenging not only its original premises but also its pervasive authority."[5] One of the most basic elements of the modernist ideology against which fundamentalists fight according to Lawrence is the nation-state. In their refusal to accept the hegemony of the nation-state, fundamentalists are often a radical political minority. Lawrence strongly argues that the logic that has led to the rise of fundamentalist movements cannot be reduced to mere politics. Yet he affirms throughout his study that fundamentalist groups embrace an ideology which often impels them into political action.

In a recent collection of essays on fundamentalism, political activism is mentioned as one of the characteristics of fundamentalism at the outset. Lionel Caplan writes that fundamentalism is "deeply involved in contemporary political processes, and so cannot be divorced from the operation and implications of power."[6] Yet this will to power is hedged by the caveat that fundamentalist groups in different cultures plug into politics in various ways. "What is also clear is that fundamentalists do not assume, nor can they be allocated in any a priori way, a consistent stance in political affairs. In some contexts they seek to subvert the existing regime, in others they are its most fervent supporters, in still others they are compelled to adopt a neutral position."[7] As a political animal fundamentalism assumes different guises in differing situations.

The fundamentalist groups considered in this essay diverge substantially in their involvement in politics. At one end of the spectrum is the Jama'at-i Islami which is an organization which was created with politics in mind. Since Pakistan became independent of the British the Jama'at has become a political party, which puts up candidates for election at every opportunity. At the opposite end of the spectrum is Bob Jones University. The founder and other leaders of the university have occasionally been outspoken in their support of conservative political candidates, but this activity has not been a consistently important feature of Bob Jones's activity. The Arya Samaj falls somewhere between the Jama'at-i Islami and Bob Jones University when it comes to involvement in politics. The Arya Samaj is not a political party, and it has never officially endorsed any party or an organization. And yet members of the Arya Samaj were active in the freedom struggle and especially in attempts to define a separate political agenda for the Hindu community. In the case of these three movements the relationship between fundamentalism and politics is a complex one indeed.

Most of these arguments about fundamentalism and politics have already been made elsewhere in this book. Why is it necessary to repeat them here? My concern is with the question that I raised at the beginning of this chapter: What might be lost in the characterization of groups in non-Western cultures as fundamentalist? Responsible scholars have argued that there is no necessary connection between fundamentalism and political radicalism. And yet I think that the intrigue of politics is one of the things that has attracted academics to the study of fundamentalism. The danger is that studies of politically oriented fundamentalists in other cultures may contribute to deeply held stereotypes amongst Westerners, particularly in America. This is especially likely when the fundamentalism described is Islamic. Anyone who has taught about Islam in a university in the United States could not have failed to notice that there is a powerful note of truth in Edward Said's devastating expose of American attitudes towards "Islam."[8] Scholars must take care when they do research on religiously motivated political activists in the Third World.

Who are fundamentalists? There are moderate Hindus in the Indian government who would surely like to characterize them as wild-eyed extremists. But the continuing popularity of political parties associated with Hindu nationalism undercuts this caricature. There are many Americans who feel that the United States has lost a sense of moral certainty, and not all who feel this way can be dismissed as on the fringe. In the same way there are many Hindus who have decried the seeming rise in corruption in Indian public life, and who search for a new foundation for political service. Some Arya Samajists believe that the Hindu tradition offers the values that can be the basis of sound government. It is interesting to note that in Pakistan it was only during the reign of General Zia that Islamizing groups like the Jama'at-i Islami began to get a serious hearing. It was certainly the case that Zia was trying to use these groups to build up an ideology to bolster his claim to power, but that may not have been all that there is to it. Pakistan still gropes for a sense of national identity.

In spite of their recent influence in the public sphere Christian fundamentalists have not had a very powerful effect on American politics for most of their history. Still, fundamentalism has dominated the religious understanding of a small proportion of the population of the United States for decades. These people have turned to fundamentalism not for a quick political fix, but because it gives them a sense of power and certainty in a world that they perceive as chaotic. By the same token the Jama'at-i Islami may not be able to convert Pakistan to its version of the Islamic ideology, and the Arya Samaj may not be able to win India to its idea of a Hindu nation. Yet these groups will continue to draw those who are searching for answers in a troubled world.

NOTES

1. Martin E. Marty, "Fundamentalism as a Social Phenomenon," *Bulletin of the American Academy of Arts and Sciences* 42, no. 2 (November 1988): 17-19.
2. R. Scott Appleby, "Report on the Fundamentalism Project," *Criterion* 27, no. 2 (Spring 1988): 7-8.
3. Ibid., 7.
4. Bruce B. Lawrence, *Defenders of God: The Fundamentalist Revolt against the Modern Age* (San Francisco: Harper and Row, 1989),

1. Italics in the original.
5. Ibid., 229.
6. Lionel Caplan, ed., *Studies in Religious Fundamentalism* (Albany: State University of New York Press, 1987), 5.
7. Ibid., 7-8.
8. I am thinking especially of Edward W. Said, *Covering Islam: How the Media and the Experts Determine How We See the Rest of the World* (New York: Pantheon Books, 1981), though the same author makes the point in other works as well.

WORKS CITED

Abbott, Freeland K. "The Jama'at-i Islami of Pakistan." *Middle Eastern Journal* 11 (1957): 37-51.

______________. "Maulana Maududi on Quranic Interpretation." *The Muslim World* 48 (1958): 6-19.

Adams, Charles J. "The Ideology of Mawlana Mawdudi." In *South Asian Politics and Religion*, ed. Donald Eugene Smith, 371-397. Princeton: Princeton University Press, 1966.

Ambedkar, B.R. *Annihilation of Caste*. 3rd ed. Jalandhar: Bheem Patrika Publications, 1968.

Ammerman, Nancy Tatom. *Bible Believers: Fundamentalists in the Modern World*. New Brunswick: Rutgers University Press, 1987.

Appleby, R. Scott. "Report on the Fundamentalism Project." *Criterion* 27, no. 2 (Spring 1988): 7-10.

Aziz Ahmad and G. E. von Grunebaum, eds. *Muslim Self-Statement in India and Pakistan, 1857-1968*. Wiesbaden: Otto Harrassowitz, 1970.

Bahadur, Kalim. *The Jama'at-i Islami of Pakistan: Political Thought and Political Action*. Delhi: Chetana Publications, 1977.

Baird, Robert D., ed. *Religion in Modern India*. Delhi: Manohar, 1981.

Barr, James. *Fundamentalism*. Philadelphia: Westminster Press, 1978.

Barrier, Norman G. "The Arya Samaj and Congress Politics in the Punjab, 1894-1908." *Journal of Asian Studies* 26 (1966-1967): 363-379.

Beale, David O. *In Pursuit of Purity: American Fundamentalism Since 1850*. Greenville, S.C.: Unusual Publications, 1986.

Berg, James, Dean of Students at Bob Jones University. Interview by author. Notes. Greenville, S. C., 31 May 1990.

Bhārtīy, Bhavānīlāl. *Navjāgaraṇ ke Purodhā: Dayānand Sarasvatī*. Ajmer: Paropkāriṇī Sabhā, 1983.

"Billy Graham's Father-in-Law Attacks Critics." *Greensboro (N.C.) Daily News*, 6 March 1966, sec. A, p. 9.

Binder, Leonard. *Religion and Politics in Pakistan*. Berkeley:

University of California Press, 1961.

Brass, Paul R. *Language, Religion and Politics in North India*. London: Cambridge University Press, 1974.

Brewer, Bartholomew F., with Alfred W. Furrell. *Pilgrimage from Rome*. New ed. Greenville, S.C.: Bob Jones University Press, 1986.

Bulletin: Catalog & Announcements. Vol. 64. Greenville, S.C.: Bob Jones University, 1990.

Caplan, Lionel, ed. *Studies in Religious Fundamentalism*. Albany: State University of New York Press, 1987.

Catholics Now at Peace. Greenville, S.C.: Bob Jones.University, 1987.

Chancellor, James Darrell. "A Comparative Approach to Religious Fundamentalism: Egyptian Sunni Islam and American Protestant Christianity." Ph. D. diss., Duke University, 1988.

The Christian Teaching of Science. Greenville, S.C.: Bob Jones University Press, 1981.

"Communalism Must Be Curbed, PM Tells Integration Council," *Statesman* (Delhi), 13 September 1986, pp. 1 and 9.

Coward, Howard G. "The Response of the Arya Samaj." In *Modern Indian Responses to Religious Pluralism*, ed. Howard G. Coward, 39-64. Albany: State University of New York Press, 1987.

Coward, Howard G., ed. *Modern Indian Responses to Religious Pluralism*. Albany: State University of New York Press, 1987.

Custer, Stewart. *Problems of Evolution*. Greenville, S.C.: Bob Jones University, 1988.

Darbari Lal and D.P. Seth, "Centenary Celebrations," no publication information.

Darling, Lynn. "Bob Jones University: Safe and Saved in South Carolina." *Washington Post*, 9 May 1982, sec. H, pp. 1 and 4.

Daskais, Jean. "Religion and Politics: Fundamentalists Helped Build Area's Republican Party." *Greenville (S.C.) Piedmont*, 14 November 1984, sec. A, pp. 1, 14-15.

Dayanand Sarasvati, Swami. *Āryābhivinay* [Arya devotions]. Included in *Dayānandīya-Laghugrantha-Saṃgrahaḥ*. Edited by Yudhiṣṭhir Mīmāṃsak. Āryasamāja-Śatābdī-Saṃskaraṇam. Bahalgarh (Sonipat): Ram Lal Kapoor Trust, 1975.

_______________.*Aryabhivinaya*. Translated by Swami Bhumananda Saraswati. 2nd ed. Bahalgarh (Sonipat): Ram Lal Kapoor

Trust, 1986.

______________.*Aṣṭādhyāyī-Bhāṣyam* [Commentary on the *Āṣṭādhyāyī*]. 2 vols. 2nd ed. Ajmer: Paropkāriṇī Sabhā, Vikram Saṃvat 2018 and 2034.

______________.*Ātma-Kathā* [Autobiography]. Maharṣi Dayānand-Nirvāṇ-Śatābdī Saṃskaraṇ. Ajmer: Vaidik Pustakālay, 1983.

______________."The Autobiography of Dayanund Saraswati Swami." *Theosophist,* October 1879, 9-13.

______________."The Autobiography of Dayanund Saraswati, Swami." *Theosophist,* December 1879, 66-68.

______________."The Autobiography of Dayānand Saraswati, Swami." *Theosophist,* November 1880, 24-26.

______________.*Dayānand-Granthmālā* [Collected works]. Nirvāṇ-Śatābdī-Saṃskaraṇ. 2nd reprint. Ajmer: Paropkāriṇī Sabhā, 1983.

______________.*Dayānandīya-Laghugrantha-Saṃgrahaḥ* [Collected minor works]. Edited by Yudhiṣṭhir Mīmāṃsak. Āryasamāja-Śatābdī-Saṃskaraṇam. Bahalgarh (Sonipat): Ram Lal Kapoor Trust, 1975.

______________.*Introduction to the Commentry* [*sic*] *on the Vedas by Maharshi Dayanand Saraswati.* Translated by Ghasi Ram. 2nd ed. Maharshi Dayanand Nirvan Centenary Publication. Delhi: Sārvadeśik Ārya Pratinidhi Sabhā, 1984.

______________.*The Light of Truth: English Translation of Svami Dayananda's "Satyārtha Prakāśa,"* Translated by Ganga Prasad Upadhyaya. 2nd ed. Ganga Prasad Upadhyaya Centenary Edition. Allahabad: Dr. Ratna Kumari Svadhyaya Sansthana, 1981.

______________.*Ṛgveda-Bhāṣyam* [Commentary on the Ṛg Veda]. Edited by Yudhiṣṭhir Mīmāṃsak. Āryasamāja-Śatābdī-Saṃskaraṇam. 3 vols. to date. Bahalgarh (Sonipat): Ram Lal Kapoor Trust, 1973-1974.

______________.*Ṛgvedabhāśyam*. 9 vols. Ajmer: Vaidik Pustakālay, Vikram Saṃvat 2019-2042.

______________.*Ṛgvedādibhāṣyabhūmikā* [Introduction to the commentaries on the Ṛg and other Vedas]. Introduction to *Ṛgveda-Bhāṣyam*. Edited by Yudhiṣṭhir Mīmāṃsak. Āryasamāja-Śatābdī-Saṃskaraṇam. Bahalgarh (Sonipat): Ram Lal Kapoor Trust, 1973.

______________.*Ṛṣi Dayānand Sarasvatī ke Śāstrārtha aur Pravacan.* Edited by Bhavānīlāl Bhārtīy and Yudhiṣṭhir Mīmāṃsak.

Bahalgarh (Sonipat): Ram Lal Kapoor Trust, 1988.

______________.*Saṃskāra-Vidhiḥ* [Rules of rituals]. Edited by Yudhiṣṭhir Mīmāṃsak. Āryasamāj-Śatābdī-Saṃskaraṇ. Bahalgarh (Sonipat): Ram Lal Kapoor Trust, 1974.

______________.*The Sanskar Vidhi (The Procedure of the Sacraments) of Swami Dayanand Saraswati*. Translated by Vaidyanath Shastri. Delhi: Sārvadeśik Ārya Pratinidhi Sabhā, n.d.

______________.*Satyārtha-Prakāśaḥ* [Light for truth]. Edited by Yudhiṣṭhir Mīmāṃsak. 2nd ed. Āryasamāj-Śatābdī-Saṃskaraṇ. Bahalgarh (Sonipat): Ram Lal Kapoor Trust, 1975.

______________.*Yajurveda-Bhāṣyam* [Commentary on the Yajur Veda]. 4 vols. 4th impression. Ajmer: Vaidik Pustakālay, Vikram Saṃvat 2029-2031.

Eggeling, Julius. *The Satapatha-Brāhmana According to the Text of the Mādhyandina School*. 5 parts. The Sacred Books of the East, ed. F. Max Mueller, vols. 12, 26, 41, 43, and 44. Oxford: Clarendon Press, 1882-1900.

Elliot, Carolyn M. "Decline of a Patrimonial Regime: The Telengana Rebellion in India, 1946-1951." *Journal of Asian Studies* 34 (1974-1975): 36.

Forbes, Richard Huntington. *Arya Samaj in Trinidad: An Historical Study of Hindu Organizational Process in Acculturative Conditions*. Ann Arbor: University Microfilms, 1985.

Geertz, Clifford. *Islam Observed: Religious Development in Morocco and Indonesia*. Chicago: University of Chicago Press, 1971.

Gilani, Syed As'ad. *Maududi: Thought and Movement*. Translated by Hasan Muizuddin Qazi. 5th ed. Lahore: Farooq Hasan Gilani, 1978.

Gold, Daniel. "Organized Hinduisms: From Vedic Truth to Hindu Nation." Paper presented at the Fundamentalism Observed conference of the Fundamentalism Project of the American Academy of Arts and Sciences. Chicago, 17 November 1988.

Gonda, Jan. *Vedic Literature (Saṃhitās and Brāhmaṇas)*. A History of Indian Literature, ed. Jan Gonda, vol. 1, fascicle 1. Wiesbaden: Otto Harrassowitz, 1975.

Graham, J. Reid. *The Arya Samaj as a Reformation in Hinduism with Special Reference to Caste*. Ann Arbor: University Microfilms, 1965.

Griffiths, Paul J. "Philosophizing Across Cultures: Or, How to Argue with a Buddhist." *Criterion* 26, no. 1 (winter 1987): 10-14.

Heimsath, Charles H. *Indian Nationalism and Hindu Social Reform*.

Princeton: Princeton University Press, 1964.

Hess, Linda, and Shukdev Singh, trans. *The Bījak of Kabir*. San Francisco: North Point Press, 1983.

Hume, Robert Ernest. *The Thirteen Principal Upanishads*. 2nd ed. Delhi: Oxford University Press, 1985.

India. *Census of India, 1911*. Vol. 14. *Punjab*. Part I. *Report*. By Harikishan Kaul. Lahore: Government of India, 1912.

India. *The Indian Penal Code (Act XLV of 1860)*. Calcutta: Government of India, 1929).

Indra Vidyāvācaspati. *Āryasamāj kā Itihās*. Delhi: Sārvadeśik Ārya Pratinidhi Sabhā, 1957.

Johnson, R. K. *Builder of Bridges: A Biagraphy of Bob Jones Sr.* Greenville, S.C.: Bob Jones University Press, 1982. First published in 1969 by Sword of the Lord.

Jones, Bob, Sr. *Comments on Here and Hereafter*. Selected and arranged by Grace W. Haight. Greenville, S.C.: Bob Jones University Press, 1942.

———. *The Second Coming of Christ*. Audio cassette of a sermon delivered on 26 October 1952. Greenville, S.C.: Bob Jones University, 1977.

———. *Three College Shipwrecks*. Greenville, S.C.: Bob Jones University, n. d.

Jones, Bob, Jr. *Cornbread and Caviar*. Greenville, S.C.: Bob Jones University Press, 1985.

———. *Fundamentals of Faith*. Greenville, S.C.: Bob Jones University Press, 1964.

———. *Pseudo-Fundamentalism*. Audio cassette of a sermon delivered on 15 November 1977. Greenville, S.C.: Bob Jones University, 1977.

———. *The Return of the Lord*. Audio cassette of a sermon delivered on 16 April 1985. Greenville, S.C.: Bob Jones University, 1985.

———. *Revival and Morality*. Greenville, S.C.: Bob Jones University, 1981. This is a reprint of an article that originally appeared in *Faith for the Family*, May-June 1981.

———. *Romanism and the Charismatic Movement*. Greenville, S.C.: Bob Jones University, 1981. This is a reprint of an article that originally appeared in *Faith for the Family*, July-August 1981.

Jones, Bob, III. *Biblical Answers to Bothersome Questions*. Greenville, S.C.: Bob Jones University Press, 1981.

______________. *The Charismatic Movement: Is It of God?* Greenville, S.C.: Bob Jones University, n. d. This pamphlet is a transcription of a sermon presented on the television program *Show My People.*

______________. *Idols, Rock Music, and Elvis Presley.* Audio cassette of a sermon. Greenville, S.C.: Bob Jones University, n. d.

______________. *The Moral Majority.* Greenville, S.C.: Bob Jones University, 1980. This is a reprint of an article that originally appeared in *Faith for the Family,* September 1980.

______________. *A Sermon a Day Keeps the Devil Away.* Greenville, S.C.: Bob Jones University Press, 1980.

______________. *What Is a Fundamentalist?* Greenville, S.C.: Bob Jones University Press, 1985. This is a reprint of an article that originally appeared in *Faith for the Family,* October 1985.

Jones, Kenneth W. *Arya Dharm: Hindu Consciousness in 19th-Century Punjab.* Berkeley: University of California Press, 1976.

______________. "The Arya Samaj in British India, 1875-1947." In *Religion in Modern India,* ed. Robert D. Baird, 27-54. Delhi: Manohar, 1981.

______________. "Politicized Hinduism: The Ideology and Program of the Hindu Mahasabha." In *Religion in Modern India,* ed. Robert D. Baird, 447-480. Delhi: Manohar, 1981.

______________. *Socio-Religious Movements in British India.* New Cambridge History of India, part 3, vol. 1. Cambridge: Cambridge University Press, 1989.

Jordens, J.T.F. *Dayānanda Sarasvatī: His Life and Ideas.* Delhi: Oxford University Press, 1978.

______________. *Swāmī Shraddhānanda: His Life and Causes.* Delhi: Oxford University Press, 1981.

Keith, Arthur Berriedale. *Rigveda Brahmanas: The Aitareya and Kauṣītaki Brāhmaṇas of the Rigveda.* Harvard Oriental Series, ed. Charles Rockwell Lanman, vol. 25. Cambridge, Mass.: Harvard University Press, 1920.

Kelley, Dean M. "The Supreme Court Redefines Tax Exemption." In *Church-State Relations: Tensions and Transitions,* ed. Thomas Robbins and Roland Robertson, 115-124. New Brunswick: Transaction Books, 1987.

Kelley Dean, M., and Donna Demac. "What's the Issue at B.J.U.?" *Christianity and Crisis,* 1 November 1982, 331-336.

Kelly, John Dunham. "Bhakti and the Spirit of Capitalism in Fiji: The

Ontology of the Fiji Indians." Ph.D. diss., University of Chicago, 1988.

Khan, M. R. *The Delusion of Grandeur: An Analysis of Maulana Maudoodi and his Jamaat*. Karachi: Lahore Book House, 1964.

Khare, H. S. "Fundamentalism." *Seminar* 322 (June 1986): 14-18.

King, Larry L. "Bob Jones University: The Buckle on the Bible Belt." *Harper's Magazine*, 8 June 1966, 53, 57-58.

Kopf, David. *The Brahmo Samaj and the Shaping of the Modern Indian Mind*. Princeton: Princeton University Press, 1979.

Lal Chand. *Self-Abnegation in Politics*. With a Foreword by Bhai Parmanand. 2nd ed. Lahore: Central Hindu Yuvak Sabha, 1938.

Lange, John Peter. *A Commentary on the Holy Scriptures*. Vol. 10 of the New Testament. *The Revelation of John*. Edited by E. R. Craven. Translated by Evelina Moore. New York: Scribner, Armstrong & Co., 1874.

Lavan, Spencer. *Unitarians and India: A Study in Encounter and Response*. Boston: Beacon Press, 1977.

Lawrence, Bruce B. *Defenders of God: The Fundamentalist Revolt against the Modern Age*. San Francisco: Harper and Row, 1989.

Lekh Rām. *Jīvancaritra: Maharṣi Swāmī Dayānand Sarasvatī*. Edited by Bhavānīlāl Bhārtīy. Translated by Raghunandansiṃh. 2d printing. Delhi: Ārṣ Sāhitya Pracār Trust, Vikram Saṃvat 2041.

Macdonell, A.A. *Vedic Mythology*. Grundriss der Indo-Arischen Philologie und Altertumskunde, ed. G. Buehler, vol. 3, part 1A. Strassburg: Karl J. Truebner, 1897.

McAllister, M. Bruce, Associate Director of Extension and Ministerial Training at Bob Jones University. Interview by author. Tape recording. Greenville, S. C., 30 May 1990.

Majumdar, R.C., ed. *British Paramountcy and Indian Renaissance*. Part 2. History and Culture of the Indian People, vol. 10. Bombay: Bharatiya Vidya Bhavan, 1965.

Marsden, George M. *Fundamentalism and American Culture: The Shaping of Twentieth-Century Evangelicalism: 1870-1925*. Oxford: Oxford University Press, 1980.

Marsden, George, ed. *Evangelicalism and Modern America*. Grand Rapids: William B. Eerdmans, 1984.

Marty, Martin E. "Fundamentalism as a Social Phenomenon." *Bulletin of the American Academy of Arts and Sciences* 42, no. 2

(November 1988): 15-29.

______________. "Fundamentalism as a Social Phenomenon." In *Evangelicalism in Modern America*, ed. George Marsden, 56-68. Grand Rapids: William B. Eerdmans, 1984.

Marty, Martin E., ed. *Fundamentalism Observed*. Chicago: University of Chicago Press, forthcoming.

Maududi, S. Abu'l-A'la, Maulana. *Fundamentals of Islam*. Lahore: Islamic Publications, 1975.

______________. *The Islamic Law and Constitution*. Translated and Edited by Khurshid Ahmad. 2nd ed. Lahore: Islamic Publications, 1960.

______________. *Purdah and the Status of Woman in Islam*. Translated and edited by al-Ash'ari. 2nd ed. Lahore: Islamic Publications, 1975.

______________. *A Short History of the Revivalist Movement in Islam*. Translated by al-Ash'ari. 2nd rev. ed. Lahore: Islamic Publications, 1972.

______________. *Towards Understanding Islam*. Translated and edited by Khurshid Ahmad. 14th ed. Lahore: Idara Tarjuman-ul-Quran, 1974.

McDonough, Sheila. *Muslim Ethics and Modernity: A Comparative Study of the Ethical Thought of Sayyid Ahmad Khan and Mawlana Mawdudi*. Comparative Ethics Series, vol. 1. Waterloo, Ontario: Wilfrid Laurier University Press for the Canadian Corporation for Studies in Religion, 1984.

Muir, J. *Original Sanskrit Texts on the Origin and History of the People of India, Their Religion and Institutions*. Vol. 3, *The Vedas: Opinions of Their Authors and of Later Indian Writers on Their Origin, Inspiration, and Authority*. 2nd ed. London: Truebner, 1873.

Mulfinger, George. *How Did Earth Get Here?* Greenville, S.C.: Bob Jones University Press, 1972.

Murty, K. Satchidananda. *Revelation and Reason in Advaita Vedānta*. Waltair: Andhra University, 1959. New York: Columbia University Press, 1959.

Mueller, F. Max. *Rig-Veda-Sanhita: The Sacred Hymns of the Brahmans*. Vol. 1. London: Truebner, 1869.

Nagar, Purushottam. *Lala Lajpat Rai: The Man and His Ideas*. Delhi: Manohar, 1977.

Olinger, Dan. *Homosexuality*. 2nd ed. Greenville, S.C.: Bob Jones University Press, 1989.

Pakistan. *Constituent Assembly of Pakistan Debates*, vol. 5 (7-12 March 1949): 1-2.

Pal, Bipin Chandra. *Memories of My Life and Times*. Vol. 2. Calcutta: Yugayatri Prakashak, 1951.

Peshkin, Alan. *God's Choice: The Total World of a Fundamentalist Christian School*. Chicago: University of Chicago Press, 1986.

Pinkston, William S., Jr. *Biology for Christian Schools*. Rev. ed. Greenville, S. C.: Bob Jones University Press, 1987.

"PM for New Ways to Combat Rise of Fundamentalism," *Hindustan Times* (Delhi), 13 September 1986, pp. 1 and back page.

"PM for Pact to Keep Communalism Out of Electoral Politics," *Indian Express* (Delhi), 13 September 1986, p. 1.

"PM's Call to Fight Fundamentalism," *Times of India* (Delhi), 13 September 1986, pp. 1 and 9.

Pollock, Sheldon. "The 'Revelation' of 'Tradition': *Śruti, Smṛti*, and the Sanskrit Discourse of Power" In *Lex et Litterae: Festschrift Botto*. Forthcoming.

Powell, J.H. "Unrequited Spring." *Atlanta Weekly*, 4 April 1982, n. p.

Prakash, Indra. *A Review of the History & Work of the Hindu Mahasabha and Hindu Sanghatan Movement*. Delhi: Akhil Bharatiya Hindu Mahasabha, 1938.

Ratan Lal, trans. *Chandapur Fair*. Ajmer: Paropkāriṇī Sabhā, 1974.

Renou, Louis. *The Destiny of the Veda in India*. Edited by Dev Raj Chanana. Delhi: Motilal Banarsidass, 1965.

Ṛgveda-Saṃhitā. Edited by N.S. Sontakke and others. 5 vols. Pune: Vaidika Saṃśodhana Maṇḍal, 1951-1984.

Riddle, Lyn Nabers. "Bob Jones University: A Mystery to Outsiders." *Greenville (S. C.) Piedmont*, 23 February 1981, sec. 2, pp. 1, 5.

Rumminger, Elmer L. *X-Rated TV*. Greenville, S. C.: Bob Jones University Press, 1973. This pamphlet is a reprint of an article that originally appeared in *Faith for the Family*, March-April 1973.

Sandeen, Ernest R. *The Roots of Fundamentalism: British and American Millenarianism, 1800-1930*. Chicago: University of Chicago Press, 1970.

Sarda, Harbilas. *Life of Dayanand Saraswati: World Teacher*. 2d ed. Ajmer: Paropkāriṇī Sabhā, 1968.

Sarup, Lakshman, ed. *The Nighaṇṭu and the Nirukta: The Oldest Indian Treatise on Etymology, Philology and Semantics*. Delhi:

Motilal Banarsidass, 1984.

Sarwat Saulat. *Maulana Maududi*. Karachi: International Islamic Publishers, 1979

Sastri, Sivanath. *History of the Brahmo Samaj*. 2nd ed. Calcutta: Sadharan Brahmo Samaj, 1974.

Shakir, Moin. "Rise of Fundamentalism—An Enquiry into its Causes." *Radical Humanist* 50, no. 5 (August 1986): 27-30, 41.

Sharma, Arvind. "Svami Dayananda Sarasvati and Vedic Authority." In *Religion in Modern India*, ed. Robert E. Baird, 179-196. Delhi: Manohar, 1981.

Shastri, J.L., ed. *Brahmasūtra-àäčkarabhāòyam*. Delhi: Motilal Banarsidass, 1980.

Shepard, William. "'Fundamentalism' Christian and Islamic." *Religion* 17 (1987): 355-378.

Shraddhanand, Swami. *Hindu Sangathan: Saviour of the Dying Race*. Delhi: Arjun Press, 1926.

Sivan, Emmanuel. *Radical Islam: Medieval Theology and Modern Politics*. New Haven: Yale University Press, 1985.

Smith, Brian K. *Reflections on Resemblance, Ritual, and Religion*. New York: Oxford University Press, 1989.

Smith, Donald Eugene, ed. *South Asian Politics and Religion*. Princeton: Princeton University Press, 1966.

Smith, Jonathan Z. *Imagining Religion: From Babylon to Jonestown*. Chicago Studies in the History of Judaism, ed. Jacob Neusner, William Scott Green, and Calvin Goldscheider. Chicago: University of Chicago Press, 1982.

Spence, O. Talmadge. *A Pentecostal Speaks to Pentecostalists*. Greenville, S.C.: Bob Jones University Press, 1973. This is a reprint of an article that originally appeared in *Faith for the Family*, September-October 1973.

Taylor, Donald. "Incipient Fundamentalism: Religion and Politics among Sri Lankan Hindus in Britain." In *Studies in Religious Fundamentalism*, ed. Lionel Caplan, 138-155. Albany: State University of New York Press, 1987.

"Text of U.S. Supreme Court Decision: *Bob Jones University* v. *United States* and *Goldsboro Christian Schools, Inc.* v. *United States*." *Journal of Church and State* 25 (1983): 605-628,

Thursby, G.R. *Hindu-Muslim Relations in British India: A Study of Controversy, Conflict, and Communal Movements in Northern India, 1923-1928*. Studies in the History of Religions (Supplements to *Numen*), vol. 35. Leiden: E. J.

Brill, 1975.

Upadhyaya, Ganga Prasad, ed. *Śatapatha-Brāhmaṇam*. 3 vols. Delhi: Research Institute of Ancient Scientific Studies, 1967-1970.

Vasu, Śrīśa Chandra, trans. and ed. *The Siddhānta Kaumudī of Bhaṭṭoji Dīkṣita*. 2nd ed. 4 vols. bound in 2. Delhi: Motilal Banarsidass, 1982.

Vaudeville, Ch. *Kabīr*. Vol. 1. Oxford: Oxford University Press, 1974.

Vogel, Claus. *Indian Lexicography*. A History of Indian Literature, ed. Jan Gonda, vol. 5, fascicle 4. Wiesbaden: Otto Harrassowitz, 1979.

Weber, Albrecht, ed. *The Vajasaneyi-Saṃhitā in the Mādhyandina and the Kānva-Śākhā with the Commentary of Mahidhara*. 2nd ed. Chowkhamba Sanskrit Series, no. 103. Benares: Chowkhamba Sanskrit Series Office, 1972.

Wisdom, Thurman, Dean of the School of Religion at Bob Jones University. Interview by author. Tape recording. Greenville, S.C., 29 May 1990.

Wisdom, Thurman. *Light on the Bible Text Debate*. Greenville, S.C.: Bob Jones University Press, 1984.

Wright, Melton. *Fortress of Faith: The Story of Bob Jones University*. Greenville, S.C.: Bob Jones University Press, 1984.

Zaehner, R.C. *The Bhagavad-Gītā*. London: Oxford University Press, 1976.

INDEX